Mendoza's Historie of the Kingdome of China Vol.1

By Juan Gonzalez de Mendoza

Translated by R. Parke

Cover Design by Alex Struik

Copyright © 2012 Alex Struik.

Alex Struik retains sole copyright to the cover design of this edition of this book.

All rights reserved. No part of this publication may be reproduced, stored in a retrieval system, or transmitted, in any form or by any means, electronic, mechanical, photocopying, recording or otherwise, without the prior permission of the copyright owner.

The right of Alex Struik to be identified as the author of the cover design of this work has been asserted in accordance with the Copyright, Designs and Patents Act 1988.

ISBN-13: 978-1479371747

ISBN-10: 1479371742

Contents

INTRODUCTION. 6

TO THE RIGHT WORSHIPFULL AND FAMOUS GENTLEMAN, M. THOMAS CANDISH, ESQUIRE, INCREASE OF HONOR AND HAPPIE ATTEMPTES..74

THE PRINTER, TO THE CHRISTIAN READER. 79

THE HISTORIE OF THE MIGHTIE KINGDOME OF CHINA, IN THE WHICH IS CONTAINED THE NOTABLE THINGS OF THAT KINGDOME, TOUCHING THAT WHICH IS NATURALL. 80

   CHAP. I. 80

   CHAP. II. 84

   CHAP. III. 86

   CHAP. IV. 90

   CHAP. V. 93

   CHAP. VI. 95

   CHAP. VII. 97

   CHAP. VIII. 99

   CHAP. IX. 102

   CHAP. X. 106

THE SECOND BOOKE. 112

   CHAP. I. 112

   CHAP. II. 116

   CHAP. III. 121

   CHAP. IV. 123

   CHAP. V. 127

   CHAP. VI. 130

   CHAP. VII. 133

CHAP. VIII. 137

CHAP. IX. 140

CHAP. X. 145

THE THIRD BOOKE AND HISTORIE OF THE GREAT AND MIGHTIE KINGDOME OF CHINA, IN THE WHICH IS CONTAYNED MANY NOTABLE THINGS WOORTHIE TO BE CONSIDERED OF, TOUCHING MORALL AND POLLITIKE MATTERS. 148

CHAP. I. 148

CHAP. II. 156

CHAP. III. 160

CHAP. IV. 162

CHAP. V. 166

CHAP. VI. 171

CHAP. VII. 175

CHAP. VIII. 180

CHAP. IX. 185

CHAP. X. 190

CHAP. XI. 197

CHAP. XII. 201

CHAP. XIII. 206

CHAP. XIV 210

CHAP. XV. 215

CHAP. XVI. 218

CHAP. XVII. 221

CHAP. XVIII. 225

CHAP. XIX 229

CHAP. XX. 233

CHAP. XXI.	237
CHAP. XXII.	242
CHAP. XXIII.	246
CHAP. XXIV.	253
FOOTNOTES:	264

INTRODUCTION.

In presenting to the members of the Hakluyt Society a reprint of the cotemporary English translation by Parke of Mendoza's interesting and now rare account of China, the editor thinks it due to his readers that some explanation should be given of the circumstances under which the original work was compiled, and that at the same time it should be shown what previous accounts had reached Europe respecting that remarkable country. The interest of the narrative itself, abounding as it does with minute and curious details of the manners and customs of so peculiar a race as the Chinese, requires no vindication: it will speak for itself. It will nevertheless interest those who appreciate the objects of the Society, to know, that the present translation was made at Hakluyt's own suggestion, shortly after the appearance of Mendoza's original work in Spanish.

It is the leading purpose of the Hakluyt Society to deal with the Archæology of Geography, and more especially so in connexion with the progress made by our own English ancestors in the advancement of [ii] that important science. In pursuance of that object, therefore, Mendoza's account of China has been selected for re-publication, as being the earliest detailed account of that country ever published in the English language. We say detailed account, because we must not omit to mention that it was preceded by a short but interesting document, published by Richard Eden in his History of Travayle in the West and East Indies, entitled "Reportes of the Province of China," of the history and contents of which we shall hereafter speak in its proper place. While, however, in the selection for re-publication, respect is paid to the earliest narratives which appeared in our own tongue, the reader's appreciation of the subject is best secured by an introductory notice of all the antecedent descriptions which may at intervals have appeared in other languages. This plan is more especially desirable with respect to those earlier glimmerings of information which Europe obtained respecting a country so removed from the civilized world, by its geographical position and ethnological peculiarities, as China, yet so marvellously in advance of it at the times of which we speak, both in its intellectual and moral developments. In such notice, meanwhile, we propose to pass by all discussion as to the much disputed question of the position of the Thinæ of Eratosthenes, Strabo, and the Periplus of the Erythræan Sea, or of the application of Marinus's Serica, as preserved to us by Ptolemy, to the kingdom of China. Upon these more uncertain data we shall dwell no longer than to state, that our own impression agrees with that of Vossius, that China is the country referred to, and[iii] that the Seres of Ammianus Marcellinus, corresponding as they so closely do in character with the modern Chinese, were intended to represent that people. That the Romans possessed some knowledge of China, would seem to be shown by a discovery made by the learned De Guignes, of a statement in a Chinese historical work, that in the year of our Lord 166, an embassy, said to have come by sea, arrived from An-thon (Antoninus) to the Emperor Yan-hi; and the use of the "serica vestis", alluded to by Horace and Propertius, would appear to confirm the impression, provided only that silk, and not muslin, were the commodity really alluded to.

On these less certain points, however, we are, as we have said, unwilling to dwell. We pass on therefore to the mention of more explicit and unquestionable record. First of these is the narrative given in an Arabic manuscript, written about the year 1173, describing the observations of two Arab merchants, who, from the style of the documents, were evidently in China a couple of centuries earlier. Their respective dates, indeed, are concluded to be 851 and 867. This curious and valuable manuscript, discovered by the learned M. Eusèbe Renaudot in the Comte de Seignelay's library, was translated by him into French, and published at Paris in 1718. A translation appeared in English in 1733. Although thus concealed from the acquaintance of Europeans till this comparatively recent date, it rightly takes its place here as comprising the two earliest accounts of China, of which we have as yet received[iv] any information. Though adulterated with some few exaggerations, and statements manifestly fabulous, they contain so many curious particulars, which even now, from the permanence of institutions and manners in China, may be considered as accurate, that no doubt can be entertained of their genuineness, or of the intelligence of the narrators.

The two narratives were written consecutively, one of them forming a sort of comment or supplement to the other.

The country is described as extensive, but, though more populous, less extensive than the Indies, and divided into many principalities. It is represented as fruitful, and containing no deserts, while India is said to contain some of great extent.

Tea, under the name of tcha, is distinctly referred to, as being universally drunk infused in hot water, and supposed to be a cure for every disease.

Porcelain is spoken of as an excellent kind of earth, of which is made a ware as fine and transparent as glass.

The Chinese are described as more handsome than the Indians, and are "dressed in silk both winter and summer; and this kind of dress is common to the prince, the soldier, and to every other person, though of the lowest degree. In winter they wear drawers, of a particular make, which fall down to their feet. Of these they put on two, three, four, five, or more, if they can, one over another; and are very careful to be covered quite down to their feet, because of the damps, which are very great and much dreaded by[v] them. In summer they only wear a single garment of silk, or some such dress, but have no turbans.

"Their common food is rice, which they often eat with a broth, like what the Arabs make of meat or fish, which they pour upon their rice. Their kings eat wheaten bread, and all sorts of animals, not excepting swine, and some others.

"They have several sort of fruits, apples, lemons, quinces, sugar-canes, citruls, figs, grapes, cucumbers of two sorts, trees which bear meal, walnuts, filberts, pistachios, plums, apricocks, services [cherries], and coco-nuts; but they have no store of palms; they have only a few about some private houses.

"Their drink is a kind of wine made of rice; they have no other wine in the country, nor is there any brought to them; they know not what it is, nor do they drink of it. They have vinegar also, and a kind of comfit like what the Arabs call Natef, and some others.

"They are not very nice in point of cleanliness. They eat also of dead animals, and practice in many other things like the Magians; and, in truth, the religion of the one and the other is much the same. The Chinese women appear uncovered, and adorn their heads with small ivory and other combs, of which they shall wear sometimes a score together. The men are covered with caps of a particular make. They are very expert mechanics, but ignorant of the arts that depend on the mathematics."

The knowledge of reading and writing is described as being general amongst them, all import[vi]ant transactions being put into writing. Idolatry is mentioned as very prevalent, and a hideous and incomprehensible statement is made, of human flesh being publicly exposed for sale in the markets. At the same time the punishment of vice is represented as most severe, and the surveillance over individuals extremely rigid, "for everybody in China, whether a native, an Arab, or any other foreigner, is obliged to declare all he knows of himself, nor can he possibly be excused for so doing". And thieves are put to death as soon as caught.

Canfu (Canton) is mentioned as the seaport of China, resorted to by Arabian shipping; and Cumdan, described as a very splendid city, supposed to be Nanking, was the residence of the monarch.

Renaudot, to whom the world is indebted for rescuing this narrative from obscurity, believes that it supplied Edrisi, the celebrated Arab geographer of the twelfth century, with the materials for the observations on China which occur in his Geographia Nubiensis; but this reproach would seem to be unfounded, inasmuch as his details are too few and vague, to warrant the conclusion that they were digested from the more lucid and ample account to which we have been referring. The most observable point of information with which Edrisi supplies us, is the fact, that the northern parts of Sin had by that time been conquered by a Tartar nation, whom he calls the Baghargar Turks. Abulfeda also, who flourished nearly two centuries later, seems to have been equally ignorant of the existence of the two Arab[vii] travellers; for he gives, as an apology for the ignorance of the geographers of that day respecting China, that no one had been there from whom they could procure information.

The incidental reference to China by Benjamin of Tudela, a Jewish traveller in the east, of the twelfth century, should not be omitted. It is but a reference, but curious enough to be quoted. It is as follows:—

"From thence (the Island of Khandy) the passage to China is effected in forty days; this country lies eastward, and some say that the star Orion predominates in the sea which bounds it, and which is called Sea of Nikpha. Sometimes so violent a storm rages in this sea, that no mariner can reach his vessel; and whenever the storm throws a ship into this sea, it is impossible to govern it; the crew and the passengers consume their provisions, and then die miserably. Many vessels have been lost in this way, but people have learned how to save themselves from this fate by the following contrivance. They take bullocks' hides along with them, and whenever this storm arises and throws them into the Sea of Nikpha, they sew themselves up in the hides, taking care to have a knife in their hand, and being secured against the sea-water, they throw themselves into the ocean; here they are soon perceived by a large eagle, called griffin, which takes them for cattle, darts down, takes them in his gripe, and carries them upon dry land, where he deposits his burthen on a hill or in a dale, there to consume his prey. The man, however, now avails himself of his knife, therewith to kill the bird,[viii] creeps forth from the hide, and tries to reach an inhabited country. Many people have been saved by this stratagem."

The first European reference to China described by a traveller from hearsay, is that given by the Minorite friar John de Plano Carpini, who, with five other brothers of the order, in 1245 was sent by Pope Innocent IV into the country of the Mongolians. The purpose of this mission was, if possible, to divert these devastating conquerors from Europe, and to instigate them rather to a war with the

Turks and Saracens. At the same time they were to inculcate, as much as might be, the Christian faith, and at all events to collect every possible information respecting a people so little known.

Carpini was absent sixteen months. A copy of his narrative, formerly belonging to Lord Lumley, is in the British Museum, and is the same which was used by Hakluyt for his Principal Navigations, from which the following extract is taken. It is after describing a battle between the Mongals and the Chinese, whom he calls Kythayans, that he describes the latter as follows:

"The men of Kytay are Pagans, hauing a speciall kinde of writing by themselues, and (as it is reported) the Scriptures of the Olde and Newe Testament. They haue also recorded in hystories the liues of their forefathers: and they haue Eremites, and certaine houses made after the manner of our churches, which in those dayes they greatly resorted vnto. They say that they haue diuers saints also, and they[ix] worship one God. They adore and reuerence Christ Jesvs our Lord, and beleeue the article of eternall life, but are not baptized. They doe also honorably esteeme and reuerence our Scriptures. They loue Christians, and bestowe much almes, and are a very courteous and gentle people. They haue no beardes, and they agree partly with the Mongals in the disposition of their countenance. In all occupations which men practise, there are not better artificers in the whole worlde. Their countrey is exceeding rich in corne, wine, golde, silke, and other commodities."

The first traveller, from whom accounts collected from personal experience respecting China were received in Europe, was William Van Ruysbroeck, commonly known by the name of De Rubruquis, a friar of the Minorite order, and sometimes called William of Tripoli, from the circumstance of the narrative of his travels having been transmitted from Tripoli to St. Louis, king of France, at whose instance they were undertaken. The cause of his mission was a rumour, which had spread through Europe, that the Mongolian chief, Mangu Khan, had embraced the Christian religion; and St. Louis being then engaged in the fourth Crusade against the Saracens, was anxious to cement an alliance with the Tartars, who were at that time in hostility with the same power on the side of Persia. This political purpose was enhanced by sanguine hopes that the Tartars were even then, or likely soon to be, converted to the Christian faith. The passage of Rubruquis was by Constantinople over the Black Sea, through the Crimea,[x] to the district of the city of the Caraci, in the Gobi Desert, where Mangu Khan was then residing.

His first reception was not of the most hospitable kind, but nine days after his arrival he succeeded in obtaining an imperial audience; and when Mangu Khan, a short time after, departed for Karakorum, a city on the east side of the river Orchon, he and his companions followed in his train. This city, of which no traces have been found in the desert for some centuries, is mentioned by Marco Polo, who visited it about eighteen years after Rubruquis, as having been the first in which these Tartars ever fixed their residence, and was at that time the capital of Mangu Khan, and the only considerable city in that part of Asia. Rubruquis, in describing it, says: "There are two grand streets in it, one of the Saracens, where the friars are kept and many merchants resort thither, and one other street of the Catayans (Chinese), who are all artificers." The explanation of this is, that the Tartars had already conquered the greater part of northern China, then known under the name of Cathay.

Rubruquis and his companions, who by this time had gained considerable favour in the eyes of the Khan, entered Karakorum with great distinction. He describes the city itself as not equal to the village of St. Denis, near Paris, the monastery of which he asserts was "tenne times more worth than the palace, and more too." The place was surrounded by a mud wall, and had four gates. The description of the palace conveys the idea of a hall,[xi] at one end of which was a raised seat for the Khan, on which he "sitteth above like a god". In this city the friar found to his surprise a French goldsmith, named Guillaume Bouchier, who is not unfrequently mentioned by early writers under the name of William of Paris, and who had constructed a piece of mechanism, the ingenuity of which deserves the highest praise, when the early period at which he worked is taken into consideration. Its description is thus given by Purchas, in a translation of the greater part of the travels of Rubruquis, inserted in the third volume of his Pilgrimes.

"Master William Parisiensis made him (the Khan) a great silver tree, at the root whereof were foure silver lions, having one pipe sending forth pure cowes milke, and the foure pipes were convayed within the tree, unto the top thereof: whose tops spread backe again downward: and upon every one of them was a golden serpent, whose tayles twine about the bodie of the tree. And one of those pipes runs with wine, another with caracosmos, that is, clarified whay; another with ball, that is, drinke made of honey; another with drinke made of rice, called teracina. And every drinke hath his vessell prepared of silver, at the foot of the tree, to receive it. Betweene those foure pipes in the top, he made an angell holding a trumpet; and under the tree, he made an hollow vault, wherein a man might be hid; and a pipe ascendeth through the heart of the tree unto the angell. He first made bellowes, but they gave not wind enough. Without the palace there is a chamber,[xii] wherein the drinkes are layd, and there are servants readie there to poure it out, when they heare the angell sounding the trumpet. And the boughes of the tree are of silver, and the leaves and peares. When therefore they want drinke, the master butler cryeth to the angell that he sound the trumpet. Then he hearing (who is hid in the vault) blowes the pipe strongly, which goeth to the angell. And the angell sets his trumpet to his mouth, and the trumpet soundeth very shrill. Then the servants hearing, which are in the chamber, every of them poure forth their drink into their proper pipe, and the pipes poure it forth from above, and they are received below in vessels prepared for that purpose. Then the butlers draw them, and carry them through the palace to men and women."[1]

Amongst the various points of information gathered by Rubruquis respecting the Chinese or Catayans, as they were so long called, occur the following important items. The characteristic principle of their religious and political creed, embodied the great truth of the existence of one supreme presiding deity, under whom the grand khan maintained the presidency over his extensive dominions, and resistance to that dominion consequently involved not only treason but heinous impiety. Another curious fact, first communicated by Rubruquis, and afterwards confirmed by Marco Polo, is that of paper currency, which was not adopted in Europe for some centuries after, being then in general use[xiii] in China. To him also we are indebted for some notion of the peculiar characters and mode of writing practised by the Chinese, who, as he says, do not write with pens as we do, but with small brushes, such as are used by our painters, and in one character or figure give a whole word.

He also speaks at length of a strong drink called Cosmos, which he describes as follows:—

"Their drinke, called Cosmos, which is mare's milk, is prepared after this manner. They fasten a long line unto two posts, standing firmly in the ground, and unto the same line they tye the young foales of those mares which they meane to milke. Then come the dammes to stand by their foales, gently suffering themselves to be milked. And if any of them be too unruly, then one takes her foale and puts it under her, letting it sucke a while, and presently carrying it away againe, there comes another man to milke the said mare. And having gotten a good quantitie of this milke together (being as sweet as cowes milke) while it is new, they powre it into a great bladder or bag, and they beat the said bag with a piece of wood made for the purpose, having a club at the lower end like a mans head, which is hollow within: and soone as they beat upon it, it begins to boyle like new wine, and to be sowre and sharpe of taste, and they beat it in that manner till butter come thereof. Then taste they thereof, and being indifferently sharpe they drinke it; for it biteth a mans tongue like the wine of raspes when it is drunke. After a man hath taken a draught thereof, it leaveth behind it a taste like[xiv] the taste of almond-milke, and goeth downe very pleasantly, intoxicating weake braynes. Likewise Karacosmos, that is to say, blacke Kosmos, for great lords to drinke, they make on this manner. First, they beat the said milke so long till the thickest part thereof descend right downe to the bottome like the lees of white wine; and that which is thinne and pure remaineth above, being like unto whay or white must. The said lees and dregs being very white, are given to servants, and will cause them to sleepe exceedingly. That which is thinne and cleere their masters drinke, and in very deede it is maruellous sweet and wholesome liquor."[2]

This limited stock of information, however, valuable as it is from the priority of its date, sinks into insignificance before the detailed and almost cotemporaneous narrative of that once reviled but now much honoured pioneer of geographical investigation, Marco Polo. In the present advanced age, when enlarged facilities have opened up to the knowledge of the world the characteristic peculiarities of remote countries and their inhabitants, we can do justice to the courage and fidelity of those who, six centuries ago, could dare to describe such apparent anomalies, while at the same time we can find an excuse for the disbelief of those who regarded them as extravagant and impudent fictions. Nor can we, indeed, conceive of any country and people, the description of which, unconfirmed by the repeated observation of many, was more calculated to excite suspicion and[xv] disbelief, while those very peculiarities, now that they are authenticated, become the staple proof of the trustworthiness of the early narrator. The father and uncle of Marco Polo, natives of Venice, had in 1254 made a trading journey to Tartary; the exploration of the east, and the importation of its rich and beautiful productions, offering a peculiar attraction to the commercial enterprise of that great and flourishing city. Marco was not born till some months after the departure of his father, but by the time of the return of the two brothers was become a young man, fifteen years having been devoted to their interesting and extraordinary peregrinations. They had crossed the Euxine Sea to Armenia, whence they travelled by land to the court of a great Tartarian chief named Barba. By him they were favorably received, and were enabled to effect advantageous sales of their merchandise. After a year, however, spent in his capital, a war broke out between him and a neighbouring chieftain, and the return of the travellers to Europe being thus intercepted, they took a circuitous course round the head of the Caspian, and so through the desert of Karak to Bokhara.

After an abode there of three years, during which they obtained a knowledge of the Tartar language, they attached themselves to the company of an ambassador going to the court of Kublai, grand Khan of the Tartars, where they arrived after a year's journey. This potent monarch gave them a gracious reception, and was curious in his enquiries concerning the affairs of Europe and the Christian religion.[xvi] Learning from them that the Pope was the person regarded with the greatest veneration in Europe, he resolved on despatching them as his ambassadors to His Holiness, with the request that he would send persons to instruct his people in the true faith. Protected by his signet they set out, and pursuing their journey across Asia, arrived in Venice in the year 1269. At this time there was a vacancy in the popedom, and the brothers remained in Venice two years before it was filled. At length, on the accession of Gregory X, they obtained letters from him, accompanied with presents to Kublai Khan, and taking with them young Marco, now seventeen years of age, and accompanied by two friars of the order of Preachers, they again departed for the east. They landed at a port in Armenia named Giuzza (Ayas), but finding that the Sultan of Babylon was at war with the province, the two friars became intimidated and returned home. The three Venetians, however, pursued their way, and after travelling for three years and a half across Asia, and encountering numerous perils and disasters, at length reached the court of Kublai. He was greatly pleased at their return, and Marco, becoming a great favourite with him, was employed by the Khan in various important missions to distant provinces. After a residence of seventeen years at the court of Kublai, the three Venetians were extremely desirous of returning to their native land, and at length obtained permission to accompany the ambassadors of a king of India, who had come to demand a princess of the Khan's family in marriage[xvii] for their sovereign. It was a voyage of a year and a half through the Indian seas before they arrived at the court of this king, named Argon. Thence they travelled to Constantinople, and finally reached Venice in 1295.

Such is the narrative of the travels and foreign residence of the three Polos, as related by Marco. They returned rich in jewels and valuable effects, after an absence of twenty-four years, which had so altered them, that nothing less than a display of their wealth was necessary to procure their recognition by their kindred. Hence, Marco gained the name of Il Millione, the house in which he had lived in Venice being still known in the time of Ramusio under the name of "La Corte del Millioni." Not long afterwards, news came to Venice that the Genoese were approaching with a powerful armament, and a number of galleys were immediately fitted out to oppose them, and Marco Polo was made sopracomito of one of them. In an engagement that ensued he fell into the hands of the Genoese Admiral Lampa Doria, and was carried prisoner to Genoa, to which circumstance we owe the advantage of possessing a permanent record of his travels. Then he spent four years in prison; but the interest excited amongst the Genoese nobles by the stirring narrative of his adventures, led them to urge him to allow an account of his travels to be drawn up from his notes and dictation. His narrative was thus taken from his mouth in his prison at Genoa, by the hand of his friend and fellow-traveller Rustichello, a native of Pisa. He[xviii] afterwards regained his liberty, but of his subsequent history little or nothing is known.

The most interesting portion of his narrative is unquestionably that which refers to China, of which he speaks under the names of Kataia and Manji; the former, as we have already stated, denoting the northern, and the latter the southern part of the empire. The northern kingdom of Kataia contained the residence of Kublai Khan, while the south, although subjugated, had not been completely incorporated into the almost boundless Tartar dominion, which had been established by Kublai's victorious ancestor, the renowned Zenghis Khan.

The route by which Polo entered China was along the northern frontier, and is thus referred to by Mr. Marsden:—"Having reached the borders of Northern China, and spoken of two places (Succuir, the modern Sucheu, and Kampion, the modern Kancheu) that are within what is named the Great Wall, our author ceases to pursue a direct route, and proceeds to the account of places lying to the north and south, some of them in the vicinity and others in distant parts of Tartary, according to the information he had acquired of them on various occasions. Nor does he in the sequel furnish any distinct idea of the line he took upon entering China, in company with his father and uncle, on their journey to the emperor's court, although there is reason to believe that he went from Kan-cheu to Sining, and there fell into the great road from Thibet to Peking." Before reaching the latter city, however, they visited Karakorum, already[xix] referred to as the capital of the Khan's dominions visited by Rubruquis. This city, Mr. Marsden says, was built by Oktar Khan, the son and successor of Jenghis Khan, about the year 1235, whose nephew Mangu Khan, made it his principal residence. No traces of it have been in existence for some centuries, but its position is noted in the Jesuits' and Danville's maps. J. Reinhold Forster, however, on the authority of Fischer's History of Siberia, observes, that it must be looked for on the east side of the river Orchon, and not on the Onghin or Onguimuren, where D'Anville has placed it.

From the length of time which had elapsed since Nicolo and Maffeo Polo had left China as Kublai's ambassadors, they were forgotten, but as soon as the Khan, who was then absent, heard of their arrival at Karakorum, he issued orders that they should be received with all honour and escorted to his presence. The appearance of young Marco produced a highly favourable impression upon the Khan, who immediately took him under his especial protection. The assiduity of Marco in studying the language and manners of the Tartars, and the wisdom and prudence which he exhibited in the exercise of the various important functions in which he was employed by the Khan, caused him rapidly to rise in the estimation and favour of that liberal-minded monarch. Upon the removal of the Khan to Khambalu, a corruption of Khambalig (capital of the Khan), and understood to be the modern Pekin, Marco followed in his train. This city was found to surpass in splendour[xx] everything that he had yet met with. The dimensions of the palace comprehended a square, each side of which was six miles long, a statement not very widely different from the truth. This enclosure, however, comprised all the royal armouries, as well as fields and meadows, stored with various descriptions of game. The roofs of the spacious halls were covered with gorgeous gilding, and painting in brilliant colours, while representations of dragons and battles were carved upon the sides. To the north of the palace stood an eminence called the Green Mountain, of about a mile in circuit, covered with the finest trees which could be collected from all parts of the empire, and which had been brought by elephants to this spot.

This account strikingly agrees with those of modern travellers, and the description of the internal government of the country, its postal arrangements, and the beneficent distribution of grain from the imperial granaries in times of scarcity, agree with since recognized Chinese history.

Marco subsequently made an excursion into the country of Manji, or Southern China, his route lying by the course of the imperial canal. In his southward progress, after passing by various cities, he at length reached Tinqui (Taitcheou), distant about three days' journey from the sea, where there is an extensive manufactory of salt, an article which forms a leading article of commerce in China. He next came to Yanqui (Yangtcheoufou), at the mouth of the river Yang-tsi-kiang, the seat of a viceroy, in which Polo[xxi] himself exercised for the space of three years the supreme jurisdiction. His subsequent route lay along the banks of the Yang-tsi-kiang, and he incidentally alludes to the noble city of Nanghin (Nanking), where he speaks of the manufacture of cloths of gold and silver, but does not seem to have visited the city itself. Taking thence a southward course, he reached Quinsai (Hang-cheou), or the city of heaven, the splendour of which still important place was at that time such, that he speaks of it in the following terms: "In the world there is not the like, nor a place in which there are found so many pleasures, that a man would imagine himself in paradise." This city, then the metropolis of Manji, was in the height of its glory, and may well be supposed to have surpassed in grandeur any city which Polo had seen; and if he is to be charged with exaggeration in describing it as one hundred miles in circumference, and to have contained one million six hundred thousand houses, and twelve thousand bridges, it must be remembered that its really immense extent was calculated to mislead the judgment of an observer, and to make him credulous of the accounts of the inhabitants. It is still a splendid and very extensive city, and it is not to be wondered at that Polo, who witnessed its unfaded glories, should have dwelt with enthusiasm on its spacious and beautiful palaces, and its waters covered with richly decorated barges. The character of the inhabitants he describes as effeminate, luxurious, and unwarlike.

In his southward journey Polo mentions many[xxii] great cities in Manji, which it would be difficult to identify with their modern nomenclature. Among these Unguen, a city of the province of Fokien, is referred to, as remarkable for its extensive manufacture of sugar, sent from thence to Khambalu; its natives being described as skilled in the art of refining it with wood ashes, from persons belonging to Babylonia (Egypt). It is also worthy of notice, that his embarcation took place at a famous port called Zaitun, which was much frequented by ships with rich cargoes from India for the supply of Manji and Kataia, and exceedingly productive in revenue to the grand Khan, who received ten per cent. on all merchandise. In spite of this impost, and the heavy freights, amounting to nearly fifty per cent., the merchants are described as making enormous profits.

The inhabitants of the place are represented as distinguished for their skill in embroidery and tapestry. This has been supposed to mean Fou-cheou-fu, Amoy, or some neighbouring port in Fokien; but it is difficult to reconcile this with the statement that one arm of the river on which this city stood reached to Quinsay, which, as we have already stated, appears to be intended for the great city of Hang-cheou.

The next in rotation on our list of eastern travellers, is Giovanni di Monte Corvino, a Franciscan monk of Calabria, who went as ambassador from Pope Nicholas IV in 1288 to the grand Khan, and died in Khambalu, that is, Pekin, holding the distinguished position of archbishop of the missions in that city. His letters refer to little more than the progress[xxiii] he made in the advancement of the Roman Catholic religion in that capital.

The next traveller in China of whom we have to speak is Oderico Mattheussi, a Minorite friar, more commonly known under the name of Oderico de Pordenone, from Pordenone in Friuli, in which place he was born about the year 1285. He undertook a journey in 1317, accompanied by several other monks, through Tartary, by Trebizond, to China, and returned by Thibet to Europe. In 1330, a year before his death, he dictated in Padua, to Guglielmo di Solagno, a monk, an account of his travels as they occurred to his memory, in the Italian language. An English translation is given by Hakluyt in his second volume, from which we quote the following extracts.

"Travelling more eastward, I came vnto a city named Fuco, which conteineth 20 miles in circuit, wherein be exceeding great and faire cocks, and al their hens are as white as the very snow, having wol in stead of feathers, like vnto sheep. It is a most stately and beautiful city, and standeth vpon the sea. Then I went 18 daies iourney on further, and passed by many prouinces and cities, and in the way I went ouer a certain great mountaine, vpon ye one side whereof I beheld al liuing creatures to be as black as a cole, and the men and women on that side differed somewhat in maner of liuing fro' others: howbeit, on the other side of the said hil euery liuing thing was snow-white, and the inhabitants in their maner of liuing were altogether vnlike vnto others. There, all maried women cary, in token that they haue[xxiv] husbands, a great trunke of horne vpon their heads. From thence I traueiled 18 dayes journey further, and came vnto a certaine great riuer, and entered also into a city, whereunto belongeth a mighty bridge to passe the said river. And mine hoste with whom I soiourned, being desirous to shew me some sport, said vnto me: 'Sir, if you will see any fish taken, goe with me.' Then he led me vnto the foresaid bridge, carying in his armes with him certaine diue-doppers or water-foules, bound vnto a company of poles, and about every one of their necks he tied a thread, least they should eat the fish as fast as they tooke them: and he caried 3 great baskets with him also: then loosed he the diue-doppers from the poles, which presently went into the water, and within lesse then the space of one houre, caught as many fishes as filled 3 baskets: which being full, mine hoste vntyed the threads from about their neckes, and entering a second time into the river they fed themselues with fish, and being satisfied they returned and suffered themselues to be bound vnto the saide poles as they were before. And when I did eate of those fishes, methought they were exceeding good.

"Trauailing thence many dayes iourneys, at length I arriued at another city called Canasia [Quinsay, or Hang-cheou], which signifieth in our language the city of heauen. Neuer in all my life did I see so great a citie; for it continueth in circuit an hundreth miles: neither saw I any plot thereof, which was not thoroughly inhabited: yea, I sawe many houses of tenne or twelue stories high, one above another. It[xxv] hath mightie large suburbs, containing more people then the citie it selfe. Also it hath twelue principall gates: and about the distance of eight miles, in the high way vnto every one of the saide gates, standeth a city as big by estimation as Venice and Padua. The foresaid city of Canasia is situated in waters and marshes, which alwayes stand still, neither ebbing nor flowing: howbeit it hath a defence for the winde like vnto Venice. In this citie there are mo then 10,002 bridges, many whereof I remembered and passed over them: and vpon euery of those bridges stand certaine watchmen of the citie, keeping continuall watch and ward about the said city, for the great Can the emperour of Catay.

"The number of his owne followers, of his wives attendants, and of the traine of his first begotten sonne and heire apparent, would seeme incredible vnto any man, vnlesse hee had seene it with his owne eyes. The foresayd great Can hath deuided his empire into twelue partes or prouinces, and one of the sayd prouinces hath two thousand great cities within the precincts thereof. Whereupon his empire is of that length and breadth, that vnto whatsoeuer part thereof he intendeth his iourney, he hath space enough for six moneths continual progresse, except his islands, which are at the least 5,000.

"The foresayd emperor (to the end that trauailers may haue all things necessary throughout his whole empire) hath caused certaine innes to be prouided in sundry places upon the high wayes, where all things pertaining vnto victuals are in a continuall readinesse.[xxvi] And when any alteration or newes happens in any part of his empire, if he chance to be farre absent from that part, his ambassadors vpon horses or dromedaries ride post vnto him; and when themselues and their beasts are weary, they blow their horne; at the noise whereof, the next inne likewise prouideth a horse and a man, who takes the letter of him that is weary, and runneth vnto another inne: and so by diuers innes, and diuers postes, the report, which ordinarily could skarce come in 30 dayes, is in one naturall day brought vnto the emperor: and therefore no matter of any moment can be done in his empire, but straightway he hath intelligence thereof."

The next traveller of whom we have to make a short mention, is the celebrated Arabian author Ibn Batuta, the date of whose journey is 1324. His point of arrival in China was Zaitun, the port already mentioned of Marco Polo's embarcation. Its identity is not easy of recognition. From this port he would seem to have travelled to Hang-cheou and back again, embarking again at Zaitun. Although his route is not distinctly traceable, the account he gives of the country appears very accurate. He particularizes the facility and safety of travelling, and the convenient, but at the same time rigid surveillance of the hostelries, in which a register was kept of all strangers who lodged in them. Silkworms and silk are mentioned, but the latter as being inferior in value to cotton. The paper money and the manufacture of porcelain are also referred to.[xxvii]

In pursuance of our chronological arrangement of travels in China, we shall here introduce the account of an embassy, though not European, sent by Mirza Shah Rokh, one of the sons of Tamerlane, to Cathay, in the year 1419. The ambassadors set out from Herat in Persia, about the month of November in that year, and reached a spot in the desert within twelve stages of Sekju (Sucheu), near the great wall in Shensi, on the 14th of June 1420. At this place they were met, by order of the khan, by some Cathayans, who erected tents or huts for their accommodation in the desert, and plentifully supplied them with roasted geese, fowls, and various kinds of meat, fruits, etc., which were served to them on china dishes; they likewise regaled them with a variety of strong liquors, together with a pot of Chinese tea. The chief person in the embassy was the Emir Sadi Khoja; and, according to the list of the names of the ambassadors and the number of their retinue, taken down by some Cathayan secretaries, the entire embassy, including merchants, amounted to eight hundred and sixty persons. In taking this list, the Cathayan officers earnestly desired that the exact number should be stated, as a want of truthfulness would involve them in discredit. Two days after their arrival, they were invited to the encampment of the dankji or governor of the borders of Cathay, by whom they were entertained with a magnificent feast. On reaching the spot, they found a square space of ground enclosed with tents, in the centre of which was a lofty awning of cloth supported on wooden[xxviii] pillars, with an imperial canopy of state at one end, where the throne was placed, as if for the emperor, with other seats on each side: on the left of this throne were placed the ambassadors, and on the right the Cathayan officers. Each ambassador had placed before him two tables, the one covered with a variety of meats and fruits, the other with cakes and bread, gracefully ornamented with silk and paper. The other persons present had but one table apiece. At the lower end of the tent stood a sideboard covered with silver and china. After the banquet they were entertained with music and a comedy, in which the actors wore masks representing the faces of animals: among these a child, enclosed in the body of an artificial stork, amused them by performing a variety of curious antics. On the next day they reached a karawl, a strongly fortified outpost, built in a defile in the mountains, through which all travellers that way must unavoidably go. Here their retinue was again carefully numbered. They next arrived at Sucheu, a large and strong square city, where they had lodgings appointed to them in a public building over the city gates, and were amply provided with every convenience and comfort for themselves and their horses, even the servants having mattresses and counterpanes allowed them for their beds.

They next came to a city called Khamchu, after which we find them crossing the river Karamoran by a bridge of boats, and arriving at a magnificent city containing many splendid temples. From the beauty[xxix] of the women, who, contrary to usual Chinese observances, were seen standing at the doors of the taverns, they designated this town in the Persian language, Rhosnabad, the city of Beauty. After passing several rivers they reached Sedinfur, a large city, in which they saw a cast image of gilt metal of immense proportions, having a great number of hands with an eye in each. This image rested on a pedestal of polished stone, and was surrounded by six tiers of balustrades.

In December 1420, after a journey of ninety-five days, they reached Kambalu or Pekin, the whole road thither from Sucheu being through so populous a country that they lodged every night in a large town. Workmen were at that time still occupied in building the walls of Kambalu. Immediately on their arrival they were conducted to the palace, and, though before sunrise, they found a multitude assembled in the outer court, amounting apparently to no less than one hundred thousand men. At sunrise, at beat of drum, the prince took his seat on a lofty throne, placed under a canopy at the outside of the palace, and amidst profound silence a number of criminals were led in, who had been brought to the capital from all parts of the empire. Each man had a board fastened to his neck, specifying his crime and his legal punishment, and was led by the hair to the emperor, who after inspecting the board pronounced sentence. Upon the dismissal of the criminals, the Persian ambassadors were introduced, and after prostrating themselves as demanded, were graciously received by the emperor. An amusing occurrence, however, had nearly destroyed all their[xxx] prospects of success. The monarch having been slightly injured by a fall from a horse which had been presented to him by the ambassadors, was so exasperated, that he condemned them all to imprisonment for life in a distant part of the empire. He afterwards, however, thought better of his resolution, and merely upbraiding Sadi Khoja, with the taunt that such a horse ought not to be presented by one sovereign to another, overlooked the offence; and on hearing that the animal was sent to him by Tamerlane as an especial favourite, his anger was entirely appeased.

Previous to their departure, a circumstance occurred which threw a gloom over the imperial court,—the most beloved of the emperor's wives died. And here, par parenthèse, we would mention a curious custom recorded in this narrative, respecting the burial of ladies belonging to the imperial family: they are interred on a certain mountain, on which all the horses belonging to them are turned out to graze at liberty for the rest of their lives; all the maidens of their retinue also are placed in attendance on the grave, and have provisions allowed them for about five years, and when these are exhausted they are left to die of famine. In addition to this loss of his favourite wife, the new palace of the emperor was struck by lightning on the night after the funeral, the flames causing fearful devastation and loss of life. These afflictions so affected the emperor, that he fell sick, and the prince his son assuming the reins of government, gave the ambassadors their audience of[xxxi] leave. On their return through Cathay they were furnished as before with every necessary, and at Sucheu, some articles which had been detained were honourably restored to them. They took their departure by a circuitous route, in consequence of intestine commotions, and passing through Khoten and Cashgar proceeded homewards to Herat, which they reached in September 1422.

Hitherto we have had to treat of travellers who in the middle ages reached China by an overland journey; we have now to allude to those who have visited that country by sea, subsequent to that grand achievement of the Portuguese, the discovery of the passage by the Cape of Good Hope.

The Portuguese themselves were, as might be expected, the first to take advantage of this expeditious route, and about the same time that they had succeeded in establishing a communication with the King of Siam they aimed at forming relations with China. On gaining information of the boundless wealth of the east and its empires in the productions of nature and art, King Manoel determined on despatching a squadron farther eastward to Bengal and

China. This squadron, consisting of eight sail, the commander of which was Fernando Peres d'Andrade, selected on account of the ability he had shown previously in India, especially at Malacca, departed, after various unsuccessful cruises, from Malacca on the 17th June 1517, and arrived on the 15th August at the Island of Tamang (called by the Portuguese Beniaga), lying three miles from the mainland, where[xxxii] all foreign ships that trade to Canton must lie at anchor and transact their business.[3] In the harbour Andrade found Edward Coelho, who, in a previous expedition, had been separated from him by a storm, had wintered at Siam, and had already been there a month. Andrade caused it to be notified to the commander of the Chinese fleet, which was stationed off the coast there for the protection of merchant ships against pirates, that he was come on a peaceful embassy from the King of Portugal to the Emperor of China. The commander bade him welcome, but referred him to the Pio (great admiral) at Nanto upon the subject of his business. After various delays and difficulties, occasioned by the numerous gradations of rank amongst the Chinese authorities, their ceremoniousness, and the mistrust, imperfectly veiled by civility, of the Chinese towards strangers, Andrade reached Canton at the close of September, and ran into the harbour with all the usual nautical ceremonies. When surprise was expressed at this, he justified himself by referring to the practice of the Chinese in this particular when their ships came to Portuguese Malacca. He then begged that he might forward to the emperor the ambassador and the presents which he had brought with him, and that the Portuguese fleet might be dismissed as soon as possible. He was answered civilly, that they would receive the ambassador, and as soon as permission was obtained from the emperor, would escort him to court. Meanwhile the commander had permission[xxxiii] to carry on trade in the town, after the ambassador had landed. Andrade now caused the ambassador, Thomas Pires, with seven Portuguese, richly dressed, to be put on shore with sound of trumpets and discharge of cannon. This Tomas Pires, erroneously called by Mendoza, Bartholomew, though a man of no rank, had been selected for this mission on account of his scientific qualifications, his tact, and experience. He was an apothecary by profession, and a practised and competent judge of the merchandize and productions of India. They not only granted him one of the best houses in the town, wherein he and his companions received visits from the most distinguished inhabitants, but also offered them maintenance, according to the custom observed with ambassadors. This, however, the commander declined, nor did he accept the invitation to come on shore, but, excusing himself, sent the factor with some assistants in his stead, and when a warehouse was granted them near the fleet, allowed the merchandize to be landed by degrees, and an interchange of traffic commenced.

Matters were in this prosperous condition, when circumstances rendered it necessary for the commander to leave Canton. Many of his people had become sick from malaria, and nine, including the factor, were dead. These and other disasters compelled Andrade to take leave of the Chinese commanders, and he went back to the island of Tamang, where he was plentifully supplied with all that he required for the repair of his ships. Before his[xxxiv] departure Andrade caused proclamation to be made in Canton, Nanto, and the harbour of Tamang, that those who had demands on the Portuguese, should apply to him in order that they might be fully satisfied. This proceeding gave the Chinese a high opinion of the integrity of the Portuguese. At the end of September 1518, Fernando Peres d'Andrade again set sail with his whole fleet, and entered the harbour of Malacca loaded with renown and riches.[4]

At his departure from Canton, he left the affairs of the Portuguese so arranged that their trade with the Chinese might be carried on securely and peacefully, and with profit to both parties. His brother, Simon d'Andrade, received from the king a commission to make another voyage to China, and departed in April 1518 from Malacca. Upon his arrival in August in the harbour of Tamu, he found that the Portuguese ambassador, Thomas Pires, had not yet left Canton, as, in spite of three applications, no order had yet been received from the court to escort him thither. At length the order came, and Pires went in the beginning of January 1520 by water as far as the mountain range Malenschwang, thence to Nankin, where the emperor was, who ordered him to Pekin, where he himself usually resided on account of the[xxxv] nearness of the Tartars, with whom he was continually at war. In January 1521, the emperor came there, and immediately dismissed the embassy. He had received unfavourable accounts of the Portuguese from the authorities at Canton and Nankin, whom the King of Bintang had influenced by an emissary; they told the emperor that, under the pretext of trading, the Portuguese explored the country with the view of taking it by force of arms, and that in this way they had made themselves masters of India and Malacca. Pires therefore was admitted no more into the palace. Meanwhile the emperor fell ill and died, and the counsellors of his successor were of opinion that Pires and all his companions should be put to death as spies. The emperor however ordered the ambassador, real or pretended, to be sent back to Canton with the presents, and to be kept in custody there until answer should be received from the Portuguese authorities at Malacca. Until then no Portuguese or Portuguese merchandise was to be admitted into the empire. The emperor further commanded that the king of Malacca, who was an ally of the emperor, and who had been driven out by the Portuguese, should be restored.

The severe conditions imposed upon the Portuguese by the emperor are not to be wondered at, for all the accounts which he had received from his authorities respecting them were prejudicial, and Simon d'Andrade himself gave frequent occasion for complaint by inconsiderate or unjust regulations, contrary both to the laws and to the received[xxxvi] opinions of the country, and provoked the Chinese against the Portuguese; and even his personal behaviour seems to have been calculated to provoke animosity.[5] At last a hot encounter took place between the Portuguese and Chinese ships, during which, fortunately for the Portuguese, a storm arose, which scattered the Chinese fleet and favoured the flight of the Portuguese, so that they happily reached Malacca at the end of October.

Thomas Pires meanwhile was, upon his arrival in Canton, thrown into prison with all his companions, and died in chains; the presents which he had brought with him were stolen. The letters, which two or three years afterwards arrived from the prisoners, contained lamentable descriptions of the oppressions they had to endure, and of the robberies which were committed in foreign ships, upon the pretence that they had Portuguese on board. The great stores of valuable merchandize, gold and silver from India, were entirely lost. Mendoza does not complete the tale of Pires's adventures, but some interesting details are given by Remusat in his Nouveaux Mélanges Asiatiques, page 205, tom. ii.[xxxvii]

The next Portuguese adventurer who comes within the range of our special notice, is Ferdinand Mendez Pinto, who from the apparent extravagance of his accounts became proverbial as an accomplished romancer. Congreve, in his Love for Love, makes Foresight thus address Sir Sampson Legend: "Ferdinand Mendez Pinto was but a type of thee, thou liar of the first magnitude." Like most of his predecessors, however, in early travel, he has by this time recovered much of his forfeited reputation, and, as in their case, some of his most remarkable statements have been confirmed by more recent explorations. Being compelled to leave his country from some accident, which he describes as casting "him into manifest peril of his life", he took to the sea. The chances of his life led him to Abyssinia, and subsequently along the coast of Arabia to India. With his adventures in these countries we have here nothing to do, but pass at once to the circumstances under which he was thrown upon the coast of China. At Goa, Pinto hired himself as a soldier to Pedro de Faria, who was proceeding as governor to Malacca. In this employ he was selected as Portuguese agent in the company of the ambassador of the Battas, on the return of the latter to Sumatra from his complimentary visit to Faria, at Malacca, the seat of government. Here he fell in with one Antonio de Faria, with whom he joined in a great commercial expedition to be sent up the Gulf of Siam.

We pass over various romantic adventures with pirates, described in his narrative, especially those with[xxxviii] one Coja Acem, a native of Guzerat, and an implacable enemy of the Portuguese, whom Faria at length overcame in a desperate encounter. The adventurers then sailed to Liampoo (Ning-po), where Faria gained intelligence of an island called Calempluy, in which were the tombs of seventeen kings of China, all of gold, and containing great treasure of various descriptions. This place they sought and reached, and having plundered, loaded their ships with the treasure. About a month after they had put to sea, they were wrecked in a furious gale in the Gulf of Nanking, and fourteen of the Portuguese alone escaped with their lives. The Chinese gave the shipwrecked pirates but a harsh reception; they were first thrust into a pond where they were almost devoured by leeches, and were afterwards sent with other criminals to Nanking, where they were punished with a severe whipping. They were subsequently sent to Peking, also chained together in parties of three, and on their arrival received thirty lashes apiece by way of welcome. Pinto gives an animated account of the magnificence of these two great capitals, but splendid as the objects he observed in them were, they would scarcely bear comparison with those which presented themselves along the great rivers and canals. The multitude of cities, together with the abundance which here prevailed, was almost incredible. The immense concourse of boats at the time of the great fairs, the mode of rearing water-fowl, their plan of hatching eggs by artificial heat, the industry and regularity of populace, and their fashion of eating[xxxix] with chop-sticks, are detailed with great exactness. Upon the whole, his remarks leave no doubt, we think, of the truth of his having been an eye-witness of what he records. Upon the subsequent occurrences of his eventful life, and his final return to Lisbon in 1558, we shall not here dwell, but proceed to the consideration of the next in order on our list of European travellers to China.

Among a series of letters in Spanish, received in 1555 from various Jesuits in the East, and appended to the 1561 edition of Francisco Alvarez's Historia de Ethiopia, occurs an account of some matters regarding the customs and laws of the kingdom of China, which a man (who was a captive there for six years) related at Malacca, in the college of the Jesuits. This valuable account, we believe, has never before appeared in English, and is here translated.

"The Chinese build their towns in the strongest situations, near rapid rivers, and chiefly at the curves, in order that they may serve in part for enclosures; and if the towns are half a league in circuit, they build walls of a league in extent, so that in case of war they may hold a considerable number of defenders. The towns are walled with stone built in mortar, for the most part; some, especially the large towns, have very strong brick walls. They contain very large buildings, and bridges of half a league, all of stone excellently wrought, and there are blocks in them so large that it appears impossible for men to have raised and set them by any contrivance. One[xl] of the things that surprised us much, was to see eight columns, upon which the government palace is built, in a town where we were for three years. We measured these columns, and two men stretching their arms round them did not touch each other; they appeared to us to be sixty feet high, little more or less; and it is very strange that men should have been able to raise them and place them where they are. The houses which are upon them are very high, all of wood, painted and gilded. An officer resides there who collects the revenue of the province, and there are similar ones in the other provinces. Each of these houses is separately enclosed by walls, within which they are accustomed to plant trees and make very pleasant gardens, with all kinds of fruit, which the Chinese are exceedingly fond of, and also of having ponds at their houses in which they breed fish for their amusement.

"What is generally considered by the nobility and principal men as the greatest distinction, is to erect edifices in front of their gates, in way of an arch going from one side of the street to the other, so that the people pass underneath; some build them of stone, others of wood, with all kinds of painting, colours of gold and blue, with pictures of various birds and other things that may gratify the sight of the passers by. And they are so curious and vain in this particular, that he who goes to the greatest expense therein, is thought most of amongst them. On the border of the arches are the name and arms of him who caused them to be erected, in letters of gold and blue.[xli]

"The houses are covered with glazed tiles of many colours, and the woodwork is much wrought. The streets are very well made and paved with stone, and the highways are all raised. I say this because they took us from that town (where we had been prisoners for three years), and we went one hundred and twenty days' journey, without going out of the kingdom, and found all the roads raised and even; and several times when we passed rivers and inquired if most of the roads that ran forward were similar, we were told that they were, and that it was a four months' journey to reach the court of the king, and the roads were all alike. They treated us very well on the journey, giving us sumpter beasts and every thing necessary.

"In all the towns there is a street of very noble houses built by order of the king, in which the officers who perform the service of visitation lodge. These officers are commissioned with the royal authority over the governing presidents (who are called in their language Taquoan). The governors of provinces and those who hold any command, are chosen for their learning and great prudence, without regard to anything else, and if the sons are as able as their fathers they succeed them in their offices, otherwise they are not admitted by the king into his service. The special governors of the towns are obliged to sit to hear and do justice to all, every morning until midday, and after having dined till sunset.

"Officers of the court come twice every year, by command of the king, to make a stay in all the[xlii] towns, principally to see if the governors do their duty well, and to remove them at once and put others in their place, if they are tyrannical, or oppress the people, or perform their functions ill. These officers examine all the walls, and if they are in bad condition, order them to be repaired. They afterwards inquire concerning the royal revenues and the expenses of the towns, moderating them if they are excessive. He who gives out money at usury loses it (if proved), and, moreover, incurs further punishment. In the towns where these officers come, they cause public notice to be given, in order that those who are aggrieved by any injustice may come before them.

"In the town I was speaking of there are six governors, one of whom takes precedence; and there are also six others whose business it is to collect the revenues, and one of them is obliged to watch the town every night with his men, that thieves may not disturb the people. Others take care to close the gates, which are very strong and fortified with iron. The governors and magistrates of every town are charged to write every moon, to the court of the king, an account of what takes place; and each has to write separately, that it may be seen if they concert what they write, and whether they speak truth; for those who lie to the king incur the punishment of death; wherefore they dread much to state anything false in their accounts. No man governs in his native place, where he has relations, that he may do justice to all without respect of persons.

"In the principal towns are many strong gaols;[xliii] we being prisoners were distributed in six of them. There are prisoners for various crimes; the most serious with them is murder. The prisoners are numerous, because the towns are populous; in every gaol there are three, four, or five hundred of them. A native of the town, where we were, told us, that in it alone there might be at that time more than eight thousand prisoners; and that was because it was a principal town, where those of the neighbouring places were assembled together. In every gaol there is a book of the prisoners therein, whom the gaoler counts every night. In that where I was, sometimes there were three hundred prisoners, at others four hundred; and although I did not see the other gaols, it appears to me from this, that there might be as many prisoners as they told me.

"The serious crimes go to the court; and for those who come from thence sentenced to death, the king gives power to the governors of the towns—if, upon a re-examination of the case, from being nearer where the offence was committed, they should find them less guilty—to spare their lives, and condemn them to banishment, or to the king's service, for so many years, or for their whole life. They take all possible pains to avoid condemning any to death. It can scarcely be expressed how much the king is feared by his subjects: they call him god and king for the strict government and justice that he maintains in his kingdom, which is necessary from the people being bad and malicious.

"In their ancient books they find that at a certain[xliv] time, white men with long beards are to take their kingdom of China; on this account they are so careful of the walls and of fortifying the towns; and the officers make a muster of the soldiers, they receive and examine them to see if they are good soldiers; they do the same with the cavalry; and to those who excel they give rewards according to their personal qualities, putting also in their heads a branch with gold and silver leaves, as a sign of honour; but those who do not satisfy them they dismiss, paying them their hire and giving them the money with reproachful words.

"The people of China are, in general, neither brave nor skilful, nor have they any natural inclination for warlike affairs; if they maintain themselves it is by the multitude of the people, the strength of the walls and towns, and the provision of ammunition. At the boundary of the kingdom of China, where it borders on the Tartars, there is a wall of wondrous strength, of a month's journey in extent, where the king keeps a great military force in the bulwarks. Where this walls comes upon mountains, they cut them in such a manner that they remain and serve as a wall; for the Tartars are very brave and skilful in war. At the time we were prisoners, they broke through a part of the wall and entered into the territory within for a month and a half's journey; but as the king prepared great armies of men provided with artful contrivances (in which the Chinese are very crafty), he kept back the Tartars, who fight on horseback. As their horses had become weak and were[xlv] dying of hunger, one of the Chinese officers commanded a large quantity of peas to be placed in the fields, and thus it was that the horses (being so hungry as they were) set themselves to eat against the will of their masters; and in this manner the army of the king of China put them in disorder and turned to drive them out. And now a strict watch is kept on the wall.

"They make great feasts in the provinces of the kingdom of China, every year on the king's birthday; and in the government palaces of every town, in a hall covered with an awning, and having the walls and the floor ornamented with very rich coloured cloths, they place a seat painted of the same colour. This hall has three doors, and it is the custom of the officers of the towns to enter by any one of them, on foot like any other man, without taking anything with him, and without a sunshade before him; in passing they make obeisance by seven or eight genuflexions, as if the king were sitting on the seat. Having finished, they go to their houses, and at this time enter on foot and by any door; for except on this day they only enter by the middle door and in very rich litters, in which their servants carry them. They hold it for greater dignity to go in these litters than on horseback, taking one or two persons on the right for state, and a sunshade on foot before them, like those which they use in India.

"They make another very great feast on the first day of the year, which is the day upon which we celebrate the feast of the Circumcision. These feasts[xlvi] last three days; on every one of which they represent scenes by day and night, for they are much addicted to the performance of farces. On these three days the gates of the town are closed, because from much eating and drinking the people are at times beside themselves. They make other very great feasts when the king nominates his son for his heir; upon which day, they declared to me, they release all the prisoners, even those sentenced to death. At the time that we were prisoners, there came news that the king intended to make his son a king, upon which the prisoners in all the gaols rejoiced much.

"These great kingdoms of China are divided by the same king into fifteen provinces, and in every one of them there is a chief town, where there is a governor, who is changed every three years; in these chief towns the treasure of the king, from the revenue of all the province, is collected. The privilege for those who shall betake themselves to the chief town is, that for crimes which they have committed elsewhere they cannot be taken; and the reason of this privilege is, that as they are continually carrying on war with the Tartars and with other kings, if they did not afford this security these persons would pass over to the enemy.

"It has been, and still is, the custom to write everything remarkable and worthy of remembrance on large stones on the highways, and in the same places where they occurred, principally in the towns at the government palaces, where the officers reside.[xlvii] These antiquities are written in the open courts, many of them in letters of gold; and the noblemen and men of quality are very curious to read them, and fond of talking of remarkable actions, and of the dignity and achievements of the former kings.

"I have heard much of the grandeur of these kingdoms, and seen somewhat (although little), which to those who have no knowledge of China would scarcely appear true; wherefore I only speak of those things that are most common among the people, leaving the rest to time, which will discover them. The noblest and most populous town is one where the king resides, which is called Paquin; the natives (for I did not see it) say that it takes seven days to traverse it by a direct road, and thirteen to go round it. It is surrounded by three enclosures and a very copious river, which entirely encompasses it, forming, as it were, the interior enclosure. Marvellous things are reported of the riches and structure of the royal residence; the designs are taken from many provinces of the same kingdom, none being allowed to go out of it. Before entering the palaces seven or eight very strong gates have to be passed, where there are very tall and stout men for guards. The king (according to what they say) never goes out of that town, and everything he eats is produced within the walls; he does not go to the outer enclosures; and they say he is never seen except by those who attend upon him, who are all eunuchs, sons of noblemen, and who when once they enter there into the residence, never more depart from it until death.[xlviii] The king has noblemen about him, very learned and of great prudence, with whom he transacts all the business of the kingdom. And these also never go without the enclosure on any account; they are called Vlaos. The manner of choosing them for that dignity is this: when there is a vacancy, the king inquires for some one distinguished in learning and for discretion, and inclined to justice; if there be one who is commonly held of this reputation, he orders him to be summoned from any province of the kingdom where he may be, and invests him with the office of Vlaos.

"The Chinese observe much exactness in their courtesies and great neatness in their apparel, both men and women; they generally go very well dressed, from the quantity of silk there is in the kingdom.

"The soil is very productive of necessaries, fruits, and very singular waters; there are very pleasant gardens, and all kinds of game and hunting. The Chinese touch no food with their hands, but all, both small and great, eat with two little sticks for cleanliness.

"Their temples are very large edifices, richly wrought, which they call Valeras, and which cost a great deal, for the statues, which are of large size, are all covered with beaten gold. The roof of the temples is gilded, and the walls ornamented with boards well wrought and painted in pictures. They are skilful workmen in carpentry. In these temples there are priests (who are obliged to remain in them always), with an appointed income. They eat neither[xlix] flesh nor fish, only herbs, principally beledas, and some fruits; on certain days they fast. If they do anything that they ought not, they are driven out and allowed to be priests no longer, and others are put in their place.

"No man can go from one province to another without taking a licence of the governor, and he who is found without one is punished; and no traveller can be (by law of the kingdom) more than three or four days in a town where he has not business; there is a man whose office it is to go about looking to this, and if any such is found, he is taken up, for they presume him to be a thief and a man of bad life. And so every one is accustomed to have some occupation, and to hold some office, even the sons of the officers and nobles. All employ their sons, of whatever condition they may be, setting them to read and write, which they vnderstand generally. Others put them to trade, and they are also in the habit of placing their sons with officers and noblemen, that they may learn how to serve. The officers are waited on with much veneration; all who speak to them do so with genuflexions, and whatever they have to ask for must be done in writing.

"The sentences which the officers pronounce are conformable to the laws of the kingdom; they judge according to the truth of the matter, which they inquire into themselves, without taking account of what the parties say; and so they are very correct in affairs of justice, for fear of the visitation, which, they say, is made every six months. Their years have[l] twelve moons, and every three years they add to the year one moon, and thus it has thirteen.

"The people of any consequence wear black silk for their dress, because coloured is held dishonourable for clothing; so much so, that no one dares to go before any officer or person of quality without a black dress; and if he has gone away from home with a coloured cloak, and he happens to have to speak to any officer, he takes a black cloak from some acquaintance whom he meets, and leaves him his own while he transacts his business. The common people always speak to the nobles cap in hand, and they may not wear black cloaks, but only very short coloured ones. The officers wear a kind of cap, different from other people, for a certain dignity is kept up amongst them as with us. In these caps they have tufts made of horsehair, stuck on every part. The king wears the same, except that they say he has two points cross-wise at the top.

"They praise and extol the richness of the king's dress, which they say is always of the colour of heaven. The officers, on the principal feasts, on the first day of January and at the beginning of the moon, dress themselves richly in coloured damask, and on the breast and back of the vesture they bear a stag and an eagle, very naturally embroidered, for they are clever designers. These garments look very well; they reach within a hand's breadth of the ground, and have very long, large, and wide sleeves. They wear boots of a blackish colour, with soles of white cloth strong as boards.[li]

"The officers and nobles, at the death of father or mother or a very near relation, wear white dresses, very cross and rough; and they gird themselves with a girdle as thick as the leg, which reaches to the ground, as does the dress also. Attached to the cap, they wear another thinner cord. When the deceased are less nearly related, they also clothe themselves all in white, from the shoes to the cap, but not so coarse and rough.

"These are the matters that are most commonly seen and known in China, where we were prisoners six years; other very remarkable things that we heard tell of I omit, because I did not see them, and because it appears to me that every day will discover more and more."

The next account of China is by Gaspar da Cruz, a native of Evora, and one of the order of Friars Preachers; he is thus described by Barbosa Machado, in his Biblioteca Lusitana. "Inflamed with an holy ardour of announcing the gospel to distant barbarians, who were given to idolatry, he set sail in the year 1548 with twelve companions, of whom the Friar Diego Bernardo was vicar-general, to the East Indies; and after building a convent at Goa, and another at Malacca, he penetrated as far as the kingdom of Camboya; but as the fruits of his labours did not correspond with his desires, he resolved upon passing on to China in the year 1556, being the first missionary who illuminated its inhabitants with the light of the faith, and had the glory of being the precursor of all those gospel labourers, who with[lii] so much labour and expenditure of blood cultivated that wild but extensive vineyard. He spent many years in this laborous undertaking, and several times incurred the risk of his life, especially on one occasion when, in a sumptuous pagoda, he threw down a multitude of idols, but at the same time confounded and silenced by the vehement efficacy of his preaching the greatest masters of Paganism. He returned to his country in 1569, and was nominated by King Sebastian, bishop of Malacca, but this dignity he did not accept. He died in 1570, through exposing himself in charitable exertions to assist the sufferers in a plague which then raged at Lisbon."

The narrative of his travels was published in black letter at Evora in 1569-70, 4to., under the title of "Tractàdo em que se contam muito por estenso as cousas de China con suas particularidades y assi do Regno dormuz." In the preface reference is made to a narrative of China by a fellow-countryman, one Francisco Henriques, but he appears merely to refer to him as having presented this relation to Sebastian I, King of Portugal, which seems to have been an unpublished manuscript. An abbreviated translation of the narrative of his travels is given by Purchas, in which he mentions "the storie of certaine Portugals, prisoners in China," one of which he nameth Galotti Perera, from whom he received great part of his Chinese intelligence. He is also referred to by Mendoza, in the first chapter of the second book, as one from whom he "follows many things in the process of his historie." This person is mentioned by Barbosa Machado under[liii] the name of Galeoti Pereyra, brother of Ruy Pereira I, first Count of Feyra, and as being captive in Funchien in China. His account appears to have been first printed in Italian at Venice, from the original Portuguese MS., and an English translation by R. Willes was given by Richard Eden in his Historye of Travaile in the West and East Indies. As this, though comparatively short, preceded the narrative of Mendoza now reprinted, and formed the main basis of the account of Gaspar da Cruz, we think it right to supply the reader with copious extracts from it, as being for these reasons a highly important and interesting document. They are as follows:

"This land of China is parted into 13 shyres, the which sometymes were eche one a kyngdome by it selfe, but these many years they haue been all subject unto one kyng. Fuquien is made by the Portugalles the first shyre, bycause there their troubles bygan, and had occasion thereby to know the rest. In this shyre be viii cities, but one principally more famous than others, called Fuquico, the other seuen are reasonably great, the best known whereof unto the Portugalles is Cinceo, in respect of a certain hauen ioyning thereunto, whyther in tyme past they were wont for merchandyse to resort.

"Cantan is the second shyre, not so great in quantitie, as well accoumpted of, both by the kyng thereof and also by the Portugalles, for that it lyeth nearer vnto Malacca than any other part of China, and was first discryed by the Portugalles before any other shyre in that prouince: this shyre hath in it seuen cities.[liv]

"Chequeam is the third shyre, the chiefest citie therein is Donchion, therein also standeth Liampo, with other thirtiene or fourtiene boroughes: countrey townes therein to many to be spoken of.

"The fourth shyre is called Xutiamfu, the principall citie therof is great Pachin, where the kyng is alwayes resident. In it are fyftiene other very great cities: of other townes therein, and boroughes well walled and trenched about, I will say nothing.

"The fyft shyre hath name Chelim: the great citie Nanquin, chiefe of other fyftiene cities, was herein of aunciente tyme the royall seate of the Chinish kynges. From this shyre, and from the aforesayde Chequeam forwarde, bare rule the other kynges, untyll the whole region became one kyngdome.

"The sixt shyre beareth name Quianci, as also the principall citie thereof, wherein the fyne claye to make vessels is wrought. The Portugalles beyng ignorant of this countrey, and fyndyng great abundaunce of that fyne claye to be solde at Liampo, and that very good cheape, thought at the first that it had been made there; howbeit, in fine, they perceiued that the standing of Quinzi, more neare unto Liampo than to Cinceo or Cantan, was the cause of so muche fine clay at Liampo: within the compasse of Quinci shyre be other 12 cities.

"The seuenth shyre is Quicini, the eight Quansi, the nienth Confu, the tenth Vrnan, the eleuenth Sichiua. In the first hereof there be 16 cities, in the next fyftiene: howe many townes the other three haue we are ignorant as yet, as also of the proper[lv] names of the 12 and 13 shyres and the townes therein.

"This, finally, may be generally sayde heereof, that the greater shyres in China prouince may be compared with mightie kyngdomes.

"In eche one of these shyres be set Ponchiassini and Anchiassini, before whom are handled the matters of other cities. There is also placed in eche one a Tutan, as you would say a gouernor, and a Chian, that is a visitor, as it were, whose office is to goe in circuit and to see iustice exactly done. By these meanes so upryghtly thinges are ordered there, that it may bee worthely accompted one of the best gouerned prouinces in all the world.

"The king maketh alwayes his abode in the great citie Pachin, as muche as to say in our language, as by the name thereof I am aduertised, the towne of the kyngdome. This kyngdome is so large, that vnder fyue monethes you are not able to traueyle from the townes by the sea syde to the court and backe agayne, no not vnder three monethes in poste at your vrgent businesse. The posthorses in this countrey are litle of bodie, but swyfte of foote. Many doe traueyle the greater parte of this iourney by water in certayne lyght barkes, for the multitude of ryuers commodious for passage from one citie to another.

"The kyng, notwithstandyng the hugenesse of his kyngdome, hath such a care thereof, that every moone (by the moones they reckon their monethes) he is aduertised fully of whatsoeuer thing happeneth therein, by these meanes folowyng.[lvi]

"The whole prouince beyng diuided into shyres, and eche shyre hauyng in it one chiefe and principall citie, whereunto the matters of all the other cities, townes, and boroughes are brought, there are drawen in euery chiefe citie aforesayde, intelligences of suche thinges as doe monethely fall out, and be sent in writing to the court. If happely in one moneth euery post is not able to goe so long a way, yet doeth there notwithstandyng once euery moneth arryue one post out of the shyre. Who so commeth before the newe moone, stayeth for the deliuery of his letters vntyll the moone be chaunged. Then lykewyse are dispatched other postes backe into all the 13 shyres agayne.

"Before that we doe come to Cinceo we have to passe through many places, and some of great importance. For this countrey is so well inhabited neare the sea syde, that you cannot go one myle but you shall see some towne, borough, or hostry, the which are so abundantly provided of all thinges, that in the cities and townes they liue ciuily. Nevertheles such as dwel abrode are very poore, for the multitude of them euery where is so great, that out of a tree you shal see many tymes swarme a number of children where a man would not haue thought to haue founde any one at all.

"From these places in number infinite, you shall come vnto two cities very populose, and beyng compared with Cinceo, not possibly to be discerned which is the greater of them. These cities are as well walled as any cities in all the worlde. As you come in to[lvii] eyther of them, standeth so great and mightie a brydge, that the lyke thereof I haue neuer seene in Portugall nor els where. I heard one of my felowes say, that he told in one bridge 40 arches. The occasion wherefore these bridges are made so great, is for that the countrey is toward the sea very plaine and low, and ouerwhelmed euer as ye sea water encreaseth. The breadth of the bridges, although it bee well proportioned vnto the length therof, yet are they equally buylt, no higher in the middle than at eyther end, in such wyse that you may directly see from ye one end to the other, the sydes are wonderfully well engraved after the maner of Rome workes. But that we did most marueyle at, was therewithall the hugenesse of ye stones, the lyke wherof as we came into the citie, we dyd see many set up in places dishabited by the way, to no small charges of theyrs, howbeit to little purpose, whereas no body seeth them but such as doe come bye. The arches are not made after our fashion, vauted with sundry stones set togeather; but paved, as it were, whole stones reaching from one piller to an other, in suche wyse that they lye both for the arches heades and galantly serue also for the hygh waye. I haue been astunned to beholde the hugenesse of these aforesayde stones, some of them are XII pases long and upwarde, the least a XII good pases long, and a halfe.

"The wayes echewhere are galantly paued with foure square stone, except it be where for want of stone they vse to laye bricke: in this voyage wee traueyled ouer certayne hilles, where the wayes were[lviii] pitched, and in many places no worse paued than in the playne grounde. This causeth us to thinke, that in all the worlde there be no better workemen for buildinges than the inhabitantes of China.

"The countrey is so well inhabited, that no one foote of ground is left untilled; small store of cattell haue we seene this way, we sawe onely certayne oxen wherewithall the countreymen doe plough theyr grounde. One oxe draweth the plough alone, not onely in this shyre, but in other places also wherein is greater store of cattell. These countrymen by arte doe that in tyllage which we are constrayned to doe by force. Here be solde the voydinges of close stooles, although there wanteth not the dunge of beastes; and the excrements of man are good marchandise throughout all China. The dungfermers seeke in euery streete by exchange to buye this durtie ware for hearbes and wood. The custome is very good for keepyng the citie cleane. There is great aboundance of hennes, geese, duckes, swyne, and goates; wethers haue they none: the hennes are solde by weight, and so are all other thinges. Two pounde of hennes fleshe, goose, or ducke, is worth two Foi of their money, that is, d. ob. sterling. Swines flesh is solde at a peny the pounde.

Beefe beareth the same pryce, for the scarcitie thereof; howbeit northwarde from Fuquieo, and farther of from the sea coast, there is beefe more plentie and solde better cheape; beefe onely excepted, great aboundance of all these viandes we haue had in all the cities we passed through. And if this countrey[lix] were lyke vnto India, the inhabitants whereof eate neyther henne, beefe, nor porke, but keepe that onely for the Portugalles and Moores, they would be solde here for nothing. But it so fallyng out that the Chineans are the greatest eaters in all the world, they doe feede uppon all thinges, specially on porke, the fatter that is, vnto them the lesse lothsome. The highest price of these thinges aforesayde I haue set downe, better cheape shall you sometymes buye them, for the great plentie thereof in this countrey. Frogges are solde at the same price that is made of hennes, and are good meate amongst them, as also dogges, cattes, rattes, snakes, and all other vncleane meates.

"The cities be very gallant, specially near vnto the gates, the which are marueylously great, and couered with iron. The gatehouses buylt on hygh with towers, the lower parte thereof is made of bricke and stone, proportionally with the walles; from the walles vpward, the buyldyng is of tymber, and many stones in it one aboue the other. The strength of theyr townes is in the mightie walles and ditches, artillarie haue they none.

"The streetes in Cinceo, and in all the rest of the cities we haue seene are very fayre, so large and so streight that it is wonderfull to beholde. Theyr houses are buylt with tymber, the foundations onely excepted, the which are layd with stone; in eche syde of the streetes are paynteles or continuall porches for the marchantes to walke vnder: the breadth of the streete is neuerthelesse suche, that in[lx] them XV men may ryde commodiously syde by syde. As they ryde they must needes passe vnder many hygh arches of triumph that crosse ouer the streetes made of tymber, and carued diuersely, couered with tyle of fine claye: vnder these arches the mercers doe vtter theyr small wares, and such as lyst to stande there, are defended from rayne and the heate of the sunne. The greater gentlemen haue these arches at their doores, although some of them be not so myghtyly buylt as the rest.

"I shall haue occasion to speake of a certayne order of gentlemen that are called Loutea; I will first therefore expound what this worde signifieth. Loutea is as muche to say in our language as Syr, and when any of them calleth his name, he answereth Syr: and as we doe say, that the kyng hath made some gentleman, so say they that there is made a Loutea. And for that amongst them the degrees are diuers both in name and office, I will tell you onely of some principalles, beyng not able to aduertise you of all.

"The maner howe gentlemen are created Louteas, and doe come to that honour and title, is by the gyuynge of a broad gyrdle not like to the rest, and a cap, at the commandement of the kyng. The name Loutea is more generall and common vnto moe, than equalitie of honour thereby signified, agreeth withall. Such Louteas that doe serue their prince in weightie matters for iustice, are created after triall made of their learning; but the other, whiche serue in smaller affayres, as capitaynes, constables, sergeantes by lande and sea, receyuers, and such lyke,[lxi] wherof there be in euery citie, as also in this, very many, are made for fauour: the chiefe Louteas are serued kneelyng.

"The Louteas are an idle generation, without all maner of exercises and pastymes, excepte it be eatyng and drynkyng. Somtymes they walke abrode in the fieldes to make the souldyers shoot at prickes with theyr bowes, but theyr eatyng passeth: they wyll stande eatyng euen when the other do drawe to shoote.

"The inhabitants of China be very great idolaters, all generally do worshyppe the heauens: and as we are woont to saye, God knoweth it, so say they at euery worde, Tien Tautee, that is to saye, the heauens do knowe it. Some do worshyp the sonne, and some the moone, as they thynke good, for none are bounde more to one then to an other. In their temples, the which they do cal Meani, they haue a great altar in ye same place as we have; true it is that one may goe rounde about it. There set they up the image of a certayne Loutea of that countrey, whom they haue in great reuerence for certaine notable thinges he dyd. At the ryght hande standeth the deuyl, muche more vglie paynted then we do vse to set hym out, whereunto great homage is done by suche as come into the temple to aske counsell, or to drawe lottes: this opinion they haue of hym, that he is malitious and able to do euyl. If you aske them what they do thynke of the soules departed, they will answeare, that they be immortall, and that as soone as any one departeth out of this life, he becometh a deuyle if he[lxii] haue liued well in this worlde; if otherwyse, that the same deuyl changeth him into a bufle, oxe, or dogge. Wherfore to this deuyl do they much honour, to hym do they sacrifice, praying hym that he wyll make them lyke vnto hym selfe, and not lyke other beastes. They haue moreouer an other sorte of temples, wherein both uppon the altars and also on the walles do stande many idoles well proportioned, but bare headed. These bare name Omithofon, accompted of them spirites, but suche as in heaven do neither good nor euyll; thought to be suche men and women as haue chastlye lyued in this worlde in abstinence from fyshe and fleshe, fedde only with ryse and salates. Of that deuyl they make some accompte, for these spirites they care litle or nothyng at all. Agayne, they holde opinion that if a man do well in this lyfe, the heauens wyll geue hym many temporall blessynges; but if he do euyll, then shall he haue infirmities, diseases, troubles, and penurie, and all this without any knowledge of God.

"In the principall cities of the shyres be foure cheefe Louteas, before whom are brought all matters of the inferiour townes throughout the whole realme. Diuers other Louteas haue the maneagyng of iustice and receyuyng of rentes, bounde to yeeld an accompte thereof vnto the greater officers. Other doo see that there be no euyll rule keept in the citie: eache one as it behoueth hym. Generally al these do impryson malefactours, cause them to be whypped and racked, hoysing them vp and downe by the armes with a corde, a thyng very vsuall there, and accompted no[lxiii] shame. These Louteas do vse great diligence in ye apprehending of theeues, so that it is a wonder to see a theefe escape away in any towne, citie, or village. Upon the sea neere vnto the shore many are taken, and looke euen as they are taken, so be they fyrst whypped, and afterward layd in prison, where shortly after they all dye for hunger and colde. At that tyme when we were in pryson, there died of them aboue threescore and ten. Yf happely any one hauyng the meanes to geat foode do escape, he is set with the condemned persones, and prouided for as they be by the kyng, in such wyse as hereafter it shalbe sayde.

"Theyr whyps be certayne peeces of canes, cleft in the middle, in such sort that they seeme rather playne then sharpe. He that is to be whipped lieth grouelong on the ground. Upon his thighes the hangman layeth on blowes myghtely with these canes, that the standers by tremble at theyr crueltie. Ten strypes drawe a great deale of blood, twentie or thyrtie spoyle the fleshe altogeather, fyftie or threescore wyll require long tyme to be healed, and yf they come to the number of one hundred, then are they incurable."

"Wee are wont to call this countrey China, and the people Chineans; but as long as we were prisoners, not hearing amongst them at any tyme that name, I determined to learne howe they were called: and asked sometymes by them thereof, for that they vnderstoode vs not when wee called them Chineans, I answered them that all the inhabitantes of India[lxiv] named them Chineans, wherefore I prayed them that they would tell mee for what occasion they are so called, whether peradventure any citie of theyrs bare that name. Heerevnto they alwayes answered mee, to haue no suche name, nor euer to haue had. Than dyd I ask them what name the whole countrey beareth, and what they would answere beyng asked of other nations what countrymen they were: It was tolde me that of auncient tyme in this countrey had been many kynges, and though presently it were all vnder one, eche kyngdome neuertheless enioyed that name it fyrst had: these kyngdomes are the prouinces I spake of before. In conclusion they sayde, that the whole countrey is called Tamen, and the inhabitantes Tamegines, so that this name China or Chineans is not hearde of in that countrey. I doe thinke that the nearenesse of an other prouince thereabout called Cochin-China, and the inhabitantes thereof Cochinesses, fyrst discouered before that China was, lying not farre from Malacca, dyd gyue occasion both to the one nation and to the other of that name Chineans, as also the whole countrey to be named China. But their proper name is that aforesayde.

"I haue hearde moreouer that in the citie Nanquim remayneth a table of golde, and in it written a kyng his name, as a memory of that residence the kynges were wont to keepe there. This table standeth in a great pallace, couered alwayes except it bee in some of theyr festiuall dayes, at what tyme they are wont to let it be seene: couered neuerthelesse as[lxv] it is, all the nobilitie of the citie goeth of duetie to doe it euery day reuerence. The lyke is done in the head cities of all the other shyres in the pallaces of the Ponchiassini, wherein these aforesayde tables doe stande, with the kyng his name written in them, although no reuerence be done therevnto but in solempne feastes.

"I haue lykewyse vnderstoode that the citie Pachin, where the kyng maketh his abode, is so great, that to goe from one syde to the other, besydes the subarbes, the which are greater than the citie it selfe, it requyreth one whole day a horsebacke, going hackney pase. In the subarbes be many wealthy marchantes of all sortes. They tolde me furthermore that it was moted about, and in the motes great store of fyshe, wherof the kyng maketh great gaynes.

"They haue moreouer one thing very good, and that whiche made vs all to marueyle at them, beyng Gentiles: namely, that there be hospitalles in all theyr cities, alwayes full of people, we neuer sawe any poore body begge. We therefore asked the cause of this: answered it was, that in euery citie there is a great circuit, wherein be many houses for poore people, for blinde, lame, old folke, not able to traueyle for age, nor hauyng any other meanes to lyue. These folke haue in the aforesayde houses, euer plentie of rice duryng theyr lyues, but nothyng els. Such as be receyued into these houses, come in after this maner. Whan one is sicke, blinde, or lame, he maketh a supplication to the Ponchiassi, and prouyng that to be true he wryteth, he remayneth[lxvi] in the aforesayde great lodgyng as long as he lyueth: besides this they keepe in these places swyne and hennes, whereby the poore be releeued without goyng a beggyng.

"The kyng hath in many ryuers good store of barges full of sea crowes, that breede, are fedde, and do dye therein, in certayne cages, allowed monethly a certayne prouision of ryce. These barges the kyng bestoweth vpon his greatest magistrates, geuyng to some two, to some three of them, as he thynketh good, to fyshe therewithall after this maner. At the houre appoynted to fyshe, all the barges are brought togeather in a circle, where the riuer is shalowe, and the crowes, tyed togeather vnder the wynges, are let leape downe into the water, some vnder, some aboue, worth the lookyng vppon: eche one as he hath filled his bagge, goeth to his owne barge and emptieth it, which done, he retourneth to fyshe agayne. Thus hauyng taken good store of fyshe, they set the crowes at libertie, and do suffer them to fyshe for theyr owne pleasure. There were in that citie where I was, twentie barges at the least of these aforesayde crowes; I wente almost euery day to see them, yet coulde I neuer be thoroughly satisfied to see so straunge a kynde of fyshyng."

The Spaniards were long behind their neighbours the Portuguese in prosecuting the important task of eastern investigation. The Papal division of the world between the discoverers of the two nations by the boundary of a certain meridian, made them follow the line of exploration to the westward.[lxvii]

The Father Andres de Urdaneta, who, previous to entering himself as a monk of the order of the Augustins, had been a skilful navigator, persuaded Philip II to realize the conquest of the Philippines, where the voyages and the life of the celebrated Magellan were brought to a close. This prince consequently issued orders to the viceroy of Mexico, to send out an expedition under the command of a native of Mexico, named Miguel Lopez de Legaspi, and desired that Andres de Urdaneta should accompany him, together with four other Augustines, viz., Diego de Herrera, Martin de Herrada, Pedro de Gamboa, and Andres de Aguirre. The fleet arrived in 1565 at the island of Zebu. On the 1st of June the same year, the Father Andres de Urdaneta returned to Mexico. In 1566 Legaspi built the town of Zebu, and the Augustines established a monastery as a station for their missions among the natives. The Spaniards, pursuing their conquests, arrived in 1571 at the island of Luzon, the most northerly and the largest of this archipelago: Legaspi here founded the city of Manilla.

The work of conversion and civilization was scarcely begun, when the island was engaged in a quarrel by the attacks of the Malays of Borneo and Mindanao. These pirates, too cunning to venture on an open struggle, landed suddenly on the coast, slaughtered or extorted money from the missionaries, and carried away several of the natives, whom they afterwards sold as slaves. In 1574 a more serious aggression diverted attention from the attacks of these pirates:[lxviii] a Chinese corsair, who was called King Limahon, appeared before Manilla. For a long time he had resisted the squadrons of his emperor, but at last, vanquished by numbers and forced to flee, he entertained the project of conquering Luzon with seventy-two vessels, which carried two thousand soldiers, bold adventurers, besides the sailors and one thousand five hundred women. They effected a landing on the 29th of November 1574, just after Lopez de Legaspi had been appointed governor-general of the Philippines. The corsairs marched against the Spanish town, which they expected to surprise; but a little corps of advanced guard, under the orders of Captain Velasquez, having given the garrison time to rally, a general battle took place, and ended in the defeat of the Chinese. Limahon in vain essayed to renew the attack: repulsed afresh, he took refuge at the mouth of the river Lingayen, in Pangasinan, the northern province of Luzon.

At the time of his attack, he had been closely followed by a Chinese captain, charged to watch him, and who had a conference with the Spanish governor. The latter thought this a favourable occasion for introducing the Gospel into China. Having sent for Alfonso de Alvarado, provincial of the Augustins, a venerable and holy old man, one of those whom Charles V had sent to the discovery of New Guinea, he told him to select missionaries for the Celestial Empire. The provincial in his joy offered to go there himself, old as he was; but the governor would by no means consent to this proposal. The choice fell upon Martin de[lxix] Herrada, or Rada, a native of Pampeluna, in Navarre, who had already filled the office of provincial, and who burned with such desire to convert the Chinese, that after having studied their language, he had made a proposal to some merchants of that nation who had come to the Philippines, that they should carry him as a slave to their country, where by this means he hoped to introduce the knowledge of the Gospel. They chose also Friar Geronimo Marin, a native of Mexico, a man equally distinguished for his piety and learning, and in company with these two missionaries, who they hoped would be able to remain a considerable time in China and to spread the knowledge of the Gospel there, they sent two soldiers, who were to bring back news respecting the progress of the mission. Besides other presents, the governor gave the Chinese captain all the slaves of his nation which the Spaniards had taken from Limahon, who was at that time held under blockade, to take them back free to their country. The 5th of July 1575, the friars landed at Tansuso [Gan-hai], whence, on their way to visit the governor of Chincheo [Tsiuen-cheu] they passed through the town of Tangoa [Tong-gan] in China.[6] The mandarin of Chincheo, of whom the captain who conducted them held his commission, gave them a good reception; but as the ambassadors were sent by a[lxx] simple lieutenant of the king of Spain, and not direct from the monarch, he insisted that they should address him on their knees. This mandarin, after having entertained them at a banquet, sent them with a good escort to the Tutan or viceroy of the province. They then made a journey of thirty leagues, carried in palanquins. At Aucheo [Focheou, so pronounced in the Fokien dialect] they met with an honourable reception. Each of the monks received a present of six pieces of silk tissue, which they crossed upon their breast in the manner of a stole, and two bouquets of silver: the other members of the embassy also had presents. As to the alliance proposed between Spain and China, and the permission requested by the missionaries for the exercise of their apostolic ministry, the viceroy referred them to the emperor. While waiting the reply from Pekin, the monks bought many books in the Chinese language, and visited the pagodas. The principal contained one hundred and eleven idols, all carved in relief and gilded. Three in particular attracted their attention. The first was a body with three heads, which looked at one another: they believed they saw in it a vague symbol of the Trinity. The second was a woman who held a little infant in her arms; they called her the Virgin Mother and the Divine Infant. The third represented to them an apostle. The monks having been to examine the gates of the city, this demand awakened the suspicions of the viceroy, who would seldom permit them to go out after. Upon his desiring to see some piece of writing[lxxi] by their hand, they copied for him the Lord's Prayer and the Ten Commandments, putting the Chinese translation to the Spanish text; and the viceroy took great pleasure in reading them. He only retarded their departure till the arrival of the visitor of the province, who desired to see them. The curiosity of this functionary once satisfied, he gave them rich presents for the Spanish governor of the Philippines, saying that they might return when they brought Limahon dead or alive. They then left Aucheo to return to Chincheo, where they made no lengthened stay, the mandarin of this town attending them to the port of Tansuso. After fresh entertainments, the Chinese captain who had brought them, was charged with the task of reconducting them to Manilla, and they embarked on the 14th of September 1575. En route, they learned that Limahon, who had been blocked up by the Spaniards, had contrived to escape with part of his troops, and had gained the island of Formosa.

The flight of Limahon disconcerted the Chinese captain who brought back the missionaries, and who feared that he should be disgraced on this account when he returned to China. This captain, to whom they explained the principal points of the Christian faith, would have embraced it, had he not feared the punishment inflicted in his country on those who forsake the national religion. He said even that they would easily succeed in converting the Chinese, if they could first gain over the emperor, by means of an embassy sent to him by the King of Spain.[lxxii]

Herrada, thus prevented from preaching, had not been idle during his stay in China; he composed a vocabulary of the Chinese language, now apparently unknown, and drew up a succinct account of his voyage, respecting which we translate some very curious remarks by the Friar Geronimo de Ramon, in his Republicas del Mundo. He says that this treatise fell into his hands, but was taken away by some one, he could not tell by whom, and never returned to him; a circumstance which caused him much annoyance, because he wished to write the Republic of China; but it turned out, he says, the better for him, for he wrote in consequence to the Licenciate Juan de Rada, Alcalde of the Upper Court of Navarre and brother of Martin, who sent him a great number of interesting papers of his brother's. He then proceeds to speak of the high respectability and credibility of De Rada, on account of his rank and distinguished piety. An original letter by De Rada, however, giving a succinct account of his embassy is inserted by the Friar Gaspar de San Augustin, in his Conquistas de las Islas Philipinas, to which we refer the reader for full accounts of all the movements of those zealous preachers of the gospel in the Philippines and in China at that early period.

De Rada's treatise formed the basis of the narrative compiled by Mendoza, which is now republished. On his return from China, his ship being stranded on the island of Bolinao, he and his companions were stript of everything and left naked; but were saved by the providential arrival of a Spanish armament, which[lxxiii] conducted them safe to Manilla, where he died in 1577.

His narrative was transmitted to Philip II, in the year 1576, by the hands of his companion, the Friar Geronimo Marin, and the king consequently nominated three ambassadors; viz., Marin, the Father Juan Gonzalez de Mendoza (the compiler of the work now reprinted, a native of Toledo, and who had left the career of a soldier for the garb of a monk of the order of St. Augustine), and Father Francisco de Ortega: all these were Augustinians. They were dispatched to Mexico for the purpose of making suitable additions to the costly presents provided by the king; but the viceroy of Mexico, instead of favouring their immediate departure, threw so many obstacles in the way, that it was not till 1584 that the embassy was carried out, and it ultimately proved a complete failure.

Meanwhile the work of evangelization was not confined to the Augustinians. Some Franciscans of the province of St. Joseph, in Spain, were sent to their assistance, and among these Pedro de Alfaro, the narrative of whose adventures is given by Mendoza in the second book of the second part.

The place and date of his birth are not recorded. We know only that he arrived in Manilla from Spain on the 2nd July 1578, with fourteen brothers of his order, of which he was the superior, to assume the post of chief "costodio" of the province of St. Gregory in Luzon, and that he built a church in that city. On his arrival, he soon became acquainted with the mission of[lxxiv] Martin de Rada in China, and conceived an earnest desire to penetrate that almost inaccessible empire. He therefore solicited permission for that purpose from Francisco de Sande, Alcalde of the royal audience of Mexico, Governor of the Philippines; but the failure of the former mission, and the fear of compromising the newly opened relations between the countries, caused a refusal. Upon this the zealous missionary resolved upon embarking without permission. He took with him Juan Bautista de Pizaro, Augustin de Tordesilla, and Sebastiano de Becotia, all three Franciscans, three Spanish soldiers, four natives of the Philippines, and a young Chinese taken from Limahon, to serve as an interpreter.

Without any nautical experience, they trusted themselves to a little boat, and managed to pass, as if by miracle, through the fleet of vessels which guarded the coast, and entered the port of Canton. On being led before a judge and asked what they sought, and how they had found their way, they freely stated the facts, and announced that their wish was to teach the way to heaven to the inhabitants of China. A native Christian, however, who acted as interpreter, considering his and their safety rather than the truth, adroitly modified their statement, and declared that they were holy men like the bonzes, that they had had no idea of visiting China, but in sailing from the Philippines to the Hilocos they had suffered shipwreck and lost most of their crew. Their only resource had been this little bark, which had unexpectedly brought them into this unknown[lxxv] port. The mandarin who examined them enquired what they had in the vessel, and was told that they had no weapons or merchandize, but only their books and articles used in their worship. He was much interested with the sight of these when they were brought, but expressed surprise that they had been saved in such a storm. The ingenious interpreter replied, that they had been saved as the most valuable objects they possessed. The result of this examination was a formal permission to land. They were not, however, allowed to preach. For some time they suffered much from want, but were at length liberally supplied from the public funds with the necessaries of life. Misrepresentations meanwhile were made respecting them, which subjected them to a second lengthy examination, which resulted in their being sent to Fucheou by order of the viceroy of that city, in order that everything they possessed might be inspected. This journey enabled them to make the observations on the country recorded by Mendoza in the second volume. The viceroy asked them some questions and handed them over to his deputy, who treated them with much courtesy. After a stay of several days in Fucheou, the Timpintao or deputy sent them back to Canton, upon arriving at which place they were ordered to prepare to leave the kingdom. This command, in their then state of destitution, overwhelmed them with dismay, and they made strenuous efforts, but without success, to gain some assistance in these trying circumstances. Some of them received a licence to go to Macao, and others[lxxvi] to Luzon. Those who resolved upon returning to the Philippines proceeded to Tsiuencheu, where they embarked, and reached Luzon on the 2nd February 1580.

The various and repeated disasters, consequent upon the zealous efforts of these adventurous friars, may well explain the failure of the mission of which Mendoza was a member. As a compensation for his failure, however, he adopted a course which was calculated to be far more practically useful. He collected the accounts of the various Portuguese and Spanish priests, which have been already alluded to; viz., Gaspar da Cruz, Martin de Rada, Pedro de Alfaro, etc., and brought them together into one volume for publication. In this task he must have received valuable assistance from his colleague in the mission, Geronimo de Marin, who, in company with De Rada, had been an eye-witness of the most important facts detailed throughout the work. To these were added, as a sort of appendix, an "Itinerario del Nuevo Mundo", in which is inserted a comparatively short account of the adventures of another party of Franciscans in China, in the year 1581, at the head of whom was Father Martin Ignazio [de Loyola], a relation of the celebrated founder of the Jesuits. It is but a repetition of similar disasters to those already recounted, the whole party narrowly escaping with their lives.

The ill success of the Augustinians and Franciscans did not deter the well-known perseverance of the Jesuits, who, of all the monkish orders, have[lxxvii] undoubtedly done the most for the diffusion of Christianity; and although it is not our province here to relate the details of their progress, it appears but an interesting sequel to the discouragements we have related, to mention the final triumph of the eminent Matteo Ricci, in the year 1600, in gaining access to the emperor at Pekin, and being finally permitted to settle in that capital. Nor can we refrain in this place, and at this particular juncture of Chinese affairs, from presenting the reader with the following translated extract from a letter written by that distinguished man in 1584, together with some observations by its recipient, one Geronimo Roman, factor of the Philippines at Macao. The document referred to was first printed by M. Ternaux Compans, in his Archives des Voyages, ou collection d'anciennes relations inédites ou très-rares, and is, as he observes, especially curious for the suggestions it contains with reference to the conquest of China. It is as follows:—

"The power of China rests rather upon the great number of towns and the multitude of inhabitants, than upon the valour of the people. There are more than sixty millions of rated persons inscribed on the royal registers, exclusive of the public functionaries and those people who are too poor to pay taxes. All the neighbouring kingdoms pay tribute to the King of China, excepting Japan, which has freed itself recently; it is on this account that the Chinese are accustomed to consider their country as the centre of the world, and to despise all other nations. They are very much dreaded by all the kings in the vicinity,[lxxviii] because they can assemble, in a moment, so considerable a fleet, that it frightens them by the number of vessels; the Chinese, however, are but poor warriors, and the military is one of the four conditions which are considered mean among them. Nearly all the soldiers are malefactors, who have been condemned to perpetual slavery in the king's service; they are only fit to war with thieves. Thus, whenever two or three Japanese vessels happen to make a descent upon the coast, the crews penetrate into the interior, even seize upon the large towns, pillage and put everything to fire and sword, and no one dares to resist them. But, being badly led themselves, they always end by falling into some ambuscade, and very few of them return to Japan. It also happens sometimes that brigands intrench themselves upon a mountain, in the interior of the country, and all the force of the empire is insufficient to dislodge them. It is said, moreover, that the Tartars ravage the frontiers of the empire; in short, it appears to me the most difficult thing in the world to regard the Chinese as warriors. They have no more spirit than women, and are ready to kiss the feet of any one who shows his teeth at them. They spend two hours every morning in combing and plaiting their hair.

Running away is no dishonour with them; they do not know what an insult is; if they quarrel they abuse one another like women, seize each other by the hair, and when they are weary of scuffling become friends again as before, without wounds or bloodshed. Moreover it is only the soldiers who are[lxxix] armed; others are not permitted to have even a knife in their houses; in short, they are only formidable from their numbers. The walls of the towns are, at most, but fit to protect them from robbers; they are built without any geometrical knowledge, and have neither revers nor ditches....

"The above is [an extract from] Father Resi [Ricci]'s letter forwarded to me by Father Ruggiero; I think it necessary to add the following observations:—

"The King of China maintains a numerous fleet on this coast, although he is not at war with any one. In an island called Lintao, which is situated near this town [Macao], there is an arsenal, the director or haytao of which is continually occupied in superintending the building and equipment of vessels. The island furnishes timber, but every other necessary for them has to be imported from the continent. There are always more than two hundred and fifty armed vessels in this province of Canton, as far as Chincheo, where a separate jurisdiction begins, and the coasts of which are guarded by another fleet. The admiral has the title of Chunpin; it is a very high rank, although inferior to the tutan; he has a numerous guard and many drums and trumpets, which make a most agreeable music to the ears of the Chinese, but an insufferable din to ours.

"These vessels go out a little when it is fine weather, but hasten back at the least wind. They have some small iron guns, but none of bronze; their powder is bad, and never made use of but in firing[lxxx] salutes; their arquebuses are so badly made that the ball would not pierce an ordinary cuirass, especially as they do not know how to aim. Their arms are bamboo pikes, some pointed with iron, others hardened by fire; short and heavy scimitars, and cuirasses of iron or tin. Sometimes a hundred vessels are seen to surround a single corsair, those which are to windward throw out powdered lime to blind the enemy, and, as they are very numerous, it produces some effect. This is one of their principal warlike stratagems. The corsairs are generally Japanese or revolted Chinese.

"The soldiers of this country are a disgraceful set. The other day they had a quarrel with some other Chinese who were carrying provisions to market, and beat them; the latter went to complain to the governor of Macao, who caused forty soldiers to be arrested and beaten with bamboos. They came out afterwards crying like children. They are mean, spiritless, and badly armed knaves. There is nothing formidable in thousands of such soldiers. Besides what can the soldiers be in a country where their position is looked upon as dishonourable and occupied by slaves. Our Indians of the Philippines are ten times more courageous.

"With five thousand Spaniards, at the most, the conquest of this country might be made, or at least of the maritime provinces, which are the most important in all parts of the world. With half a dozen galleons, and as many galleys, one would be master of all the maritime provinces of China, as well as of[lxxxi] all that sea and the archipelago which extends from China to the Moluccas."

Mendoza's work was first published at Rome in 1585, in a small octavo form, under the following title:

"Historia de las cosas mas notables, ritos y costumbres del gran reyno de la China, sabidas assi por los libros de los mesmos Chinas, como por relacion de religiosos y otras personas que an estado en el dicho reyno. Hecha y ordenada por el mvy R. P. Maestro Fr. Joan Gonzalez de Mendoça de la orden de S. Agustin, y penitenciario appostolico a quien la Magestad Catholica embio con su real carta y otras cosas para el Rey de aquel reyno el año 1580. Al illustrissimo S. Fernando de Vega y Fonseca del consejo de su Magestad y su presidente en el Real de las Indias. Con vn Itinerario del nueuo Mundo. Con privilegio y licencia de su Sanctidad. En Roma, a costa de Bartholome Grassi, 1585, en la stampa de Vincentio Accolti."

This edition, of which there is a copy in the British Museum, having on its title-page the autograph of Sir Hans Sloane—is described by Brunet as "rare". The text comprises four hundred and forty pages: it is preceded by the Latin Privilege of Pope Sixtus V, dated June 13th; Mendoza's dedication to Fernando de Vega, dated Rome, June 17th; a note or post-script "al lector", in which Mendoza alludes to the recent receipt of letters from Father Andres de Aguirre, provincial of the Philippines, conveying the startling intelligence that the King of China and his subjects were ready and willing to embrace the Catholic[lxxxii] faith; this is followed by Mendoza's Preface to the reader, and two sonnets in Spanish, the first entitled: "Soneto de ... en la reduçion del Reyno de la China a la Iglesia Catholica." This interesting and important little volume is also remarkable as being the first European work in which Chinese characters were printed.

We learn from Brunet that two editions of the original Spanish were published the following year (1586), one at

Madrid, the other at Barcelona: it was again printed at Medina del Campo in 1595, and at Antwerp in 1596.

An Italian translation by Francesco Avanzo was published at Venice in 1586, 8vo.; at Rome and Genoa in the same year, 4to.; and again at Venice in 1587, in 12mo.; 1588 and 1590 in 8vo.

The English and French translations appeared in the same year, viz., 1588; the rare black-letter English version now reprinted, being made by Parke at the instance of Hakluyt himself, as we learn from the translator's dedication to the celebrated navigator Thomas "Candish" (Cavendish), which is dated on new-year's day, 1589.

The French translation, which was made by Luc de la Porte, was reprinted at Paris in 1589 and 1600; and with a slightly varied title at Geneva in 1606, at Lyon in 1606, and at Rouen in 1604.

A Latin version by Marcus Henning was published at Frankfort in 1589, 8vo.; and that by Joachimus Brulius appeared at Antwerp in 1655, 4to.

Adelung (Fortsetzung zu Jöchers Lexikon) states that[lxxxiii] a German version was published at Frankfort in 1589, 4to.

On his return, as a recompense for his services, Mendoza was made bishop of Lipari in 1593. In 1607 he went to America with the title of Vicar Apostolic, and in the same year was made bishop of Chiapa; and in 1608 was translated to the bishopric of Popayan. He was the author of several other works, historical and theological. The year of his death is not exactly known, but it was about the year 1620. Ossinger, in his Bibliotheca Augustiniana, describes him as a most eminent historian, a very eloquent orator, and a highly accomplished preacher.

THE HISTORIE OF THE GREAT AND MIGHTIE KINGDOME OF CHINA, AND THE SITUATION THEREOF:

Togither with the great riches, huge citties, politike gouernement, and rare inuentions in the same.

Translated out of Spanish by R. Parke.

TO THE RIGHT WORSHIPFULL AND FAMOUS GENTLEMAN, M. THOMAS CANDISH, ESQUIRE, INCREASE OF HONOR AND HAPPIE ATTEMPTES.

It is now aboue fiue and thirty yeares passed, right worshipfull, since that young, sacred, and prudent Prince, king Edward the sixt of happie memorie, went about the discouerie of Cathaia and China, partly of desire that the good young king had to enlarge the Christian faith, and partlie to find out some where in those regions ample vent of the cloth of England, for the mischiefs that grew about that time neerer home aswell by contempt of our commodities, as by the arrestes of his merchantes in the Empire, Flanders, France, and Spaine: forsseeing withall how beneficiall ample vent would rise to all degrees throughout his kingdome, and specially to the infinite number of the poore sort distressed by lacke of worke. And although by a voyage hereuppon taken in hande for this purpose by Sir Hugh Willobie and Richard Chauncellour, a discouerie of the bay of Saint Nicolas in Russia fell out, and a trade with the Muscouites, and after another trade for a time with the Persians by way of the Caspian sea ensued, yet the discouerie of the principall intended place followed not in his time, nor yet since, vntill you tooke your happie and renowmed voyage about the worlde in hande, although sundrie attemptes, at the great charges of diuers honorable and well disposed persons, and good worshipfull merchants and others haue beene made since the death of that good king, in seeking a passage thither both by the North-east, and by the Northwest. But since it is so (as wee[2] vnderstande) that your worshippe in your late voyage hath first of our nation in this age discouered the famous rich ilandes of the Lu Zones, or Philippinas, lying neare vnto the coast of China, and haue spent some time in taking good view of the same, hauing brought home three boyes borne in Manilla, the chiefe towne of the said Ilands, besides two other young fellowes of good capacitie, borne in the mightie Iland of Iapon, (which hereafter may serue as our interpretors in our first traficke thither), and that also your selfe haue sailed along the coast of China, not farre from the Continent, and haue taken some knowledge of the present state of the same, and in your course haue found out a notable ample vent of our clothes, especially our kersies, and are in preparing againe for the former voyage, as hee that would constantly perseuer in so good an enterprise: we are to thinke that the knowledge and first discouerie of the same, in respect of our nation, hath all this time beene by the Almightie to you onely reserued, to your immortall glorie, and to the manifest shew of his especiall fauour borne towards you, in that besides your high and rare attempt of sailing about the whole globe of the earth, in so short a time of two yeares and about two monethes, you have shewed your selfe to have that rare and especiall care for your countrie, by seeking out vent for our clothes, that ought vpon due consideration to moue many thousands of English subiects to pray for you, and to loue and honor your name and familie for euer. For as you haue opened by your attempt the gate to the spoile of the great and late mightie, vniuersall, and infested enimie of this realme, & of al countries that professe true religion: so haue you by your great care wrought a way to imploie the merchants of Englande in trade, to increase our Nauie, to benefite our Clothiers, and (your purpose falling out to your hoped effect) to releeue more of the poorer sort, then all the hospitals and almes houses can or may, that haue beene built in this realme, since the first inhabiting thereof.

And sir, if to this your late noble attempt, it might please you, by your incouragement, and by the help of your purse to adde[3] your present furtherance for the passage to be discouered by the northwest, (for proofe whereof there bee many infallible reasons, and diuerse great experiences to be yeelded) our course with our commodities to the rich Iland of Iapon, to the mightie empire of China, and to the Ilandes of the Philippinas, for the vent that you haue found out, should be by the halfe way shortened, and you should double and manyfolde treble the credite of your fourmer late enterprise, and make your fame to mount, and yourself to liue for euer in a much higher degree of glorie, then otherwise it might be, or that by any other mean you could possibly deuise: In which action so highly importing the generall state of this lande I haue perfect experience that many worshipfull and wealthie marchants of this citie and other places would most willingly ioyne their purses with yours: and to play the blabbe, I may tell you they attende nothing with greater desire and expectation, then that a motion hereof being made by some happie man, your selfe and they might friendly and seriously ioyne together for the full accomplishing of this so long intended discouerie: And to descende to some particulars, there is one speciall reason that giueth an edge vnto their desires, proceeding from the late worthie attemptes of that excellent and skilful pilot M. John Dauis, made for the search of the aforesaid northwest passage these three late yeares, hauing entred into the same foure hundred leagues further than was euer hitherto thoroughly knowen, and returned with an exact description thereof, to the reasonable contentment for the time, of the aduenturers, and chiefly of the worshipfull M. William Sanderson, whose contributions thereunto, although they haue beene verie great and extraordinarie, yet for the certaine hope or rather assurance that he conceiueth vpon the report of the Captaine himselfe and all the rest of any skill employed in these voyages, remayneth still constant, and is readie to disburse as yet to the freshe setting on foote of this enterprise entermitted by occasion of our late troubles, euen this yeare againe, for the finall perfection of so profitable and honorable a discouerie, a farre greater portion then in reason would[4] be required of any other man of his abilitie. And albeit, sir, that you haue taken in your late voyage, besides the knowledge of the way to China, the intelligence of the gouernement of the countrie and of the commodities of the territories and prouinces of the same, and that at the full, according to the time of your short abode in those partes, yet neuerthelesse for that of late more ample vnderstanding hath beene in more length of time, by woonderfull great endeuour taken by certaine learned Portingals and Spaniardes of great obseruation, and not long agoe published in the Spanish tongue, I haue for the increase of the knowledge of the subiectes of Englande, and specially for the illuminating of the mindes of those that are to take the voyage next in hande to Iapan, China, and the Philippinas, translated the same worke into English, and committed it to print, passing ouer Paulus Venetus, and sir John Mandeuill, because they wrote long agoe of those regions: which labour, to say trueth, I haue vndertaken at the earnest request and encouragement of my worshipfull friend Master Richard Hakluit late of Oxforde, a gentleman, besides his other manifolde learning and languages, of singular and deepe insight in all histories of discouerie and partes of cosmographie: who also for the zeale he beareth to the honour of his countrie and countrimen, brought the same first aboue two yeares since ouer into this court, and at this present hath in hande a most excellent and ample collection of the sundrie trauailes and nauigations of our owne nation, a matter long intended by him, and seruing to the like beneficiall and honorable purpose, which I hope will shortly come to light to the great contentation of the wiser sort.

In the meane season, hauing nowe at length finished according to my poore skill and leasure this my translation, I thought best to dedicate and commende the same to your worshipfull patronage, as the man that I holde most worthie of the same, and most able of our nation to iudge aright of the contentes thereof, and to correct the errors of the author whensoeuer you shall meete with them: beseeching you to accept in good part the trauaile and good meaning[5] of the translator: and so wishing vnto you health, increase of knowledge, with fortunate and glorious successe in your further couragious attempts, I leaue you to the protection of the Almightie.

    From London the first of Ianuarie 1589.

    Your worships alwaies to command,

        Robert Parke.

THE PRINTER, TO THE CHRISTIAN READER.

Whereas (good courteous Reader) in this historie describing the kingdome of[6] China with the countries there adiacent, thou shalt finde many times repeated, and that in some things too gloriously, the zeale of certaine Spanish Friers that laboured in discouerie of the saide China, and the declaration of certaine myracles (but falsely reported) by them to haue beene wrought, togither with examples of diuerse their superstitious practices: which happily may giue offence vnto some in reading: thou must vnderstande that this is to be rather imputed vnto the first writer of this historie in Spanish, than to any fault of mine: for the Spaniardes (following their ambitious affections) doo vsually in all their writinges extoll their owne actions, euen to the setting forth of many vntruthes and incredible things: as in their descriptions of the conquestes of the east and west Indies, etc., doth more at large appeare. Notwithstanding all which, our translator (as it seemeth) hath rather chosen to be esteemed fidus interpres, in truely translating the historie as it was, though conteyning some errors, then to be accounted a patcher or corrupter of other mens workes.

But howsoeuer either our first authour, or the translator, haue shewed themselues affectioned, sure I am that the knowledge of this kingdome will not onely be pleasant, but also verie profitable to our English nation: and by playing the good Bee, in onely accepting herein that which is good, I doubt not, but the reading of this historie will bring thee great contentment, and delight.

Vale.

THE HISTORIE OF THE MIGHTIE KINGDOME OF CHINA, IN THE WHICH IS CONTAINED THE NOTABLE THINGS OF THAT KINGDOME, TOUCHING THAT WHICH IS NATURALL.

CHAP. I.

The description of the kingdome and the confines that it hath belonging.

This great and mightie kingdome of China, which we do meane to treat of in this Historie, hath beene discouered by cleere and true notice, within this tenne yeares, by Spanyards that were dwellers in the Ilands Philippinas, that are three hundreth leagues distant from the said kingdome: Notwithstanding, that long time before, there was relation giuen, by way of the Portingall Indias, by such as dwelt in Macao, and did trafike to Canton, a citie of the same kingdome of China. But this was by relation so, that the one nor the other could satisfie, for that there was founde varietie in that which was true, till the yeere of 1577. Frier Martin de Gorrada,[7] prouincial of the Augustine friers, who were the first discouerers of the said Ilands Philippinas, and ministred first the holy baptisme amongst them, with his companions, frier Hieronimo Martin, Pedro Sarmiento, and Myghell de Loarcha, cheefe officers of the citie of Marrila[8] in the[8] said Ilands, by the order and commandement of Guido de Labassares, gouernour thereof, did enter into the saide kingdome of China, led and gouerned by a captaine belonging to the king of the said kingdome, called Omoncon.

Of the comming of this Omoncon vnto the Ilands Philippinas, and of his hardines to carrie the aforesaid vnto the firme land, he being commanded to the contrarie vpon paine of death, and how he was receiued, and great courtesie shewed, and of other things verie curious, you shall finde in the second part of this historie, where as is the substance and whole relation of all that was brought vnto the king of Spaine.

You shall vnderstande that this mightie kingdome is the Orientalest part of all Asia, and his next neighbour towards the Ponent is the kingdome of Quachinchina,[9] whereas they doo obserue in whole all the customes and rites of China. The greatest part of this kingdome is watred with the great Orientall Ocean sea, beginning at the Iland Aynan,[10] which is hard by Quachinchina, which is 19 degrees towards the North, and compassing towards the South, whereas their course is northeast. And beyond Quachinchina towards the North, the Bragmanes[11] do confine, which are much people, and verie rich, of golde, siluer, and pretious stones, but in especiall, rubies: for there are infinit. They are proude and hawtie men, of great corage, wel made, but of browne colour: they haue had (but few times) warre with them of China, in respect for that betwixt both the kingdomes, there are great and mightie mountaines and rockes that doth disturbe them. And harde vnto this nation ioyneth the Patanes[12] and[9] Mogores,[13] which is a great kingdome, and warlike people, whose head[14] is the Gran Samarzan:[15] They are the true Scythas or Massagetas, of whom it is affirmed that they were neuer ouercome by any other nation: they are a people well proportioned and white: by reason they dwel in a cold countrie. Betwixt the West and the South is the Trapobana, or Samatra, a kingdome very rich of gold, pretious stones, & pearles: and more towards the South, are the two Iauas, the great and the lesse, and the kingdome of the Lechios:[16] and in equall distance, are the Iapones: yet notwithstanding those that are more indifferent to this kingdome are the Tartarians, which are on the selfe firme land or continent, and are alonely diuided by a wal, as shal be declared in the 9 chapter of this booke. These Tartarians haue had many times wars with them of China: but at one time (as you shall perceive) they got the whole kingdome of China, and did possesse the same for the space of 93 yeares, till such time as they of China did rebell and forced them out again. At this day they say that they are friends one with another, and that is, for that they bee all Gentiles, and do vse all one manner of ceremonies and rites. They doo differ in their clenes[17] and lawes, in the which the Chinas doth exceede them very much. The Tartarians are very yellow and not so white: and they go naked from the girdlested vpwards, and they eate raw flesh, and do annoint themselues with the blood of raw flesh, for to make them more harder and currish, by reason whereof they doo so stinke, that if the aire doth come from that part where they be, you shall smel them afar off by the strong sauor. They haue for certainty, the truth of[10] the immortalitie of the soule (although it be with error), for they say that the soule doth enter into other bodies, and that soule that liued well in the first bodie, doth better it from poore to rich, or from age to youth: and if it liued evill, to the contrarie in worse. The sons of the Tartarians do very much obserue and keepe the commandement in obeying their parents, for that they doo wholly accomplish the same without failing any iot of their will, vnder paine to be seuerly and publikelie punished. They confess one God, whom they worship, and haue him in their houses carved or painted, and every day they doe offer vnto it incense, or some other sweet smelles: they do call him the high God, and do craue of him vnderstanding and health. They haue also another god, which they say is son vnto the other; they do call him Natigay: this is their god of terestriall things. They haue him likewise in their houses, and every time they go to eate they doo annoint his face with the fattest thing they haue to eate: that being doone they fall to eating, hauing first giuen their gods their pitance. They are a kinde of people that verie seldome doo fable a lie, although their liues should lie thereon, and are verie obedient vnto their king: but in speciall in their warres, in the which euerie one doth that he is appointed to doo: they are led by the sound of a drome or trumpet, with the which their captaines do gouerne them with great ease, by reason that they are trained vp in the same from their youth. And many other things are amongst them, in the which they do resemble them of China, (who) if they did receiue the faith of our Lord Jesu Christ, it is to be belieued that the Tartarians would do the same, for that they are taken for men very ducible, and do imitate verie much them of China.[11]

CHAP. II.

Of the temperature of the kingdome of China.

The temperature of this mightie kingdome is diuersly, by reason that almost the whole bignesse therof is from the south to the north, in so great a length that the iland of Aynan being neere vnto this land, in 19 degrees of altitude, have notice of some prouinces that are in more than 50 degrees, and yet they do vnderstand that beyond that there bee more vpon the confines of Tartaria. It is a strange thing to be seene, the strange and great difference betwixt the colours of the dwellers of this kingdome. In Canton, a mightie citie, whereas the Portingales had ordinarie trafficke with them of China, for that it was nigh vnto Macao, where as they had inhabited long since, and from whence they do bring all such merchandise as is brought into Europe. There is seene great diuersities in the colours of such people as doe come thither to trafficke, as the said Portingales do testifie.

Those which are borne in the citie of Canton, and in al that cost, are browne people, like vnto them in the citie of Fez or Barbarie, for that all the whole countrie is in the said paralel that Barberie is in. And they of the most prouinces inwards are white people, some more whiter than others, as they draw into the cold countrie. Some are like vnto Spanyards, and others more yealow, like vnto the Almans,[18] yelow and red colour.

Finally, in all this mightie kingdome, to speake generally, they cannot say that there is much cold or much heat, for that the geographers do conclude and say it is temperate, and is vnder a temperate clime, as is Italy or other temperate countries, wherby may be vnderstood the fertilitie of the same, which is (without doubt) the fertilest in all the world,[12] and may compare with the Peru and Nuoua Espannia, which are two kingdomes celebrated to be most fertill: and for the verification, you shall perceiue in this chapter next folowing, wherin is declared such things as it doth yeeld and bring forth, and in what quantitie. And yet aboue all things (according unto the sayings of fryer Herrada,[19] prouinciall, and his companions, whose relation I will follow in the most part of this hystorie, as witnesses of sight), vnto whom we may giue certaine credite, without any exception. They say that the countrie is so full of youth that it seemeth the women are deliuered euery moneth, and their children, when they are little, are extreame faire; and the country is so fertill and fat, that it yeldeth fruit three or four times in the yeere, which is the occasion that all things is so good cheape, that almost it seemeth they sell them for nothing.

CHAP. III.

Of the fertilitie of this kingdome, and of such fruits and other things as it doth yeld.

The inhabitants in this countrie are perswaded, of a truth, that those which did first finde and inhabite in this lande, were the nevewes of Noe (who, after they had traueiled from Armenia, wheras the arke stayed, wherin God did preserue their grandfather from the waters of the flood), went seeking a land to their contentment; and not finding a countrie of so great fertilitie and temperature like vnto this, wherein was all things necessarie for the life of man, without comparison: they were compelled, with the aboundance thereof, to inhabite therein, vnderstanding that if they should search throughout all the world, they should not finde the[13] like; and I thinke they were not deceiued, according as now it is to be seene, and what may be considered in the proces of this chapter, of such fruits as the earth doth yeeld. And although there is declared here of such as shall suffice in this worke, yet is there left behind a great number more; of whose properties, as well of herbes and beasts, which of their particulars may be made a great volume, and I doo beleeue that in time there will be one set forth.

The great trauell and continual laboure of the inhabitants of this countrie, is a great helpe vnto the goodnes and fertilitie therof, and is so much that they do neither spare nor leaue mountains nor vallies, neither riuers, but they do sow and plant all such things as they perceiue that the place wil yeeld, according unto the goodnesse thereof: as orchards with fruite, great fields of wheat, barlie, rice, flaxe and hempe, with many other things: all which traueile vnto them is verie easie, remembering with what great libertie they do inioy their goods, and the great and infinit number of people that there is, as well for handie craftes as for to till and cultiuate the grounde. In all this mightie countrie they do not suffer vacabunds nor idle people, but all such (ouer and aboue that they are greeuouslie punished), they are holden for infamous: neither doo they consent nor permit any of them that are naturally borne there to go out of their countries into other strange countries; neither haue they any wars at this present, which was the thing that in times past did consume much of their people. The king dooth content himselfe onely with his owne kingdome (as one that is helde the wisest in all the world). Beside all this, they are naturally inclined to eate and drinke wel, and to make much of themselves in apparel, and to haue their houses well furnished with household stuffe; and to the augmenting hereof, they do put themselues in great labor and trauaile, and are great dealers and trafickers: al which, with the fertilitie of the countrie aboue said, is the occasion that iustlie it might[14] haue the name to be the most fertilest in all the whole world.

This country doth yeeld all kind of herbs, as doth Spaine, and of many kindes mo: also all manner of fruites, like as in Spaine, with diuers other sorts, the names whereof are not yet knowne, for that they do differ very much from ours; but yet the one and the other are of a marueilous excellent tast, as they doo say. They haue three sorts of orenges, the one verie sweete, which doth exceede sugar in their sweetnesse: the other sort not so sweet as the first: the third sort are somewhat sower, but verie delightfull in the tast. Also they haue a kinde of plummesExcellent plummes., that they doo call lechias,[20] that are of an exceeding gallant tast, and neuer hurteth any body, although they shoulde eate a great number of them. It yeldeth great aboundance of great melons, and of an excellent sauour and tast, and verie bigge. Also a kinde of russet appels that be very great, of a good tast. I doo not heere declare of other fruites, nor of their names, because I will not seeme tedious vnto the reader, nor spende the time herein, but will treat of other things of more importance.

In all parts of this kingdome there is great store of sugarExcellent white sugar good cheape., which is the occasion that it is so good cheape: for you shall have a quintal of verie excellent white and good sugar, when it is most deerest, for the value of sixe ryals of plate. There is great abundance of honie, for that their delight is in hiues, by reason whereof not only honieHonie and wax., but waxe is very good cheape; and there is so great quantity therof, that you may lade ships, yea fleetes thereof. They do make great store of silkeExcellent good silke., and excellent good, and give it verie perfite colours, which dooth exceed very much the silke of Granada, and is one of the greatest trades that is in all that kingdome.

The veluets, damaskes, sattens, and other sortes of webs, which is there made, is of so small a price, that it is a wonder to speake it, in especiall unto them that doo know how their[15] prises be in Spaine and in Italie. They do sell none of their silkes there by the yard, neither any other kinde of websterie, though it be lynnen; but by the waight, wherein there is least deceit. They haue great store of flaxeGreat store of flaxe and hempe., wherwith the common people doo apparell themselues: also hempe for the cawlking of their ships, and to make ropes and hasers. And on their drie and tough landes, although they be stonie, they gather great stoore of cotton woollCotton, wool, wheat, and barlie, rie, oates.. They doo sowe wheate, barlie, rye, and oates, and manie other kindes of graine; and the one and the other doo yeelde great increase. In the marrish groundes (of which there be many), by reason of moyst and great aboundance of riuers that be in this countrie, they doo sowe riceGreat abundance of rice., which is a common victuall or maintiniment vnto all people of the kingdome, and vnto them that dwell neere them; and they doo gather so greate aboundance that when it is most dearest you shall haue a haneg[21] for a ryall of plate: of the which, and of all other graines aforesaid, the countrie was woont to yeeld them, and foure times in the yeere there increase.

On their high grounds, that are not good to be sowne, there is great store of pine trees, which yeelde fruite very sauorie: chestnutsChestnuts. greater, and of better tast, then commonly you shall finde in Spaine: and yet betwixt these trees they do sow maiz, which is the ordinarie foode of the Indians of Mexico and Peru, and great store of panizo,[22] so that they doe not leaue one foote of grounde vnsowen. And of trueth, almost in all the whole countrie, you shall not finde any ground that is barren or without profite, what by the naturall vertue of the country, and also by the manuring and helping of it.[16]

CHAP. IV.

Here I do proceed in the fertilitie of this kingdome, and of such things as it doth yeeld.

Besides the fertilitie of this countrie beforesaide, all the fields be verie faire to behold, and yeelde maruelous odoriferous smelles, by reason of the great quantitie of sweete flowers of diuers sorts. It is also garnished with the greene trees that be planted by the riuers sides and brookes, whereof there is great quantitie. And there is planted there orchards and gardens, with banketing houses of great pleasure, the which they doo vse verie much for their recreation and auoiding the troubles of minde. The Loytias, or gentlemen, doo vse to plant great forrests and thicke woods, whereas doo breed many wilde boores, bucks, hares, and conyes, and diuers other beastsAll kind of beasts.: of whose skins they make very excellent furresExcellent furres, muske., but in especiall of martas ceuellias,[23] of which there is a great number. There is great aboundance of muske, the which they do make of a little beast that doth feede of nothing else but of a roote which is of a maruellous smell, that is called camarus, as big as a man's finger. They do take them and beat them with blowes till they be brused all to peeces; then they do put them in a place whereas they may soonest putrifie; but first they do bind very fast such parts whereas the blood may run out of their brused bones, all to peces, remaining within them. Then after, when they thinke they be putrified, then they do cut out smal peeces, with skinne and all, and tie them vp like bals or cods, which the Portugals (who doth by them) do call papos: and this is the finest that is brought out of all Indies (if there be no deceit vsed in it), for many times they will put amongst it small peeces of lead, and other things of weight. There is also great store[17] of kyne, that are so little worth that you may buy a very good one for eight rials of plate; and beefesGreat store of beefes., that are bought for halfe the mony: one whole venison is bought for two rials; great store of hogs, whose flesh is as holsome and good as our mutton in Spaine. There is great aboundance of goatesDeere, hogs, and goates., and of other beasts that are to be eaten, which is the occasion that they are of little value. The flying foules that doo breed about the lakes and riuers are of so great quantitieGreat store of wildfoule. that there is spent daily, in small villages in that countrie, many thousands, and the greatest sort of them are teales. The fashion how they do breed and bring them vp shal be declared in a chapter particularly; for that which is said shal not seeme impossible. They be sold by waightFoule solde by waight., and likewise capons and hens, and for so smal value that two pounds of their flesh being plucked, is worth ordinarily two Foys, which is a kinde of mony like vnto the quartes[24] of Spaine; hogs flesh, two pounds for a Foy and a halfe, which is six marauadiz. Likewise all other victuals after the same rate, as it doth plainly appeare by the relation made by the friers.

There are also many herbs for medicines, as very fine reubarbeReubarbe and other medicinall hearbs., and of great quantitie, and wood called Palo de China; great store of nutmegs, with the which they may lade fleetes, and of so lowe a price that you may buy foure hundreth for a ryall of plate; and cloues, sixe pound for halfe a ryall of plate; and the Foure hundred of nutmegs for six-pence. Cloues, sixe pound for 3 pence; the like of pepper. like in pepper. Synamon, one rowe, which is 25 pound, for four ryals of plate, and better cheape. I do leaue to speake of many other hearbs medicinable and profitable for the vse of man: for that if I should write the particular vertue of euerie of them, it would require a great volume. Of fish, both swimming and shell fish of all sorts, that they haue with them is to be wondred at: not onely vpon the sea coasts, but also in the remote places of that kingdome, by reason of the great riuers, which be nauigable vnto such places. Besides all this it[18] is verie rich of mines of golde and siluer, and other mettals, the which (gold and siluer excepted) they do sell it so good cheape that a quintal of copper, Mines of gold and siluer and other mettals. Iron and Steele 4 shilling a quintal. Siluer is worth more than gold. Great store of pearles. yron, or steele is to be bought for eight rials of plate. Gold is better cheape there then it is in Europe, but siluer is more woorth. There is founde great store of pearles in all this kingdome: but the most part of them are not rounde, by the which you may gather and vnderstande the goodnesse and fertilitie of the same. And that the first that did discouer and inhabite that kingdome were not deceiued, for that they founde all things necessarie vnto the preseruing of the life of man, and that in aboundance: for the which, with iust reason, the inhabitants may thinke themselues to possesse the best and fertilest kingdome in all the whole world.

CHAP. V.

Of the antiquitie of this kingdome.

As before is said, this kingdome is of so ancient antiquity, that there is opinion that the first that did inhabite this countrie, were the neuewes of Noe. But the light which is found in the histories of China, is that from the time of Vitey, who was their first king, and did reduce their kingdome vnto an empire, and hath and doth indure vnto the king that now rayneth: as you shall vnderstand in the place where we shall make mention of the kings of that countrie, whereas you shal vnderstand by iust computations, that vnto this day, there hath rayned, naturall and vsurped, to the number of 243 kings243 kings.. The sonne doth succeede the father in the kingdome, and for want of a sonne, the next kinsman doth succeed: and for that they do take (after the vse of the emperors of Turkie) so many wiues as pleaseth them: it seldome falleth out to lacke heires, for that the first sonne that is borne of either of his wiues is right heire vnto the kingdome: and the rest of his sonnes he doth appoint them[19] cities where as they do dwel priuately: and there they are prouided of all things necessarie for them, conformable vnto their degrees, with expresse commission vpon paine of death neuer to go out of them, neither to returne vnto the court, except they be sent for by the king. So after this conclusion, all those that are kinsfolke vnto the king, are resident and kept in a mightie and populous citie, called Causi,[25] whereas those whome the king and his counsel do thinke and see to be men of great wisdome, or giuen to martiall affaires, they doo commande that they neuer goe forth of their houses, to auoide occasions of suspition whereby might grow alterations and treasons against the king. The dwelling places of these prouinces, are mightie and of a huge bignesse: for that within the compasse of them, they haue all manner of contentment necessary for them: as gardens, orchards, fishing ponds of diuers sorts, parkes and groues, in the which are all kinde flying foules, fish and beasts, as are to be found in the mountaines and riuers. And it is walled round about with a stone wall, so that euery house of these seemeth to be a towne. They giue themselues much vnto musike, wherewith they doo passe away the time. And for that they are giuen to pleasure and ease, they are commonly corpulent and fatte, verie faire conditioned and quiet, liberall vnto strangers. These princes, in what place soeuer they are, the gouernours of the cities are bound to visite them euery festiuall day. Likewise if they doo passe on horsebacke by their doores, they must alight and walke on foote while they haue passed it: and if they be borne in a litle chaire, likewise to come out of the same, and to walk on foote with silence, till they be past. And for that they shall not plead ignorance, the gates of these princes houses are all painted red: so that they being brought vp from their youth, in this straight, close, and idle life, it is not vnto them tedious, but dooth rather reioyce in the same.[20]

CHAP. VI.

The bignesse of this kingdome of China, and of such measures as they do vse in trauaile.

This mightie kingdome, which we commonly call China, without knowing any cause or foundation wherefore we should so cal it, those countries neere ioyning vnto the same, do call it Sangley: and they in their naturall toonge do cal it Taybiner,[26] the which is to be vnderstood, nothing but a kingdome: and is the most biggest and populous that is mentioned in all the world, as it shalbe apparant in the discourse of this hystorie, and in the wonderfull things that shalbe treated of in the next chapter following. All the which is taken out of the bookes and hystories of the said Chinos, whereas they do make mention of the mightinesse thereof, and of the 15 prouinces that are comprehended in the same: the which bookes and hystories were brought vnto the citie of Manilla, printed and set forth in China, and were translated into the Spanish toong, by interpreters of the saide nations. And for that they were baptised and became Christians, they remaine as dwellers amongst vs in these ilandes, the better to obserue and keepe the lawes of baptisme, and to flie the paine and punishment the which they should receiue for dooing the same: for that they turned Christians and receiued the faith without the license of the king and counsell, which is forbidden vppon paine of death, and is executed with great violence, and without remission. This mightie kingdome is in circuit or compasse about 69516 die,[27] which is a kind of measure that they do vse: which being reduced into the Spanish account, is almost[21] 3000 legues, and in length 1800 leagues, this is to be vnderstood the whole 15 prouinces: the which are garnished with many cities and townes, besides a great number of villages, as you may

The China is in compass 3000 leagues and 1800 leagues long.

plainely see in the chapter following. By the said booke, it is found that the Chinos haue amongst them but only three kind of measures: the which in their language are called lii, pu, and icham, which is as much as to say, or in effect, as a forlong, league, or iorney: the measure which is called lii, hath so much space as a mans voice in a plaine grounde may bee hearde in a quiet day, halowing or whoping with all the force and strength he may: and ten of these liis maketh a pu, which is a great Spanish league: and ten pus maketh a dayes iourney, which is called icham, which maketh 12 long leagues. By the which account it is founde that this kingdome hath the number of leagues as afore is saide: yet, by the account of other bookes, they do finde it bigger and of more leagues. Yet frier Martin de Herrada, prouinciall of the Austen friers in the Ilands Philippinas, who is an excellent geometrician and cosmographer, did cast the account with great diligence, by their owne descriptions, and doth finde it to amount vnto the sum aforesaid, to be 1800 leagues long and 3000 leagues in compasse, beginning at the prouince of Olam, which is that towards the south, and nearest vnto Malacia,[28] and so alongst the countrie towards the north east for the space of 600 leagues.

CHAP. VII.

Of the 15 prouinces that are in this kingdome.

This mightie kingdome is diuided into fifteene prouinces, that euery one of them is bigger then the greatest kingdome[22] that we doo vnderstand to be in all Europe. Some doo esteeme those cities to be metropolitans, where as is resident, the gouernors, presidents, or viz rées, which in their natural toong are called Cochin: of the prouinces, two of them, which are called Tolanchia and Paguia, are gouerned by the king in person with his royall counsel. The occasion why the king is alwayes resident or abiding in one of these two prouinces which are two of the mightiest and most popularst of people, is not for that in them he is most at his content, or receiue more pleasure in them then in any of the other: but onely for that they doo confine vpon the kingdome of Tartaria, with whom in times past they had ordinary and continuall wars: and for that the king might with more ease put remedie in such harmes receiued, and defend with better oportunitie the rage of his enimie, he did ordaine and situate his pallace and court in them two. And for that it hath beene of antiquitie many yeeres past, it hath remained hitherto, and appeareth to continue still the habitation of the kings of that kingdome, as by desert for the excellencie of the clime, and aboundance of all things necessarie.

The names of the fifteene prouinces are as followeth:—Paguia,[29] Foquiem,[30] Olam,[31] Sinsay,[32] Sisuam,[33] Tolanchia,[34] Cansay,[35] Oquiam,[36] Aucheo,[37] Honan,[38] Xanton,[39] Quicheu,[40] Chequeam,[41] Susuam,[42] and Saxij.[43] Almost all these prouinces,[23] but in particular tenne of them which are alongst the sea costs, are full of deepe riuers of sweete water and navigable, vpon whose branches are situated many cities and townes, whereof you may not onely haue the number of them, but also their names: for that these Chinos are so curious people, that in their books are named besides the cities and townes, the banketing houses and houses of pleasure, which the gentlemen haue for their recreation. And for that it will be more trouble than profite to inlarge any further in this matter, I will refer it vnto the next chapter, where I will intreate of the cities and townes that either of these prouinces hath, and pass ouer all the rest, as not necessarie; for our intent is to set forth the bignes of this kingdome.

CHAP. VIII.

Of the cities and townes that every one of these prouinces hath in himselfe.

These fifteene prouinces, which with better truth might be called kingdomes, according vnto the greatnes of them, as you may perceiue by the number of cities and townes that each of them hathe, besides villages, the which if I should adde herevnto, would be an infinite number.

The number of cities and townes that euery prouince hath. First, the prouince of Paguia, where as ordinarily the king and his counsel is resident, hath 47 cities and 150 townes.

Canton hath 37 cities and 190 townes.

Foquien hath 33 cities and 99 townes.

Olam hath 90 cities and 130 townes.

Synsay hath 38 cities and 124 townes.

Sisuan hath 44 cities and 150 townes.

Tolanchia hath 51 cities and 123 townes.

Cansay hath 24 cities and 112 townes.

Ochian hath 19 cities and 74 townes.

Ancheo hath 25 cities and 29 townes.

Honan hath 20 cities and 102 townes.
Xaton hath 37 cities and 78 townes.

Quicheu hath 45 cities and 113 townes.

Chequeam hath 39 cities and 95 townes.

Susuan hath 42 cities and 105 townes.

By which account appeareth to be 591 cities and 1593 townes, beside villages and houses of pleasure, which are an infinite number: by the which you may consider that this kingdome doth deserve to be called great, and compared with the best and principalst that is heard of in al the whole world. The Chinos do vse in their pronunciation to terme their cities with this sylable, Fu, that is as much as to say, citie, as Taybin fu, Canton fu, and their townes with this sylable, Cheu. They have some villages that are so great, that it lacketh but onely the name of a towne. All their cities for the most part are situated by the riuers sides: such as are nauigable, the cities are moted rounde about, which make them to bee verie strong, not only the cities but townes are walled round about with high and strong wals of stone, one faddome high, and all the rest is of bricke, but of so hard a substance that it is not to be broken almost with pickaxes. Some cities hath their wals so broad, that 4 and 6 men may walke side by side on them: they are garnished with many bulwarks and towers, a small distance the one from the other, with their battlements and faire galleries, where as many times their vizroyes doeth goe to recreate themselues with the gallant sight of the mountains and riuers, with their fields so odoriferous. There is betwixt the wals of their cities and the mote of the same a broade space, that six horsemen may ride together; the like space is within, betwixt the walles and the houses, whereas they may walke without impediment. Their wals are kept in such good reparation, by reason of their great care and diligence, that[25] they seeme to be but new made, and yet in some cities there is founde mention of two thousand yeeres since the first foundation. In every city the king doth ordaine a justice, and giveth him great rents onely to visit them, and make them to be renewed and repaired where as is requisite, and is done vpon the kings cost: for out of his rents in such cities and townes is given them all that is needful to be asked. The high waies in all this kingdome are made and kept plaine with great care and diligence, and the entering into the cities and townes are very sumptuous and with great maiestie, they have three or foure gates bound with yron very strong. Their streetes very well paved, and so broad that 15 horsemen may ride together in them, and so straight, that although they be very long, yet you may discouer the end. On both the sides are portals, vnder which be their shops full of all sorts of merchandises very curious, and of all occupations that you will desire: In the streets, a good space the one from the other, are made manie triumphall arkes of extreme bewtie: they are made of masons worke, very curiously painted after the fashion of the old antiquitie of Rome. All their houses ordinarily haue three doores, that in the middest is great, the other be lesser, but of a maruellous gallant proportion. The king is always resident in the citie of Suntien,[45] The mightie citie called Suntien, or Quinsay.[44] which in their language is as much to say, the citie of heauen. Of which citie the Chinos do declare many things which seemeth to be true, for that if you do talke with many of them, and at sundrie times and places, yet doo they not varie the one from the other: and according to their report, it should be the greatest in all the worlde, in these dayes. They who do make it to be least, do affirme, that to goe from gate to gate, leauing the suburbs, had need of a summers day and a good horse to do it: it is also called Quinsay, as Marcus Paulus doth call it.[26]

CHAP. IX.

Of the wonderfull buildings in this kingdome, and of mightie wall or circuit in the same of 500 leagues long.

In this kingdom in al places, there be men excellent in architecture: and the necessaries that they haue to build with is the best that is in the world. For as it is said in the chapter past, they haue a kinde of white earth of the which they make brickes, of so great hardnesse and strength, that for to breake them, you must haue pickaxes, and vse much strength: and this is the cause that in all the kingdome there is mightie buildings and verie curious. Putting apart the kings pallace where hee is resident in Tabin[46] (for of that you shall haue a particular chapter), in all such cities that bee the heads of the prouinces, is resident a vizroy or gouernour, and dwelleth in the house that (in euery such citie) the king hath ordained on his proper cost: all the which, to conclude, are superbious and admirable, and wrought by marueilous art, and are as bigge as a great village, by reason that they haue within them great gardens, water ponds and woods compassed about: in the which (as it is declared in the 4 chapter) is great quantitie of hunt and flying foules. Their houses commonly be verie gallant and after the manner of Rome, and generallie at the doores and gates of them are planted trees in gallant order: the which maketh a gallant shadow and seemeth well in the streets. All these houses are within as white as milke, in such sort that it seemeth to be burnished paper. The floares are paued with square stones, verie broad and smooth; their seelings are of an excellent kind of timber, verie well wrought and painted, that it seemeth like damaske and of[27] the colour of gold, that sheweth verie well: euerie one of them hath three courts and gardens full of flowers and herbes for their recreation. And there is none of them but hath his fish poole furnished, although it bee but small. The one side of their courts is wrought verie gallant, like as it is in counting houses, vpon the which they haue many idols carued, and wrought of diuers kinds of mettals: the other three parts or angles of their courts are painted with diuers things of verie great curiositie. But aboue all things they are marueilous cleane, not only in their houses, but also in their streets: in the which commonly they haue three or foure necessarie or common places of ease, verie curiously ordained and placed; for that the people, being troubled with their common necessitie, shall not foule the streetes, and therefore they haue this prouision: the like is vsed in all wayes throughout the kingdom. Some cities there be, whose streets be nauigable, as in Bruxels in Flanders, Mexico in the Indians, and as in Venice in Italie; which is the occasion that they are better serued and prouided, for that their barkes and boates doo enter laden with all kinde of victuals harde to their doores.

The highways throughout all this kingdome, are the best and gallantest paued that euer hath beene discouered: they are verie plaine, yea vnto the mountaines, and they are cut by force of labour and pickaxes, and maintained with brick and stone, the which by report of them which hath seen it, is one of the worthiest things that is in all the realme. There are many mightie bridges, and of a wonderfull making, and some wrought vpon boats, as it is in Syvill: but in especiall vpon such riuers as are broad and deepe. In the citie of Fucheo,[47] there is a towre right against the house of the kings chiefe receiuer, and it is affirmed by those that haue seene it, to surmount any building that hath beene[28] amoungst the Romans: the which is raised and founded vppon fortie pillars, and everie pillar is of one stone, so bigge and so high that it is strange to tell them, and doubtfull to the hearers to beleeue it: for which cause I thinke it best not to declare it in particular, as I do in all things where as I doo finde it difficult to be beleeued, and where I haue no certaine author to verifie the truth.

There is in this kingdome a defence or wall that is fiue hundred leaguesA wal of 500 leagues long. long, and beginneth at the citie Ochyoy,[48] which is vppon the high mountaines, and runneth from the west vnto east. The king of that countrie which made it was called Tzintzon, and it was for his defence against the Tartaries, with whom he had warres; so that the wall doth shut vp all the frontier of Tartaria. But you must vnderstande that foure hundred leagues of the saide wall is naturall of it selfe, for that they be high and mightie rockes, verie nigh together: but in the other hundred leagues is comprehended the spaces or distance that is betwixt the rockes, the which he caused to be made by mens handes of verie strong worke of stone, and is of seuen fathom brode at the foote of it, and seuen fathom high. It beginneth at the partes of the sea, in the prouince of Canton,[49] and stretcheth foorth by that of Paguia and Cansay, and doth finish in the prouince of Susuan.[50] This king, for to finish this wonderful[29] worke, did take of euerie three men one thorough his kingdome, and of fiue, two; who for that they trauailed in their labour so long a iourney, and into different clymes (although that out of those provinces that were nearest there came great store of people), yet did they almost all perish that followed that worke.

The making of this superbious and mightie worke, was the occasion that his whole kingdome did rise vp against the king, and did kill him, after that he had raigned fortie yeares, and also a sonne of his that was called Agnitzi. The report of this wall is helde to be of a verie truth, for that it is affirmed by all the Chinos that doo traficke to the Islands Philippinas and to Canton, and Machao, and be all confirmable in their declaration as witnesses, because they haue seene it: and it is the farthest parts of all the kingdome, whereas none of vs vnto this day hath beene.

CHAP. X.

Of the dispositions, countenance, with apparell and other exercises of the people of this countrie.

Both men and women of this countrie are of a good disposition of their bodies, well proportioned and gallant men, somewhat tall: they are all for the most part brode faced, little eyes and flat noses, and without bearde saue only upon the ball of the chinne: but yet there be some that haue great eyes and goodly beardes, and their faces well proportioned, yet of these sorts (in respect of the others) are verie few: and it is to bee beleeued that these kinde of people doo proceede of some strange nation, who in times past when it was lawfull to deale out of that countrie, did ioyne one with another.

Those of the prouince of Canton (which is a whot[51] country)[30] be browne of colour like to the Moores: but those that be farther within the countrie be like unto Almaines,[52] Italians and Spanyardes, white and redde, and somewhat swart. All of them do suffer their nailes of their left hande to grow very long, but the right hand they do cut: they haue long haire, and esteeme it very much and maintaine it with curiositie: of both they make a superstition, for that they say thereby they shall be carried into heauen. They do binde their haire up to the crowne of their heade, in calles of golde verie curious, and with pinnes of the same.

The garments which the nobles and principals do vse, bee of silke of different colours, of the which they haue excellent good and verie perfite: the common and poore people doo apparell themselues with another kinde of silke more courser, and with linnen, serge, and cotton: of all the which there is great abundance. And for that the countrie for the most part is temperate, they may suffer this kinde of apparell, which is the heauiest that they doo vse: for in all the whole kingdome they have no cloth, neither doo they suffer it to be made, although they have great aboundance of woolle, and very good cheape: they Great abundance of wool and good cheape.do vse their coates according vnto our old vse of antiquitie, with long skirts and full of plaites, and a flappe ouer the brest to be made fast under the left side, the sleeues verie bigge and wide: upon their coates they doo vse cassockes or long garments according vnto the possibilitie of either of them, made according as wee doo vse, but only their sleeues are more wider. They of royall bloode and such as are constituted vnto dignitie, do differ in their apparell from the other ordinarie gentlemen: for that the first haue their garments laide on with gold and siluer downe to the waste, and the others alonely garnished on the edges, or hem: they do vse hose verie well made and stitched, shoes and buskins of veluet, verie curious. In the[31] Shooes and buskines of veluet. winter (although it be not very colde,) they haue their garments furred with Great abundance of Marters furres. beasts skins, but in especiall with Martas Ceuellinas, of the which they haue great aboundance (as aforesaid) and generally they do vse them at all times about their necks. They that be not married doo differ from them that be married, in that they do kirrle their haire on their foreheade, and wear higher hattes. Their women do apparell themselues verie curiouslie, much after the fashion of Spaine: they vse many iewels of gold and precious stones: their gownes haue wide sleeues; that wherewith they do apparel themselues is of cloath of gold and siluer and diuers sortes of silkes, whereof they haue great plentie, as aforesaid, and excellent good, and good cheape: and the poore folkes doo apparell themselues with veluet, vnshorne veluet and serge. They haue verie faire haire, and doo combe it with great care and diligence, as do the women of Genouay, and do binde it about their heade with a broad silke lace, set full of pearles and precious stones, and they say it doth become them verie well: they doo vse to paint themselues, and in some place in excesse.

Amongst them they account it for gentilitie and a gallant thing to haue little feete, and therefore from their youth they so swadell and binde them verie straight, and do suffer it with patience: for that she who hath the least feete is accounted the gallantest dame. They say that the men hath induced them vnto this custome, for to binde their feete so harde, that almost they doo loose An il vse and custome. the forme of them, and remaine halfe lame, so that their going is verie ill, and with great trauell: which is the occasion that they goe but little abroad, and fewe times doo rise vp from their worke that they do; and was inuented onely for the same intent. This custome hath indured manie yeares, and will indure many more, for that it is stablished for a law: and that woman which doth breake it, and not vse it with her children, shalbe counted as euill, yea shalbe punished for the same. They[32] are very secreat and honest, in such sort that you shall not see at any time a woman at her window nor at her doores: and if her husband doo inuite any person to dinner, she is neuer seene nor eateth not at the table, except the gest be a kinsman or a very friende: when they go abroade to visite their father, mother, or any other kinsfolkes, they are carried in a little chaire by foure men, the which is made close, and with lattises rounde about made of golde wyre and with siluer, and curteines of silke; that although they doo see them that be in the streete, yet they cannot be seene. They haue many servants waiting on them. So that it is a great maruell when that you shall meete a principall woman in the streete, yea you will thinke that there are none in the citie, their keeping in is such: the lameness of their feet is a great helpe therevnto. The women as well as the men be ingenious;

they doo vse drawne workes and carued works, Ingenious people. excellent painters of flowers, birds and beasts, as it is to be seene vpon beddes and bords that is brought from thence. I did see my selfe, one that was brought vnto Lysborne in the yeare 1582, by Captaine Ribera, chiefe sergant of Manilla, that it was to be wondred at the excellencie thereof: it caused the kings maiestie to haue admyration, and he is a person that little wondreth at things. All the people did wonder at it: yea the famous imbroiderers did maruaile at the curiousnesse thereof. They are great inuenters of things, that although they haue amongst them many coches and wagons that goe with sailes, and Wagons with sailes. made with such industrie and policie that they do gouerne them with great ease: this is crediblie informed by many that haue seen it: besides that, there be many in the Indies, and in Portugall, that haue seene them painted vpon clothes, and on their earthen vessell that is brought from thence to be solde: so that it is a signe that their painting hath some foundation. In their buying and selling they are verie subtill, in such sort that they will depart a haire. Such merchants as do keepe[33] shoppes (of whom in euery citie there is a great number) they haue a table or signe hanging at their doore, whereon is written all such merchandise as is within to be sold.

That which is commonly sold in their shops is cloth of golde and siluer, Cloth of gold tissue and silke. cloth of tissue, silkes of diuers sorts and excellent colours: others there be of poorer sort that selleth serges, peeces of cotton, linnen and fustian of all colours; yet both the one and the other is verie goode cheape, for that there is great aboundance, and many workemen that do make it. The apothecarie that selleth simples, hath the like table: there be also shops full of earthen Porsilan. vessels of diuers making, redde, greene, yellow, and gilt; it is so good cheape that for foure rials of plate they giue fiftie peeces:

very strong earth, the which they doo breake all to peeces and grinde it, and put it into sesternes with water, made of lime and stone; and after that they haue well tumbled and tossed it in the water, of the creame that is vpon it they make the finest sort of them, and the lower they go, spending that substance that is the courser: they make them after the forme and fashion as they do here, and afterward they do gild them, and make them of what colour they please, the which will never be lost: then they put them into their killes and burne them. This hath beene seene and is of a truth, as appeareth in a booke set foorth in the Italian toonge, by Duardo Banbosa,[53] that they do make them of periwinkle shelles of the sea: the which they do grinde and put them under the ground to refine them, whereas they lie 100 years: and many other things he doth treat of to this[34] effect. But if that were true, they should not make so great a number of them as is made in that kingdome, and is brought into Portugall, and carried into the Peru, and Noua Espania,[54] and into other parts of the world: which is a sufficient proofe for that which is said. And the Chinos do agree for this to be true. The finest sort of this is neuer carried out of the countrie, for that it is spent in the seruice of the king, and his gouernours, and is so fine and deere, that it seemeth to be of fine and perfite cristal: that which is made in the prouince of Saxii[55] is the best and finest. Artificers and mechanicall officers doo dwell in streets appointed, whereas none do dwell amongst them, but such as be of the same occupation or arte: in such sort that if you doo come at the beginning of the All occupations be in streets by themselves. street, looke what craft or art they are there, it is to be vnderstood that all that streete are of that occupation. It is ordayned by a law and statute, that The son inherits his fathers occupation. the sonne shall inherite his fathers occupation, and shall not vse any other without licence of the justice: if one of them bee verie rich and will not worke, yet he cannot let but haue in his shop men that must worke of his occupation. Therefore they that do vse it, by reason that they are brought vp in it from their youth, they are famous and verie curious in that which they do worke, as it is plainelie seene in that which is brought from thence to Manilla, and into the Indies, and vnto Portugall. Their currant monie of that kingdome is made of golde and siluer, without any signe or print, but goeth by waight: so that all men carrieth a ballances with them, and little peeces of siluer and golde, for to buy such things as they haue neede of. And for[35] things of a greater quantitie they haue bigger ballances in their houses, and waights, that are sealed, for to giue to euery man that which is theirs: for therein the iustices haue great care. In the gouernement of Chincheo[56] they haue copper monie coyned, but it is nothing woorth out of that prouince.[36]

THE HISTORIE OF THE MIGHTIE KINGDOME OF CHINA, WHEREIN SHALBE DECLARED, OF THE RELIGION THAT IS AMONGST THE PEOPLE, AND OF THEIR IDOLS THAT THEY DO WORSHIP, AND OF OTHER THINGS TOUCHING THAT THEY DO VSE ABOUE NATURE.

THE SECOND BOOKE.

CHAP. I.

Of the number of gods that they doo worship, and of some tokens and paintings that is found amongst them that do represent a mysterie of our Christian religion.

In the two prouinces, Paguina an[d] Tolanchia, wheras we haue said, the king of the countrie is ordinarily resident, for that they do bound vpon Tartary, with whom they haue continuall warres: and againe the most principall and politike people be in those places, ouer and aboue all the other.

Amongst the figures of all their idols that they do haue, the Chinos doo say that there is one of a strange and maruellous making, vnto whom they do great *A strange* reuerence: they doo paint him a bodie with three *image.* heads, that doth continually looke the one on the other: and they say that it dooth signifie, that all three be of one good will and essence, and that which pleaseth the one pleaseth the other: and to the contrarie, that which is grieuous and displeaseth the one, is grieuous and displeaseth the other two: the which being[37] interpreted Christianly, may be vnderstoode to be the mysterie of the holy *A mysterie of* the Trinitie. Trinitie, that wee that are Christians doo worship, and is part of our faith: the which, with other things, seemeth somwhat to be respondent to our holy, sacred, and Christian religion: so that of verie truth we may presume that Saint S. Thomas preached in this kingdome. Thomas the Apostle[57] did preach in this kingdome, who as it is declared in the lesson on his day, The martyrdom of Saint Thomas. whereas he was martyred in the city of Calamina, for his faith and holy Gospel that he preached.

It is verified that when this glorious apostle did passe into the Indies, hee trauelled through this kingdome of China, where as it appeareth he did preach the holy Gospel and mysterie of the Holy Trinitie: whose picture in the manner aforesaid doth indure vnto this day, although those people, by the great and long blindnesse which they are in with their errors and idolatrie, doo not perfectly knowe what that figure with three heads doth represent or signifie. The better for to beleeue that which is said, or at least to vnderstande that it is so, is that it is found in the writings of the Armenians, that amongst them are in reputation and of great authoritie: and there it saith, that this glorious apostle did passe through this kingdome of China, when he went into the Indies, where he was martyred, and that he did preach there the holy Gospell, although it did profite verie little, for that the people were out of order, and occupied in their warres: and therefore this apostle did passe into the Indies, and left some of the countrie (although but a few) baptised and[38] instructed, that when it should please God, they might haue occasion to perseuer in that which was taught them.

They haue also amongst them (as it is said) certaine pictures, after the fashion and with the ensignes of the twelue apostles, which is a helpe to the verifying of that aforesaide: although if you doo aske of the people who they are, they doo answere that they were men, and great philosophers that did liue vertuouslie, and therfore they are made angels in heauen. They doo also vse amongst them the picture of a woman verie faire with a man childe in her armes, whereof they say shee was deliuered and yet remained a virgine, and was daughter vnto a mightie king: they do reuerence her verie much, and do make prayer vnto her: more then this, they cannot say of this mysterie, but that she liued a holy life and never sinned.

Frier Gaspar de la Cruz, a Portugall of the order of Saint Dominicke, was in the citie of Canton, where he did write many things of this kingdome,[58] and with great attention, whom I do follow in many things in the proces of this hystorie, and he saith, that he being vpon a small island that was in the middest of a mightie riuer, there was a house in manner of a monasterie of religious people of that country, and being in it, he saw certaine curious things of great antiquitie: amongst them he saw a chappel, like vnto an oratorie or place of prayer, verie well made, and curiouslie dressed: it had certaine staires to mount into it, and compassed about with gilt grates, and was made fast: and looking vpon the altar, the which was couered with a cloth verie rich, hee sawe in the midedst of the same an image of a woman of a meruailous perfection, with a childe hauing her armes about hir necke, and there was burning before her a[39] lampe: he being amased at this sight he did demande the signification: but there was none that could declare more thereof then that which is said before. Of this which hath been said, it is easily to be beleeued how that the Apostle S. Thomas did preach in this kingdom, for that it is seene these people haue conserued these traditions many yeares past, and doo conserue the same: which is a signe and token that they had some notice of the true God, whose shadows they do represent. There is amongst them many errors, and without any foundation, and is not of them to be seene nor perceiued til such time as by faith they shall knowe the right God: as may bee seene in the chapters, where we shall speake of these matters.

CHAP. II.

I do prosecute the religion they haue, and of the idols they do worship.

Ouer and aboue that which is saide, these idolators and blind people (being men so prudent and wise in the gouernment of their common wealth, and so subtill and ingenious in all arts) yet they do vse many other things of so great blindnes and so impertinent, that it doth make them to wonder, which attentiuelie doo fall in the consideration: yet is it not much to be meruailed at, considering that they are without the cleere light of the true Christian religion, without the which the subtilest and delicatest vnderstandings are lost and ouerthrowne. Generally amongst them they doo vnderstand that the heauen is the creator of all things visible and inuisible: and therefore they do make a shew of it in the first caract or letter of the crosse row, and that the heauen hath a gouernour to rule all such things as are comprehended[40] there aboue: whom they call Laocon Izautey,[59] which is to be vnderstood in their language: the gouernour of the great and mightie God, this they do worship as the principall, next vnto the sun. They say that this gouernour was not begotten, but is eternal, and hath no body, but is a spirit. Likewise they do say that with this there is another of the same nature, whom they call Causay,[60] and is likewise a spirit, and vnto this is giuen power of the lower heauen, in whose power dependeth the life and death of man. This Causay hath three subiectes whom he doth commande, and they say they bee likewise spirites, and they doo aide and helpe him in things touching his gouernment. They are called Tauquam, Teyquam, Tzuiquam, either of them hath distinct power the one ouer the other: they say that Tauquam hath charge ouer the raine, to prouoke water for the earth, and Teyquam ouer humane nature to bring forth mankinde, ouer warres, sowing the ground, and fruites. And Tzuiquam ouer the seas and all nauigators. They doo sacrifice vnto them, and doo craue of them such things as they haue vnder their charge and gouernment: for the which they do offer them victuals, sweate smels, frontals and[41] carpets for their altars: likewise they promise many vowes, and represent plaies and comedies before their idols, the which they do verie naturallie.

Besides this, they haue for saints such men as haue surmounted other in wisdome, in valour, in industrie, or in leading a solitarie or asper life: or such as haue liued without doing euill to any. And in their language they cal them Pausaos, which be such as we do call holy men.

They likewise doo sacrifice vnto the diuell, not as though they were ignorant that he is euill, or condemned, but that he shoulde doo them no harme, neither on their bodies nor goods. They haue manie strange gods, of so great a number, that alonely for to name them is requisite a large hystorie, and not to be briefe as is pretended in this booke. And therefore I will make mention but of their principals, whom (besides those which I haue named) they haue in great reuerence.

The first of these they doo call Sichia, who came from the kingdome of Trautheyco,[61] which is towards the west: this was the first inuenter of such religious people, as they haue in their countrie both men and women, and generally doth liue without marrying, in perpetuall closenesse; and all such as doo immitate this profession do weare no haire, which number is great, as hereafter you shall vnderstand: and they greatly obserue that order left vnto them.

The next is called Quanina, and was daughter vnto the king Tzonton, who had three daughters; two of them were married, and the third, which was Quanina, hee woulde also haue married, but she would neuer consent thereunto: saying that she had made a vow to heauen to liue chast, whereat the king her father was verie wroth, and put her into a place like vnto a monastrie, whereas she was made to[42] carrie wood and water, and to worke and make cleane an orcharde that was there. The Chinos do tell many tales of this maide, for to be laughed at: saying, that the apes came from the mountaines for to help her, and how that saints did bring her water, and the birds of the aire with their bylles did make cleane her orchard, and that the great beastes came out of the mountaines and brought her woode. Her father perceiuing that, imagining that she did it by witchcraft, or by some art of the diuell (as it might well bee), commanded to set fire on that house whereas she was: then she seeing that for her cause that house was set on fire, she would haue destroyed her selfe with a siluer pinne, which she had to trim vp her haire: but vpon a sodanne at that instant there fel a great shower of raine and did put out the fire, and shee departed from thence and hid her selfe in the mountaines, whereas she liued in great penance and led a holy life. And her father, in recompense of the great sinne and evill he committed against her, was turned to a lepar, and full of wormes, in such sort that there was no phisition that could cure him: by reason whereof hee was constrained to repaire vnto his daughter to seeke cure (which being aduised of the same by reuelation of a deuine spirit); then her father, being certified thereof, did craue pardon at her handes, and did repent him verie much of that which he had done, and did worshippe vnto her, the which she seeing, resisted her father therein, and put a saint before him, that he should worship it and not her, and therewith shee straight waies returned vnto the mountaines, whereas she died in great religion. This they haue amongest them for a great saint, and doe pray vnto her to get pardon for their sinnes of the heaven, for that they do beleeve that she is there.

Besides this, they haue another saint which they call Neoma, and was borne in a towne called Cuchi, in the prouince of Ochiam. This they saye was daughter vnto a principall man of that towne, and would neuer marrie, but[43] left her owne naturall soyle and went vnto a little iland, which is right ouer against Ingoa, whereas she liued a verie straight life, and shewed manie false miracles. The occasion why they haue her in reputation of a saint is: There was a certaine captaine of the king of China, whose name was Compo; he was sent vnto a kingdome not farre from thence to make warre against the king. It so chaunced that he, with his nauie, came to an anker at Buym, and being readie to departe, hee would haue wayed his ankers, but by no meanes he could not mooue them: being greatly amazed thereat, and looking foorth, he sawe this Neoma sitting on them. Then the captaine came vnto her, and told her with great humilitie, that he was going to warres by commandement of the king. And that if so be she were holie, that she would giue him counsell what were best for him to do: to whom she answered and sayd, that if he would haue the victorie ouer them that hee went to conquer, that he should carrie her with him. He did performe that which she said, and carried her with him vnto that kingdome, whose inhabitantes were great magicians, and threw oyle into the sea, and made it seeme that their shippes were all on fire. This Neoma did worke by the same art, and did vndoe that which the other did practise or imagine, in such sort, that their magicke did profitte them nothing, neither could they doe anie harme vnto them of China. The which being perceiued by them of ye kingdome, they did yeeld themselues to be subjectes and vassales vnto the king of China. The captaine beleeued this to be a myracle, yet notwithstanding he did coniure her (as one of good discretion), for that thinges might fall out to the contrarie; and the better to certifie his opinion, whereby hee might the better giue relation thereof vnto the king, he said: Ladie, turne me this rodde the which I haue in my hand drie, to become greene and florishing, and if you can so do, I will worship you for a saint. Then she at that instant did not onely make it greene,[44] but also to haue an odoriferous smell. The which rod he put vpon the poope of his ship for a remembrance, and for that he had a verie prosperous and good viage, he did attribute it vnto her. So that vnto this day, they haue her in reputation of a saint, and carrie her picture vppon the poope of their ships, and such as be trauellers to the sea doo offer vnto her sacrifices.

These aforesaide they doo esteeme for their principall saints, yet besides all these they haue an infinite number of carued idols, which they doo place vpon alters in their tempels: the quantity of them is such that in my presence it was affirmed by frier Geronimo Martin, he that entred into China, and is a man of great credite woorthy to giue credite vnto, that amongst many other things, he was in one of their temples in the cittie of Vcheo, where as hee did count one hundred and twelue idols: and besides this they haue manie in the high wayes and streetes, and vppon their principall gates of the citie, the which they haue in small veneration, as you shall perceiue in this chapter following: whereby it is plainlie to be seene, in what subiection they are vnto errours and idolatrie, such as doo lacke the trueth of true Christian religion.

CHAP. III.

How little they doo esteeme their idols whome they worshippe.

These miserable idolaters doo so little esteeme their idols, that it is a great hope and confidence, that at what time soeuer the gospel shal haue any entry into that country, straightwayes they will leaue off all their superstitions: in particular in casting of lots, which is a thing much vsed throughout all that kingdome: also this will be a great helpe thereunto, for that they are generally men of good vnderstanding, and ducible and subiect vnto reason, in so[45] ample sort (as is declared by that religious Dominicke aforesaid), he being in Canton in a temple whereas they were sacrificing vnto their idols, being mooued with great zeale to the honour of God, did throw certaine of them downe to the grounde. When these idolaters did see his boldnesse, which seemed vnto them to be without reason, they laide hands on him with an infernall furie, with determination for to kill him: then he did request of them that before they did execute it, that they would heare what he would say: the which his petition seemed vnto the principals that were there to bee iust, and commanded all the people to withdrawe themselues, and to heare what he woulde say. Then he, with the spirit that God did put in him, said, that they should aduertise themselues, for that God our Lorde and creator of heauen and earth, had giuen vnto them so good vnderstandings, and did equall them vnto the politikest nations in all the world: that they should not imploy it vnto euil, neither subiect themselues to worship vnto stones and blocks of wood, which haue no discourse of reason, more then is giuen them by the workmen that did make them, and it were more reason the idols should reuerence and worship men, because they haue their similitude and likenesse: with these words, and other such like in effect, they were all quieted, and did not only approoue his saying to be true, but did giue him great thankes, excusing themselues: saying, that vntill that time there was none that euer did giue them to vnderstand so much, neither how they did euill in doing their sacrifices, and in token of gratefulnes (leauing their idols on the ground, and some broken all to pieces) they did beare him company vnto his lodging. Hereby you may vnderstand with what facilitie, by the helpe of almightie God, they may be reduced vnto our Catholicke faith: opening (by the light of the gospel) the doore which the diuell hath kept shut by false delusions so long time, although the king, with all his gouernors and[46] ministers, hath great care that in all that kingdome there be none to induce nouelties, neither to admit strangers or any new doctrin without license of the said king, and of his roial counsel, vpon pain of death, the which is executed with great rigor. They are people very ducible and apt to bee taught, and easie to bee turned from their idolatrie, superstition, and false gods: the which they haue in smal veneratiō as aforesaid. With great humility they do receiue and approue corrections of their weaknes, and do know the vauntage that is betwixt the gospell and their rights and vanities, and do receiue the same with a verie good will, as it hath beene and is seene in manie Chinos that haue receiued baptisme in the citie of Manila, vpon one of the Ilands Philippinas, whereas they do dwell, and leaue their owne naturall countrie for to enioy that which they vnderstande to bee for the saluation of their soules. So that those who haue receiued baptisme are become verie good Christians.

CHAP. IV.

Of lots which they doo vse when they will doe anie thing of importance, and howe they doe inuocate or call the diuell.

The people of this countrie do not alonely vse superstitions, but they are also great augurisers or tellers of fortunes, and do beleeue in auguries, as a thing most certaine and infallible, but in especiall by certaine lots which they They cast lottes. do vse at all times, when they beginne any jorney, or for to doe anything of importance, as to marie a sonne, a daughter, or lend anie money, or buy any lands, or deale wt merchandise, or any other thing whose end is incertaine or doubtfull. In all these matters they do vse lottes, the which they do make of two sticks, flat on the one side, and[47] round on the other, and being tyed togither with a small threede, throwe them before their idols. But before they do throwe them, they do vse great ceremonies in talke, and vse amorous and gentle wordes, desiring them to giue them good fortune. For by them they doe vnderstand the successe to be good or euill in their iourney, or any other thing that they do take in hande. Likewise they do promise them, if they do giue them good fortune, to offer vnto them victuales, frontalles, or some other thing of price. This being done, they throwe downe their lots, and if it so fall out that the flat side be vpper, or one flat side and the other round, they haue it for an euill signe or token. Then they returne vnto their idols, and say vnto them manie iniurious words, calling them dogs, infamous, villaines, and other names like in effect. After they haue vttered vnto them all iniuries at their pleasure, then they beginne againe to fawne vpon them, and intreat them with milde and sweet words, crauing pardon of that which is past, and promising to giue them more gifts then before they did, if their lot do fal out wel. Then, in the like manner as before, they do proceed, and throw the lots before the idols: but if it fal not out according vnto their expectation, then they returne againe with vituperous and vile words: but if to their desire, then with great praises and promises. But when that in matters of great importance, it is long before their lots do fall well, then they take them They throw their gods under their feet. and throwe them to the grounde, and treade vppon them, or else throwe them into the sea, or into the fire, whereas they let them burne a while: and sometimes they doo whippe them vntill such time as the lottes doo fall as they would haue them, which is the rounde side vpwards, and is a token of good successe vnto that for which they do cast their lottes. Then if the lottes doo fall out vnto their content, they doo make vnto them great feastes with musicke and songes of great praise, and doo offer vnto them geese, duckes, and boyled rise. But if the[48] thing whereon they doo cast their lottes bee of importance, then they doo offer A hogs head for a sacrifice. vnto them a hogges heade boyled, dressed with hearbes and flowers, the which is esteemed aboue all other thinges, and therewith a great pot with wine. Of all that they doo offer, they doo cut off their billes, and the clawes of the fowles, and the hogges snowte, and do throw vpon it graines of rise, and sprinkling it with wine, they set it in dishes vpon the altar, and there they do eate and drinke, making great feast and cheere before their idols.

Another kind of lots. Another kinde of lots they doo vse, in putting a great number of little stickes into a pot, and vpon everie one of them is written a letter: and after that they haue tumbled and tossed them together in the pot, they cause a child to put in his hand and take out one, and when they haue seene the letter, they seeke in a booke which they haue for that purpose the leafe that beginneth with that letter, and looke what they doo finde written therein, they do interpret of it conformable vnto the thing that they cast their lots for.[62]

Generally in all this country when they finde themselues in any trouble, they Inuocation to the diuell. do inuocate and call vpon the diuell, with whom they do ordinarily talke (euen as we do cal vpon God in our neede): of him they doo demande what way and order they might take to cleere themselues thereof, as they did in the presence of frier Pedro de Alfaro, of the order of Saint Francis, in the yeare of our Lorde 1580, at such[49] time as he came from China, as may be seene in his relation. The order that they haue in inuocating or calling on the diuell, is as followeth. They cause a man to lie vpon the ground, his face downwards, then another beginneth to reade vpon a booke singing, and part of them that are present do answere vnto him, the rest do make a sound with little bels and tabers; then within a little while after, the man that lieth on the ground beginneth to make visages and iestures, which is a certaine token that the diuell is entered within him: then do they aske of him what they doo desire to know; then he that is possessed doth answere, yet The diuell telleth lies. for the most part they bee lies that hee doth speake; although hee doo keepe it close, yet doth hee giue diuers reasons vnto that which hee dooth answere, for that alwayes they doo answere either by worde or by letters, which is the remedie they have when that the diuell will not answere by worde. And when that he doth answere by letters, then do they spread a redde mantle or couerlet vpon the ground, and throw thereon a certaine quantitie of rice dispersed equally in euery place vpon the couerlet; then do they cause a man that cannot write to stand there with a sticke in his hand; then those that are present do begin to sing and to make a sounde as at the first inuocation, and within a little while the diuell doth enter into him that hath the sticke, and causeth him to write vpon the rice, then do they translate the letters that are there formed with the sticke, and being ioyned altogether, they finde answere of that they do demaunde; although for the most part it falleth out as aforesaide, as vnto people that do communicate with the father of all lying, and so do their answeares fall out false and full of leasings. If that at any time he do tell them the truth, it is not for that he dooth it by nature or with his will, but to induce them vnder the colour of a truth to perseuir in their errors, and they do giue credite vnto a thousand lies: in this sort doo they inuocate the diuell, and it is so ordinarie a thing throughout al the kingdome, that there is nothing more vsed nor knowne.[50]

CHAP. V.

Of the opinion they haue of the beginning of the worlde, and of the creation of man.

Although the Chinos be generally verie ingenious, and of a cleere vnderstanding, yet in their owne respect they say that all other nations in the worlde be blinde, except the Spaniards, whom they have knowne but of late time; they haue amongst them both naturall and morall philosophie, the which is read publikely amongst them, and also astrologie.

But nowe touching the beginning of the worlde, and the creation of man: they have many errors, wherof some of them shalbe declared in this chapter, taken out of their owne books, and specially out of one that is intituled the beginning of the world.

Strange opinions. They say that at the beginning, the heaven, the earth, and the water were a masse or lumpe ioyned in one. And that there is one resident in heaven, whom they call by name Tayn, hee by his great science did separate heaven and earth the one from the other, so that the heaven remained hie in the state that it is, and the earth following his naturall inclination, as grave and heauie, did remaine whereas it is. They say that this Tayn did create a man of nothing, who they call Panzon,[63] and likewise a woman, who they call Pansona. This Panzon, by the power that was given him by Tayn, did create of nothing another man, who they call Tanhom,[64] with thirteen other brothers. This Tanhom was a man of great science, in so ample sort, that hee did give name vnto all created things, and did know by the assignement and doctrine of Tayne the vertue of them all, and to apply them[51] to heale all manner of diseases and sicknesses: this Tanhom and his

brethren, but especially the eldest, who was called
Teyencom,[65] he had twelve; his first begotten, called
Tuhuncom, had nine, so had al the rest very many. They do
believe that the linage and generation of these did indure
for more than ninty thousand yeeres, and in the end and
conclusion of them did end all humaine nature; for that it
was the will of Tayn, who did first create the man and
woman of nothing, for to be reuenged on certaine iniuries
that they did vnto him, and for euery one that he had
shewed vnto them, they did almost knowe so much as
himselfe, and would not acknowledge any superioritie, as
they did promise him, at such time as hee did give vnto him
the secreat of all his science. At that time did the heauen
fall downe, then did Tayn raise it vp againe, and created
another man vpon the earth named Lotzitzam;[66]
Marvellous varieties. hee had two hornes, out of the which
proceeded a verie sweete sauour, the which sweet smell did
bring forth both men and women. This Lotzitzam vanished
away, and left behind him in the world manie men and
women, of whom did proceede all nations that now are in
it. The first that this Lotzitzam brought foorth was called
Alazan, and lived nine hundred yeares; then did the heauen
create another man called Atzion, whose mother, called
Lutin, was with childe with him, onely in seeing a lyons
head in the aire: he was borne in Truchin in the province of
Santon, and liued eight hundred yeares. At this time was
the worlde replenished with much people, and did feede on
nothing but on wilde hearbs and raw things: then was there
borne into the worlde one called Vsao, who gave them
industrie to make and do many things, as to vse the trees to
make defence to save them from wilde beasts, which did
them much harme, and to kill them, and make garments of
their skinnes. After him came one called Huntzui, who did
inuent the vse of The first invention of fire. fire, and
instructed them what they should doo, and how to rost[52]
and boyle their victuals, and how to barter and sell one

thing for another. They did understande one another in their contradictions by knots made vpon cords, for that they had not the vse of letters nor any mention thereof. After that, they say that a certain woman, called Hautzibon, was deliuered of a son named Ocheutey,[67] who was the inuentor of many things and ordained mariage, and to play on many Strange opinions. and diuers instruments. They do affirme that he came from heauen by myracle for to doo good vpon the earth: for that his mother going by the way did see the print of a mans foote, and putting her foote on it, she was straight wayes invironed with a lightning, with whom she was conceiued, and with child with this son. This Ocheutey had a son called Ezoulom,[68] who was the inuentor of phisicke and astrology, but, in especiall, matters touching lawe and iudgement. Hee showed them how to till the lande, and inuented The invention of plough and spade. the plough and spade; of this man they do tell manie wonderfull and maruellous things, but amongst them all, they say that he did eate of seuen seuerall kindes of hearbes that were poyson, Sic. orig. and did him no harme; he liued 400 hundred yeares; his son was called Vitey, the first they had amongst them; hee reduced all The first king of China. things to be vnder gouernement, and to haue it by succession, as shalbe declared in the chapter whereas I will treate of the king of this mightie kingdome that now liueth. These and many other varieties and toyes they saie of the beginning of the world, whereby may be vnderstood how little men may do without the fauour of God, and the light of the catholike faith, yea, though they be of the most subtilest and finest wit that may be imagined.[53]

CHAP. VI.

How they hold for a certaintie that the soule is immortall, and that he shal haue another life, in the which it shalbe punished or rewarded according vnto the workes which he doth in this world; and how they pray for the dead.

By that aforesaid it appeareth to be of a truth that the apostle S. Thomas did preach in China, and we may presume that all which wee haue seene dooth remaine printed in their hearts from his doctrine, and beareth a similitude of the truth and a conformity with the things of our catholike religion. Now touching this that wee will treate of in this chapter, of the immortalitie that they believe of the soule, and of the rewarde or punishment which they shall have in the other life, according vnto the workes doone in company with the bodie, which appeareth to be the occasion that they do not live so euill as they might, not hauing the knowledge of this truth.

I do hope by the power of his diuine maiestie that they wil easily be brought vnto the true knowledge of the gospel. They say and do affirme it of a truth, that the soule had his first beginning from the heauen, and shall neuer haue The soul is immortal. ende, for that the heauen hath given it an eternall essence. And for the time that it is within the body that God hath ordained, if it do liue according to such lawes as they have, without doing euill or deceit vnto his neighbor, then it shalbe caried vnto heaven, wheras it shal liue eternally with great ioy, and shalbe made an angel: and to the contrarie, if it liue ill, shall go with the diuels into darke dungeons and prisons, whereas they shall suffer with them torments which neuer shall haue end. They doo confesse that there is a place whither such soules as shalbe made angels doo go to make themselues cleane of al such euil as did cleaue vnto them, being in the bodie: and for that it should be speedelier doone, the good[54] deeds which are done by their parents and friends doo helpe them verie much. So that it is very much vsed throughout al the kingdome to make orations and praiers for the dead,[69] for the which they have a day appointed in the moneth of August. They do not make their offrings in their temples, but in their houses, the which they doo in Strange obsequies. this manner following. The day appointed, all such as do beare them companie vntill their sacrifices are concluded for the dead, which are such as we do cal here religious men, euery one hath his companion and walketh the streets, and dooth report the daies and houses where they will be, for that it cannot be doone altogether. So when they come vnto the house whereas they must doo their offices, they enter in, and do prepare that euery one do make oration and sacrifice according to their fashion for the dead of that house, vnderstanding that by their helpe they shalbe made cleane from their euils, which is an impediment that they cannot be angels nor inioy the benefite which is ordained for them in heauen. One of these that is like vnto a priest, dooth bring with him a taber, and other two little bords, and another a little bell. Then they do make an altar, wheron they do set such idols as the dead had for their saints liuing; then do they perfume them with frankensence and storax and other sweet smels: then do they put fiue or six tables ful of victuals for the dead and for the saints: then straightwayes, at the sound of the taber, little bords, and bels (which is a thing more apt for to dance by, as by report of them that have heard it), they begin to sing certaine songs which they haue for that purpose: then do the nouices goe vp vnto the altar, and do offer in written paper those orations which they did sing to the sound of[55] those instruments. This being done, they sit down and begin anew to sing as before. In the end of their prayers and songs, he who doth this office, doth sing a prayer, and in the end thereof (with a litle borde that he hath in his hand for the purpose) he striketh a blow vpon the table, then the other do answere in the same tune, declining their heades, and doe take certaine painted papers, and guilt papers, and doe burne them before the altar. In this sort they are all the night, which is the time that ordinarily they do make their sacrifices, the which being done, the priests and those that be in the house, do eat the victuals that was set vpon the tables, wherein they doo spend the residue of the night till it be day. They say that in doing this they do purifie and make cleane the soules, that they may goe and become angels. The common people do beleeue of truth that the soule that liueth not well, before they go into hell (which shall not be before the end of the world, according as they do thinke in their error), in recompence of their euill life, the heauens doo put them into the bodies of buffes and other beasts; and those which liue well, into the bodies of kings and lords, whereas they are very much made of and well serued. These and a thousande toies in like sort, making that the soul dooth mooue out of one into another, as certaine old philosophers did affirme it to bee, who were as blind and as far from the truth as they.

They make their sacrifices in the night.

Great superstition.

CHAP. VII.

Of their temples, and of certaine manner of religious people, both men and women, and of their superiors.

There are found in this kingdome many moral things, the which do touch verie much our religion, which giueth vs to[56] vnderstand that they are people of great vnderstanding, in especiall in naturall things, and that it should be of a certainty, that the holy apostle of whom we have spoken, did leaue amongst them by his preachings occasion for to learne manie things that do shew vnto vertue; one of the which is, that there is found amongst them many monasteries in their cities and townes, and also in the fieldes, wherein are manie men and women that do liue in great closenes and obedience, after the fashion of other religious monasteries. They haue amongst them (that is knowne) onely foure orders, euery one of them hath their generall, who dwelleth ordinarily in the citie of Suntien, or Taybin, whereas is the king and his counsell. These their generals they doo call in their language tricon, who doo prouide for euery prouince a prouinciall, to assist and visite all the conuents, correcting and amending such faults as is found, according vnto the institution and manner of liuing. This prouinciall doth ordaine in euery conuent one, which is like vnto the prior or guardian, whom al the rest do reuerence and obey. This generall is for euer till he doo die, except they doo finde in him such faults that he doth deserue to be depriued; yet they do not elect their prouincials as we do vse, but it is doone by the king and his counsell, always choosing him that is knowne to be of a good life and fame, so that fauour carrieth nothing away. This generall is apparelled all in silke, in that colour that his profession dooth vse, either black, yeallow, Gallant colours for religious men. white, or russet, which are the fower colours that the foure orders doo vse: hee neuer goeth foorth of his house, but is carried in a little chaire of iuorie or golde, by foure or sixe men of his habite. When any of the conuent doth talke vnto him, it is on their knees; they haue also amongst them a seale of their monasterie, for the dispatching of such businesse as toucheth their religion. These haue great rentes giuen them by the king for the sustayning of themselues and their suruants. All their conuents hath great rentes in general; part[57] giuen them by the king, and part of charitie, giuen them in those cities or townes whereas they haue their houses, the which are many and verie huge. They doo aske their charitie in the streets, singing with the sounde of two little bords, and other instruments. Every one of them when they do begge, doth carrie in their hands a thing, wherein are written certaine praiers, that they say is for the sins of the people; and all that is giuen them in charitie they lay it vpon the said thing, wherewith they do vnderstand (in their blind opinion) that their spirit is cleare of all sinne. In general their beards and heads are shauen, and they weare one sole vesture, without making any difference, according vnto the colour of their religion. They do eate altogether, and haue their sels according to the vse of our friers, their vestures or apparel is ordinary of serge of the said foure colours. They haue beads to pray on, as the papists vse, although in another order; they doe assist al burials for to haue charity; they do arise two houres before day to pray, as our papists[70] do their mattins, and do continue in the same vntill the day doo breake: they doo praie all in one voice, singing in verie good order and attention, and all Gallant bels. the time of their praying they do ring belles, whereof they haue in that kingdome the best and of the gallantest sounde that is in all the world, by reason that they are made almost all of steele; they pray vnto the heauen, whom they take for their god, and vnto Sinquian, who they say was the inuenter of that their manner of life, and became a saint.

They may leaue their order at all times at their pleasure, giuing their generall to vnderstand thereof.

But in the time that they are in that order they cannot marrye, neither deale with anye woman, vpon paine to bee punished asperly.[71] At such time as one doth put himselfe in religion, the father or next kinsman of him that taketh[58] the order, doth inuite all them of the conuent, and doth make them a great and solemne banket; yet you must vnderstand that the oldest sonne of any man cannot The eldest sonne is prohibited to take orders. put himself in any monasterie, but is prohibited by the lawes of the countrie, for that the eldest sonne is bound to sustaine his father in his old age. When that any of these religious men do die, they doo wash him, and shaue him, before they do burie him, and do all weare mourning apparell for him. The religious man or woman that is once punished for any fault, cannot afterward turne and receiue the habite at any time. They haue a certaine marke giuen vnto them in token of their fault, and that is a borde put about their necke, so that it is seene of all people. Euerie morning and euening they do offer vnto their idolles frankensence, benjamin, wood of aguila,[72] and cayolaque,[73] the which is maruelous sweete, and other gummes of sweet and odoriferous smels. When that they will lanch any ship into the water after that it is made, then these religious men, all apparelled with rich roabes of silke, do go to make sacrifices vpon the poopes of them, wheras they haue their oratories, and there they doo offer painted papers of diuers figures, the which they doo cut in peeces before their idols, with certaine ceremonies and songes well consorted, and ringing of little belles, they do reuerence vnto the diuell. And they do paint him in the fore castle, for that he shall do no harme vnto the shipps: that being done, they do eate and drinke[59] till they can no more. And with this they thinke it is sufficient for the shippe, that all such viages as shee shall make shall succeede well, the which they haue amongst them for a thing most certaine: and if they did not blesse them in this order, all things would fall out to the contrarie.

CHAP. VIII.

The order that they haue in burying of the dead, and the mourning apparell they haue.

A strange kind of buriall. It seemeth vnto me not farre from our purpose, to declare in this place, how they vse in this kingdome to burie the dead, and it is surely a thing to be noted: the manner is as foloweth. When that any one doth die, at the very instant yt he yeeldeth vp ye gost, they do wash his bodie all ouer from top to toe, then do they apparell him with the best apparell that he had, all perfumed with sweet smels. Then after he is apparelled, they do set him in ye best chaier that he hath; then commeth vnto him his father and mother, brethren and sisters and children, who kneeling before him, they do take their leaue of him, shedding of many teares, and making of great moane, euery one of them by themselues. Then after them in order commeth all his kinsfolkes and friends; and last of all his servants (if he had any), who in like case do as the other before. This being done, they do put him into a coffin or chest, made of verie sweete wood (in that countrie you haue verie much); they do make it very close, to avoid the euil smel. Then do they put him on a table with two bankes, in a chamber verie gallantly dressed and hanged with the best clothes that can be gotten, couering him with a white sheete hanging downe to the ground, whereon is painted the dead man or woman, as[60] naturall as possible may be. But first in the chamber whereas the dead bodie is, or at the entrie, they set a table with candles on it, and full of bread and fruits of diuers sorts. And in this order they keepe him aboue ground 15 dayes, in ye which time euery night commeth thether their priests and religious men, whereas they sing praiers and offer sacrifices, with other ceremonies: they bring with them many painted papers, and do burne them in the presence of the dead bodie, with a thousand superstitions and witch-craftes: and they do hang vpon cordes (which they haue for the same purpose) of the same papers before him, and many times do shake them and make a great noyse, with the which they say it doth send the soule straight vnto heauen.

In the end of the 15 daies, all which time the tables are continually furnished with victuals and wine, which the priests, their kinsfolkes and friends, that do come to visite them, do eat. These ceremonies being ended, they take the coffin with the dead bodie, and carrie him into the fields, accompanied with all his kinsfolks and friends, and with their priests and religious men, carrying candles in their hands, wheras ordinarily they do burie them on a mountaine, in sepulchres, that for the same purpose in their life time they caused to be made of stone and masons worke: that being doone, straight waies hard by ye sepulture, they do plant a pine tree, in ye which place there be many of them, and they be neuer cut downe except they be ouerthrowne with the weather, and after they be fallen they let them lie till they consume of themselues, for that they be sanctified. The people yt do beare him company to the graue, do go in uery good order like a procession, and haue with them many instruments, which neuer leaue playing till such time as the dead is put into the sepulcher. And that burial which hath most priests and musicke is most sumptuous, wherin they were woont to spend great riches. They sing to the sound of the instruments many orations vnto[61] their idols, and in the end they do burne vpon the sepulcher many papers, whereon is painted slaues, horse, gold, siluer, silkes, and many other things, the which they say, that the dead body doth possesse in the other world whether he goeth to dwell. At such time as they do put him into the grave, they doo make great bankets and sports with great pastime, saying of a truth, that looke what soeuer they doo at that time, the angels and saints that are in heauen doe the like vnto the souls of the dead that is there buried. Their parents, familiars, and servants, in all this time doo weare mourning apparell, the which is verie asper,[74] for that their apparell is made of a verie course wolle, and weare it next vnto their skins, and girt vnto them with cords, and on their heads bunnets of the same cloth, with verges brode like vnto a hat hanging downe to their eyes; for father or mother they do weare it a hole yeare, and some two yeares, and if his son be a gouernor (with licence of the king), he doth withdraw himself many times, leauing the office he hath, the which they esteeme a great point of honor, and have it in great account, and such as are not so much in aliance do apparell them in died linnen certaine monethes. Likewise their parents and friendes, although these doo weare it but for the time of the buriall.

CHAP. IX.

Of their ceremonies that they vse in the celebrating the Marriages.

The people of this kingdome haue a particular care to giue state vnto their children in time, before that they be ouercome or drowned in vices or lasciuious liuing. The which care is the occasion, that in this countrie, being so[62] great, there is lesse vice vsed than in any other smaller countries: whose ouer much care doth cause them many times to procure to marrie their children being verie yoong: yea, and to make consort before they bee borne, with signes and tokens, making their writings and bandes for the performance of the same in publike order. In all this kingdome—yea, and in the Ilands Philippinas—it is a customable vse, that the husband doth giue dowrie vnto the wife with whom he doth marrie; and at such time as they doe ioyne in matrimonie, the father of the bride doth make a great feast in his owne house, and doth inuite to the same the father and mother, kinsfolkes and friends, of his sonne in lawe. And the next day following, the father of the bridegroome, or his next parent, doth the like vnto the kinsfolkes of the bride. These bankets being finished, the husbande doth giue vnto his wife her dowrie in the presence of them all, and she doth giue it vnto her father or mother (if she haue them) for the paines they tooke in the bringing her vp. Whereby it is to be vnderstoode, that in this kingdome, and in those that doe confine on it, those that haue most daughters They that haue most daughters are most richest. are most richest; so that with the dowries their daughters do giue them, they may well sustaine themselues in their necessitie; and when they die, they doo giue it that daughter that did giue it them, that it may remaine for their children, or otherwise vse it at their willes. A man may marrie with so manie They may marrie with many wiues.

wiues as he can sustaine, so it be not with his sister or brothers daughter; and if any doo marrie in these two degrees, they are punished very rigorously. Of all their wiues, the first is their legitimate wife, and all the rest are accompted but as lemanes or concubines. These married men doo liue and keepe house with his first wife, and the rest he doth put in other houses; or if he be a merchant, then he doth repart them in such villages or townes whereas hee doth deale in, who are vnto him as seruantes in respect of the first. When the father doth die, the eldest sonne, by[63] his first wife, doth inherite the most part of all his goods, and the rest is reparted in equall partes amongest the other children, both of his first wife and of all the other wiues. For lacke of a sonne by his first wife, the first borne of the other wiues doth inherite the most part: so that few times, or neuer, there is none that dieth without heyres, eyther by his first wife, or by the others. And if it so fall out that any of these his wiues do commit adulterie (the which seeldome chaunceth, by reason of their keeping in, and great honestie, as also it is great infamie vnto the man that doth offer any Honest women. such thing), then may the husband, finding them togither, kill them: but after that first furie being past, he cannot but complaine of the adulterers vnto the Justic, and although it be proued verie apparent, yet can they giue them no more punishment but beate them cruelly vpon their thyghes, as is the custome and lawe of the countrie, as shalbe declared vnto you in his place. Then may the husband afterwardes sell his wife for a slave, and make money of her for the dowrie he gaue her. Notwithstanding, there be amongst them that for interest will dissemble the matter—yea, and will seeke opportunities and occasion. Yet if such be spied or knowen, they are righteously punished. They say in the prouinces that bee neere vnto Tartaria, and in the selfe same Tartaria they doo vse a custome and manner of marriage very strange, that is: the vizroys or gouernors doo limit and appoint a time when that all men and women shall meete together, such as will marrie, or receive the order of religion.

A strange kind of marriage. The time being accomplished, all such as would be married, do meete together in a citie of that prouince appointed for that purpose; and when they come thither, they doo present themselues before 12 auncient and principall men, appointed there by the king for the same purpose, who doo take a note of their names, both of men and women, and of what state and degree they are, and of their substance for[64] to dowrie their wiues with whom they shalbe married. Then do they number all the men and women that be there, and if they do find more men than women, or, to the contrarie, more women than men, then they cast lots, and do leaue the number that doth so beare in register til the next yeare; yt they may be the first that shalbe married. Then sixe of those ancient men do put the men in three parts; the rich they put in one part, without any consideration of gentilitie or beautie, and those that are rich in a meane in an other parte, and the poor in the thirde part. In the meane time that these sixe men be occupied in the reparting of the men, the other sixe doe repart the women in three parts—to say in this manner, the most fairest in one part, and them not so faire in an other, and the fowlest in an other. This diuision being made, then do they marrie them in this order: vnto the riche men they doo giue the fairest, and they doo giue for them the prise that is appointed by the judges, and vnto them that are not so rich they do giue them that are not so faire, without paying for them anye thing at all; and vnto the poore men they giue the fowlest, with all that which the rich men do pay for the faire women, diuiding it into equall partes. Sure it is a notable thing if it bee true. This being done, they are all married in one daie, and holpen (although peraduenture not all content), the marriages being doone, there is greate feastes made, in such houses as the king hath ordeyned in euerye citie for the same purpose, the which are furnished with beds, and all other necessaries belonging thereunto, for that the new married people may be serued of all that is needful for the time that the feast do indure. This solemnitie beeing finished, which they saye doth indure fiftie dayes, these newe married people doo goe vnto their owne houses. You must vnderstande that this custome of marriage is ordeyned for the common and poore people, and not for lords nor gentlemen, who are not bound to obey this ordinaunce, but to marrie whereas they like best, euerie one[65] to seeke and marrie with his equall, or else by an order which the king hath set downe vnto the viceroys and gouernors, what to be done therein.

When that the King of China is married, then dooth he choose thirtie concubines, the principallest persons in all his kingdome, the which hee dooth keepe and maintayne within his pallace so long as hee doth liue. But after that hee is dead, and his funerall ended, as is accustomed, then doth the heire or successor of the kingdome apparell these thirtie women maruelous gorgeously, with many iewelles; then doth hee cause them to set in an estrado, or rich pallet, gallantly dressed and furnished, in one of the three halles (as shall be declared in the second chapter of the third booke), with their faces couered, in such sort as they may not be seene nor knowen; and being set in this order, then doth there enter in thirtie gentlemen of the principallest of the kingdome, (those whom the king left named in his testament), the which goeth by antiquitie, or according vnto order set by the king; and eyther of them doth take one of these ladies by the hand, and looke howe they found them, so they doo carrie them with their faces covered till they bring them home to their houses, whereas they haue them for their wiues, and do maintaine and keepe them all the dayes of their liues. Towards the mainteyning of them, the king doth leaue in his testament great reueneues, and the successor in the kingdome doth accomplish and performe the same with great diligence and care.

In old time, when that the kinges of China would marrie one of his children or kingsfolkes, he did make in his pallace a great and solemne banket, to the which he did inuite all the principallest lordes and gentlemen of his court, commaunding to bring with them their sonnes and daughters, who did accomplish the same, striuing who should apparell their children most richest and most gallantest. The banket being done, the young princes do go whereas are these[66] young ladies, euerie one placed in order according to their age, and there he doth chuse his wife according to his owne will or desire, and where he liketh best. But at this time, this custome is left off, for that the princes and gentlemen do marry with their kinsfolkes, so that it be not in the first or seconde degree: yet many times they do not keepe the second.

CHAP. X.

How that in all this mightie kingdome there is no poore folks walking in the streets nor in the temples a begging, and the order that the king hath giuen for the maintayning of them that cannot worke.

Manie things of great gouernment hath beene and shall be declared in this historie worthy to be considered: and in my opinion, this is not the least that is contained in this chapter, which is such order as the king and his counsell A good order to avoid idle people. hath giuen, that the poore may not go a begging in the streetes, nor in the temples whereas they make orations vnto their idols: for the auoiding therof the king hath set downe an order, vpon great and greeuous penaltie to be executed vpon the saide poore, if they do begge or craue in the streetes, and a greater penaltie vpon the citizens or townes men, if they do giue vnto any such that beggeth; but must incontinent go and complaine on them to the justice, who is one that is called the justice of the poore, ordayned to punish such as doo breake the lawe, and is one of the principallest of the citie or towne, and hath no other charge but only this. And for that the townes be great and many, and so full of people, and an infinite nomber of villages, whereas it cannot be chosen but there is many borne lame, and other misfortunes, so that he is not idle, but alwaies occupied in giuing order to remedie the necessities of the poore without I would the like were with vs. breaking of the lawe. This iudge, the first day that hee doth enter into his office, hee commandeth that whatsoeuer children be borne a creeple in any part of his[67] members, or by sicknes be taken lame, or by any other misfortune, that incontinent their fathers or mothers doo giue the iudge to vnderstande thereof, that he may prouide for all things necessarie, according vnto the ordinance and will of the king and his counsell; the which is, the man child or woman child, being brought before him, and seene the default or lacke that it hath, if it be so that with the same it may exercise any occupation, they giue and limit a time vnto the parents, for to teach the child that occupation ordayned by the iudge, and it is such as with their lamenes they may vse without any impediment, the which is accomplished without faile; but if it so be, that his lameness is such that it is impossible to learne or exercise any occupation, this iudge of the poore doth command the father to sustaine and maintaine him in his owne house all the dayes of his life, if that hee hath wherewithall; if not, or that hee is fatherlesse, then the next rich kinsman must maintaine it; if he hath none such, then doth all his parents and kinsfolkes contribute and pay their partes, or giue of such thinges as they haue in their houses. But if it hath no parentes, or they be so poore that they cannot contribute nor supply any part therof; then doth the king maintaine them in verie ample manner of his owne costes in hospitalles, verie sumptuous, that he hath in euerie citie throughout his kingdome for the same effect and purpose: in the same hospitalles are likewise maintayned all such needie and olde men as haue spent all their youth in the A very good order. wars, and are not able to maintaine themselues: so that to the one and the other is ministered all that is needefull and necessarie, and that with great diligence and care: and for the better accomplishing of the same, the iudge doth put verie good order, and dooth appoint one of the principallest of the citie or towne, to be the administrator, without whose licence, there is not one within that hospitall that can goe foorth of the limittes: for that license is not granted vnto anie, neyther doo they demand it, for that there they are prouided of all thinges[68] necessarie so long as they doo liue, as well for apparell as for victualles. Besides all this, the olde folkes and poore men within the hospitall, doo bring vpp hennes, chickens, and hogges for their owne recreation and profit, wherein they doo delight themselves. The iudge doth visite often times the administrator by him appointed. Likewise the iudge is visited by an other that commeth from the court, by the appointment of the king and the counsell to the same effect: and to visite all such hospitalles as bee in the prouinces limited in his commission, and if they doo finde any that hath not executed his office in right A mirror for vs to look vpon. and iustice, then they doo displace them, and punish them verie rigorouslie: by reason whereof all such officers haue great care of their charges and liue vprightly, hauing before their eyes the straight account which they must giue, and the cruell rewarde if to the contrarie.

The blinde folkes in this countrie are not accounted in the number of those that of necessitie are to bee maintayned by their kinsfolkes, or by the king; for they are constrayned to worke; as to grind with a querne[75] wheate or rice, or to blowe smythes bellowes, or such like occupations, that they haue no neede of their sight. And if it be a blind woman, when she commeth vnto age, she doth vse the office of women of loue, of which sorte there are a great number in publike places, as shall be declared in the chapter for that purpose. These haue women that doo tende vpon them, and doo paint and trim them vp, and they are such that with pure age did leaue that office. So by this order in all this kingdome, although it be great, and the people infinite, yet there is no poore that doo perish nor begge in the streetes, as was apparent vnto the Austen and Barefoote fryers, and the rest that went with them into that countrie.[69]

THE THIRD BOOKE AND HISTORIE OF THE GREAT AND MIGHTIE KINGDOME OF CHINA, IN THE WHICH IS CONTAYNED MANY NOTABLE THINGS WOORTHIE TO BE CONSIDERED OF, TOUCHING MORALL AND POLLITIKE MATTERS.

CHAP. I.

How manie kinges hath beene in this kingdome, and their names.

In the fourth chapter of the first booke, I did promise particularly to declare howe many kinges haue beene in this kingdome, and their names. Nowe to accomplish the same, I will beginne and declare the succession of them from Vitey, the first king of China. Vitey (who was the first that did reduce the kingdome to one empire gouernment) vnto him that dooth reigne at this daye, remitting that which shall lacke vnto the chapter aforesaide: whereas shall be found the number of the kinges, and how many yeares since the first beginning of this kingdome, and the manner of the succession.[76]

This Vitey was the first king of China (as it appeareth by[70] their histories, where as they doo make particular mention). But amongest other thinges that they do declare of the kinges person, they do say that he was in height so much as seuen measures, which is accustomed in China; and euerie Which is foure yeardes quarter and halfe. measure is two thirdes of a Spanish vare, which is by good account foure vares[77] and two terses[78] in length: he was sixe palmes broade in the shoulders, and was as valiant in his deedes as in bignesse of his bodie: he had a captaine called Lincheon, who was not onely valiant, but politike and of great wisedome, by reason whereof with his valour and strength he did subiect vnto Vitey all the whole countrie that he doth now possesse, and caused all people to feare him. They do attribute that The first inuention of garments and dying of colours. this Vitey did first inuent the vse of garmentes for to weare, and by the dying of all manner of colours, of making of shippes: hee likewise inuented the sawe to sawe tymber; but aboue all thinges he was a great architector, and an inuenter of buildinges, whereof hee made verie manie and verie sumptuous, which doo indure vnto this day in the remembraunce of his name: he did also inuent the wheele to turne silke, the which is vsed to this day in all the kingdome: hee was the first that did use to weare golde, pearles, and precious stones for iewelles, and to weare cloth of golde, siluer, and silke in apparell: he did repart all the people of the countrie into cities, townes, and villages, and did ordaine occupations, and commaunded that no man should vse any other but that which his father did vse, without his particular licence, or the gouerners of his kingdome. And that should not be granted without great occasion for the same.

All of one occupation were put in streetes by themselues,[71] the which order is vsed vnto this day throughout al the kingdome; so that if you doo desire to know what occupation is in anye street, it is sufficient to see the first house thereof, although it be very long: for it is verie certaine that they be all of one occupation and not mingled with any other. Amongst all other things he ordeyned one thing of great consideration, that was, no woman to be No woman to be idle. idle, but to worke, either in her husbands occupation, or in sowing or spinning.

This was a law so generall amongst them, that the queene her selfe did obserue and keepe it.

A strange kind of hearb. They saye that he was a great astrologician, and had growing in the court of his pallace a certaine hearbe, the which did make a manner of demonstration when that any did passe by it, whereby it did shewe if any were euill intentioned against the king. Many other things they do declare which I let passe, because I would not be tedious vnto the reader, referring the dreames and fondnesse of these idolaters vnto the iudgement of your discretion: for vnto the discreete is sufficient to touch of euerie thing a little. He had foure wiues, and by them fiue and twentie sonnes; he reyned a hundreth yeares: there was betwixt this king and he which did build the great wall (that was spoken of in the ninth chapter of the first booke) one hundred and sixteene kinges, all of the lynage of this Vitey. All the which did raigne, as appeareth by their histories, two thousand two hundreth and fiftie seuen yeares. I do not here declare their names, because I would not be tedious, although they be particularly named in their histories; but here I will set downe them that I finde necessarie to be spoken of for the succession vnto him that now reygneth.

The last king of the lynage of this woorthie Vitey, was called Tzintzon: this did make the mightie and great wall aforesaide. Finding himselfe to be greatly troubled with the king of Tartarie, who did make warre vppon him in many places of his kingdom, he did ordaine the making thereof,[72] and for the furnishing of the same, he did take the third man of the countrie to the worke; and for that manie people did die in this tedious worke, by reason they went so farre from their owne houses, and in diuers climes cleane contrarie vnto that where as they were bred and borne: it grew that the king was hated and abhorred of all people, in such sort that they did conspire his death, which in effect they did accomplish and slew him, after he had reigned fortie yeares: and also his sonne and heyre, who was called Aguizi. After the death of this Tzintzon and his sonne, they did ordaine for their king one that was called Anchosan, a man of great valour and wisedome; hee reigned twelue yeeres: a sonne of his did succeede him in the kingdom, called Futey, and he reigned seuen yeares. After the death of this king, who died very young, his wife did reigne and gouerne, and was of his owne lineage: she did maruellously gouerne that kingdome for the space of 18 yeares, and for that shee had no issue naturall of her bodie, a sonne of her husbands yt he had by an other wife did succeede in the kingdome, and reigned three and twentie yeares: a son of his did succeede him, called Cuntey, and reigned 16 yeares and eight monthes: a son of his called Guntey, did reigne 54 yeares: a sonne of his did succeede him called Guntey, and reigned thirteene yeares: his sonne, called Ochantey, did succeede him, and reigned 25 yeares and three monthes: his son, called Coanty, succeeded him, and reigned 13 yeares and two monthes. After him reigned his sonne Tzentzey 26 yeares and 4 monthes: then succeeded his son called Anthrey, and reigned no more but 6 yeares; his sonne, Pintatey, did inherite and reigned 5 yeares. This Pintatey when he died was not married, and therefore a brother of his did succeede him, called Tzintzuny, and reigned but 3 yeares and 7 monethes: after him succeeded a younger brother called Huy Hannon, and reigned sixe yeares: his sonne, called Cubun, did succeed him, and reigned 32 yeares:[73] his sonne, Bemthey, did inherite and reigned 18 yeares: after him his son, Vnthey, and reigned 13 yeares: Othey succeeds him, and reigned 17 yeares; his sonne, called Yanthey, reigned but 8 monethes, and left a sonne, called Anthey, who reigned 19 yeares, whose eldest sonne, called Tantey, died incontinent after his father, and reigned only 3 monthes, and his brother, called Chyley, reigned one yeare; his son, called Linthey, reigned 22 yeares; his sonne, called Yanthey, did succeede him, and reigned 31 years. This Yanthey (the historie saieth) was a man of small wisedome, which was the occasion that he was abhorred and hated of those of his kingdome. A nephew of his, called Laupy, did rebell against him; he had two sociates for to helpe him, gentlemen of the court; they were two brethren and verie valiant, the one was called Quathy, the other Tzunthey; these two did procure to make Laupy king. His vncle the king vnderstoode thereof, and was of so litle valor and discretion, that he could not, neither durst he put remedie in the same, which caused commotions and common rumors amongst the people. But in especiall there was foure tyrantes ioyned in one, and all at one time, they wer called, Cincoan, Sosoc, Guansian, and Guanser. Against these Laupy did make warre vnder colour to helpe his vncle, but after a while, that the warre indured, he concluded and made peace with Cincoan, and he married with one of his daughters, who straight wayes made warre against the other three tyrants with the helpe of his father in lawe.

At this time this mightie kingdome was diuided in three partes, and beganne the tyrannie as you shall vnderstande: the one and principall part fell vpon Laupy by the death of his vncle, the other to Sosoc, and the other vnto Cincoan his father in law. In this sort remained the kingdome in diuision a while, til such time as Cuthey, sonne vnto Laupy, did reigne in his fathers steede. Then did there a tyrant rise vp against him, called Chimbutey, and slew him: he by[74] his great valour did bring the kingdome all in one as before, after that it had bin in diuision 41 yeares, and reigned after that alone 25 yeares: his sonne, named Fontey, did succeede him, and reigned 17 yeares. And to make short of this linage, there was 15 kinges, and reigned 176 yeares; against the last of them, who was called Quioutey, there did arise against him tyrannously Tzobu. Of this linage there was eyght kinges, who reigned 62 yeares: against the last of them, called Sutey, there arose one called Cotey, of whose lynage there was fine kings, and reigned twentie foure yeres; the last of them, called Otey, was slaine by Dian. There was of this lynage foure kings that reigned 56 yeres: against the last of them rose vp Tym, and there was of this race fiue kinges, and reigned one and thirty yeares: against the last of this house rose vp Tzuyn. And there was of this linage three kings, and reigned seuen and thirtie yeares, against the last of these rose vp Tonco. This and all the rest of his lynage did gouerne maruelous well; which was the occasion that they endured the longer time. There was of them one and twentie kinges, and reigned 294 yeares; the last of them, called Troncon, did marrie with one that had beene his fathers wife, called Bausa, a verie faire woman: hee tooke her out of a monasterie, where she was a nunne, onely to marrie with her: she vsed such policie that he was slaine, and did gouerne the kingdome after, alone, one and fortie yeares. The historie sayth that she was dishonest, and that with extremitie, and vsed the companie of the best and principallest of the realme; and not content with that, she married with one of base lynage, one fit for her purpose, because she was so vicious. They say that before she did marrie, she caused to be slaine the sonnes she had by her first husbande, for that she had a desire that a nephew of hers should succeede her in the kingdome. Then those of the kingdome perceiuing her intent, and wearie of her by reason of her ill liuing, sent out to seeke a bastard sonne of her husbandes,[75] who was fledde away, and with a common consent they raysed him for king. He was called Tautzon: he caused cruell and rigorous iustice to be done vpon his stepmother, as was reason for her euilles, and an example to all those of the kingdome, who by a president of her ill liuing beganne to straggle: there was of his lynage seuen kinges, that reigned 130 yeares: against the last, called Concham, arose Dian; of this linage there were but two kinges, and reigned eighteene yeares. Against the second and last arose Outon, and was of his linage three kinges, and reigned but fifteene yeares: against the last there arose Outzim; of this there was but two kinges, and reigned nine yeares and three monethes; there arose against the last Tozo: he and his sonne reigned foure yeares: with the sonne of this one Auchin did fight and slewe him in the combat, and succeeded him in the kingdome: hee with other two of his lynage reigned tenne yeares; against the last of these arose vp one of the lynage of Vitey, the first king, and slewe him; hee was called Zaytzon; there was of this lynage seuenteene kinges, and reigned with all peace and quietnesse three hundred and twentie yeares: the last of this lynage was called Tepyna, with whom did fight the gran Tartaro called Vzon, who entred into China with a mightie armie, and got all the kingdome; and it was possessed with nine Tartare kings, the which reigned 93 yeares, and intreated the inhabitantes with great tyrannie and seruitude: the last of these was called Tzintzoum; this was more cruel vnto the Chinos then any of the rest, which was the occasion that all the kingdome did ioyne together in one, and did elect a king, called Gombu, a man of great valour and of the lynage of ancient kinges past, who by his great woorthinesse and ioyning much people together, did so much that hee did driue all the Tartaros out of the kingdome, with the death of many thousands of them, who obstinately and without iustice did with all tyrannie keepe that kingdome in possession: there[76] was of this lynage twelue kinges with this that now reigneth: the eleuen kinges past reigned two hundreth yeares: he that now possesseth the kingdome is called Boneg, who by the death of his elder brother that died by a fall hee had from his horse, did inherite the kingdome: he is of 21 yeares of age (as they saye) and hath his mother aliue, of whom, as yet, there is nothing written: so that I can write nothing in particular, but that they say he is a gallant gentleman, and welbeloued of his subiects, and a great friende vnto iustice. He is married with a cosen of his, and hath one sonne.

Those of his linage hath got of the Tartares many countries since they were driven out of China, the which are on the other side of the mightie wall. God for His mercie's sake bring them to the knowledge of His holy lawe, and accomplish a prophesie that they have amongst them, by the which they are given to vnderstand that they shall be ruled and brought in subiection by men with great eyes and long beards—a nation that shall come from countries farre off, by whom they shalbe commanded, which signifieth to be Christians. The king of this countrie is had in so great reputation amongest his subiects, that in all the prouinces where he is not resident, in the chiefe cities whereas are the vizroyes or gouernors, they haue a table of gold, in the which is portred the king that nowe reigneth, and couered with a curtin of cloth of gold, verie riche, and thether goeth euery day the loytias, which are the gentlemen, men of lawe, and ministers of justice, and do by dutie reuerence vnto it, as though the kinge were personally present. This table and picture is discouered the first day of their feasts which they doo celebrate, and is at the newe moone of euery month, on the which day all people do repair and do reuerence vnto the picture with the same respect as they would doo if he were present: they do call the king Lord of the Worlde, and Sonne of Heaven.[77]

CHAP. II.

Of the court and pallace of the king, and of the citie where as he is resident; and how that in all the kingdome there is not one that is lord over subiects by propertie.

The habitation of this king, and almost of al his predecessors, hath bin and is commonlie in the citie of Taybin or Suntien: the occasion is (as they saye) for that it is neerest vnto the Tartarians, with whom continually they have had wars, that they might the better put remedie in any necessitie that shoulde happen, or, peraduenture, for that the temperature or clime of that place is more healthfull than the other prouinces, or the dwelling to be of more pleasure, as it is giuen to vnderstand by that worde Suntien, which in their language is as much to say the celestiall citie; it is of such bignesse that, for to crosse it ouer from gate to gate, a man must traueile one whole day, and A citie of a daies iourney long. have a good horse, and put good diligence, or else he shal come short: this is, besides, the subburbes, which is as much more ground. Amongst the Chinos is found no varietie in the declaration of this mightie city, and of the great riches that is in it, which is a signe to be of a truth for that they agree all in one. There is so much people in it, what of citizens and courtiers, that it is affirmed that, vpon any vrgent occasion, there may be ioyned together two hundreth thousand men, and the half of them to bee horsemen. At the entring into this citie toward the orient, is situated the mightie and sumptuous pallace of the king, where he remaineth ordinarily, although hee hath other two: the one in the midst of the citie, and the other at the end towards the west. This first pallace they do testifie is of such huge bignesse, and so much curiositie, that it is requisite to haue foure days at the least to view and see it all. First it is compassed[78] about with seuen walles, very huge; and the space that is betwixt one wall and other doth contain ten thousand souldiers, which doo watch and gard the king's house dayly: there is within this pallace three score and nineteen halls, of a marueilous rich and curious making, wherein there are many women that do serue the king in the place of pages and squires; but the principallest to be seen in this pallace is foure halles very rich, whereas the king giueth audience vnto such ambassadours as come vnto him from other kingdomes or prouinces, or vnto his owne people when they call any court of parliament (which is very seldome), for that he is not seene by his commons out of his owne house but by great chance, and yet when they doo see him, for the most part it is by a glasse window. The first of these hals is made al of mettal, very curiously wrought Foure curious halles. with manie figures: and the seconde hath the seeling and the floore wrought in the order of masons' worke, all of siluer of great value: the third is of fine golde, wrought and inamiled verie curiously. The fourth is of so great riches, that it much exceedeth all the other three: for that in it is represented the power and riches of that mightie kingdome: and therefore in their language they do cal it the hall of the king's treasure; and they do affirme that it deserueth to haue that name—for that there is in it the greatest treasure that any king hath in all the world, besides many iewels of an inestimable price, and a chaire (wherein he dooth sit) of great maiesty, made of iuory, set full of precious stones and carbuncles, of a great price, that in the darkest time of the night the hall is of so great clearenesse as though there were in it many torches or lights: the wals are set full of stones of diuers sorts, verie rich and of great vertue, wrought verie curiously: and to declare it in fewe words, it is the richest and principalst thing to be seene in all the kingdome, for therein is the principallest thereof.[79]

In these foure halles are heard such ambassadours as are sent from other countries, according vnto the estate and qualitie of the king and prouinces from whence they come:

so that according as they are esteemed, so are they entertained into one of these foure hals. If that from whence they come is from a king of small power, he hath audience in the first hall: if he be of a reasonable power, in the second hal, and in this order in the rest. Within this mightie pallace, the king hath all that any humane vnderstanding can desire or aske (touching this life), in pleasure for to recreate his person, and for their queene: for that neuer (or by great chance) they go foorth of the same: and it hath beene a customable vse amongst the kings of that countrie, that it is as a thing inherited by succession never to go forth. They say, their reason why they doo keepe themselues so close and not to go abroade, is to conserue the mightie estate of their estade,[79] and also to auoide for being slaine by treason (as many times it falleth so out); for which occasion you haue had kings, that in all the time of their reigne haue not gone out of their pallace but onely the day of their oath and crownation: and besides this their close keeping, yet haue they tenne thousande men continually (as aforesaide) in garde of the pallace both day and night, besides others that are in the courtes, staires and halles, and other places. Within the gates and wals of this mightie pallace they haue gardines, orchards, woodes, and groues, whereas is all manner of hunt, and foule, and great pondes full of fish. And, to conclude, they haue all manner of pleasures and delites, that may be inuented or had in any banketting house in the fielde. In all this kingdome there is not one that is lorde ouer any subiect or vassales (as they of Turkie), neither haue they any iurisdiction proper, but that which is his patrimonie and moueables, or that which the king doth giue them in recompence of good seruice or gouernment, or for any[80] other particular respect: all the which dooth end with the person, and is returned againe vnto the king, except he will giue it vnto the sonne of him that is dead, in curtesie more then by obligation or duetie: giuing to vnderstande that it is to auoyd inconueniences and occasions of treasons, which might grow if that there were any lords that were rich or of power, and not for couetousnes or any other intent. Those whom he dooth put in authoritie, whether they are vizroyes, gouernours, or captaine generals, or whatsoeuer they be, hee giueth vnto them large wages, sufficient to sustaine them in their office, in so ample sort, that it is rather ouerplus vnto them then lacke; for that he will not that their necessitie compell them to take presents or bribes, which thing doth Punished for taking bribes. blinde them, that they cannot do iustice vprightly: and vnto him that doth receiue or take any such (although it be but of smal prise) he is cruelly punished.

CHAP. III.

The number of such subiects as doo pay vnto the king tribute in all these fifteene prouinces.

Vnderstanding the greatnesse of this kingdome of China, and the infinite number of people that is therein, it is an easie thing to bee beleeued, the number that euery prouince hath of such as do pay tribute, as is taken out of the booke that the officers haue, whereby they do recouer that tribute: and it is affirmed, that there are as many more, such as are free and do pay no tribute. The loytians and ministers of iustice, all sorts of soldiers, both by sea and land (which is an infinite number), are free and do pay nothing; the number as followeth.

The prouince of Paguia[80] hath two millions seuen hundred and foure thousand that doth pay tribute to the king.[81]

The prouince of Santon, 3 millions and 700 thousand tributers.

The prouince of Foquien, two millions foure hundred and seuen thousand tributers.

The prouince of Olam, two millions two hundred and foure thousand tributers.

The prouince of Sinsay, three millions three hundred and foure score thousand.

The prouince of Susuan, two millions and fiftie thousand.

The prouince of Tolanchia, there where as the king is resident, and is the biggest of them al, sixe millions fourescore and ten thousand.

The prouince of Cansay, two millions three hundred and fiue thousand.

The prouince of Oquiam, three millions and eight hundred thousand.

The prouince of Ancheo, two millions eight hundred and foure thousand.

The prouince of Gonan, one million and two hundred thousand.

The prouince of Xanton, one million nine hundred fortie and foure thousand.

The prouince of Quicheu, two millions thirtie and foure thousand.

The prouince of Chequeam, two millions two hundred and fortie foure thousand.

The prouince of Sancii, which is the least of all the prouinces, hath one million sixe hundred threescore and twelue thousand tributers.

By this account it is found, that the tribute payers are verie many: and it is approoued in manie places of this historie whereas they do treate of the greatnes of this kingdome, that it is the mightiest and biggest that is to bee read of in all the world. God, for His mercies sake, bring them to the knowledge of His lawe, and take them out from the tyrannie of the diuell, wherein they are wrapped.[82]

CHAP. IV.

The tribute that the king hath in these fifteene prouinces, according vnto the truest relation.

Although this kingdome is great and very rich, yet there is none that doth pay so little tribute ordinarily vnto their king as they do, neither amongst Christians, Moores, nor Gentiles, that we know. The extraordinary and personall seruice is very much, that in some respect wee may say that they are more slaues than free men, for that they do not possesse one foote of land; but they pay tribute in respect whereof, as also for the great misusing of them by their gouernours, will bee a great part and occasion to inuite them to receiue the lawe of the gospell, and that with great facilitie to inioy the libertie of the same.

The ordinarie tribute that euery one dooth pay that dooth keepe house, is two Mases[81] euery yeare, which is as much as two Spanish rials of plate. This tribute is verie little, yet the Loytians (which is a great part of the kingdome) do pay none, neither their gouernours nor ministers, captaines nor souldiours: the multitude of the people is so great, and the kingdome so bigge, that alonely that which they giue for expences of the king and his court is woonderfull, with customes, dueties, portages, and other rents: not accounting that which is paide vnto garisons and souldiers of that kingdome, neither in that which is spent in repairing of walles of particular cities, and in men of warre at sea, and campes[83] by land, to gouernoures and iustices, which doth not enter into this account.

The rent of the king. The rent which remaineth vnto the king ordinarily is this that followeth, and is taken with great regard out of the booke of his excheker. Yet the Chinos do say that it is much lesse then that they do pay at this time;

for that this is of old antiquitie, when as the tributes were lesse: the tributes as followeth.

Pure gold. Of pure golde, from seuenteene to two and twentie killates,[82] they giue him foure millions, and two hundred fiftie sixe thousand and nine hundred Taes:[83] euerie one is worth ten rials and foure and twentie marauadies Spanish mony.

Fine siluer. Of fine siluer, three millions one hundred fiftie three thousand two hundred and nineteene Taes.

Pearles. The mines of pearles, whereof you haue many in this kingdome (although they are not verie round), is woorth vnto him commonly two millions sixe hundred and thirtie thousand Taes.

Precious stones. Of precious stones of all sorts, as they come from the mines, one million foure hundred three score and ten thousand Taes.

Muske and amber. Of muske and amber, one million and thirtie fiue thousande Taes.

Of earthen dishes and vessell, fourscore thousand Taes. Besides all this, the king doth put forth verie much ground to his subiects, and they do pay him with part of the croppe that they gather, or with the cattle that they bring vp on ye same grounde.

Rice. The quantitie that they pay him is as followeth. Of cleane rice (which is a common victuall throughout all the kingdome, and of the countries adioyning to them) they pay him three score millions, one hundred three score and eleuen thousand, eight hundred thirtie and two hanegges.

Barle. Of barley, twentie nine millions, three hundred foure[84] score and eleuen thousand, nine hundred fourescore and two hanegges.

Wheate. Of wheat like vnto that in Spaine, thirtie three millions, one hundred twentie thousand and two hundred hanegges.

Salt. Of salt, twentie fiue millions three hundred and fortie thousand foure hundred hanegges, which is made in his owne salt pits, and is of a great rent.

Mayz. Of wheat called Mayz, twentie millions two hundred and fiftie thousand hanegs.

Millo. Of millio,[84] twentie foure millions of hanegges.

Panizo. Of Panizo,[85] fourteene millions and two hundred thousande hanegges.

Other graine. Of other different graine and seeds, fortie millions and two thousand hanegges.

Peeces of silk. They doo pay him in peeces of silke, of fourteene vares long the peece, two hundred fiue thousand and fiue hundred ninetie peeces.

Raw silke. Cotton wool. Of raw silke in bundles, fiue hundred and fortie thousande pounds. Of cotton wool, three hundred thousand pounds.

Mantels. Of mantles wrought of all colours, eight hundred thousand and foure hundred mantles. Of Chimantas[86] made of rawe silke, that waieth twelue pound a peece, three hundred thousand sixe hundred and eightie of them. Of mantles made of cotton of fourty vares, sixe hundred seuenty eight thousand, eight hundred and seuentie. Of Chimantas of cotton, three hundred foure thousand sixe hundred forty and eight. All this aforesaide is for expenses of the court, which is great. The Chinos yt come vnto the Philippinas do affirme the same, and do not differ in the report, which is a signe to be true: likewise they do receiue of it in his tresurie, whereas is many millions, and cannot be otherwise, considering his great rentes.[85]

CHAP. V.

Of the men of war that are in the fifteene prouinces, as wel footmen as horsemen, and of the great care they haue in the gard of the kingdome.

Looke what care and diligence this mightie king hath, that iustice should be ministred with right and equitie: so likewise (yea and much more) he hath touching matters that may preuent wars, which be offered by princes adiacent vnto him, or any other whatsoeuer. But in especiall with the Tartarians, with whom they haue had continuall wars many years. (Although at this day) that the Tartarians doo feare him very much: in such sort as he thinketh it best to keepe him for his friende, and doth acknowledge vnto him a certain manner of vassalage. And although at this present and long time since, he hath bin and is without any occasion of wars, that should come vpon a sodain; yet hath he had manie and grieuous enimies to defend himselfe from, or to offend them, as you shall perceiue in this that followeth. For besides that he hath in euery prouince his president and counsell of war, captaine generall, and others ordinarie to take vp people, and ordaine their campes and squadrons as well by sea as by land, to serue at all assaies when that occasion shall serue; so likewise he hath in euery city captaines and souldiers for their particular Great care for to defend their countrie. garde and defence, and doo range and watch to set their garde in order both day and night, as though their enimies were at the gates. This military order they do vse and maintaine, in such sort that no nation knowne may be compared vnto them. Although, speaking generally, (according vnto the relation of certaine Spanish souldiers that were there, and did manie times see them) there be other nations that do exceed them both in valiantnesse, courage, and worthinesse of mind.[86]

They haue at the gates of all their cities their squadrons, who let[87] the entrie and going out of any whatsoeuer, except he haue licence of the iustice of that citie or towne, brought them in writing: the which gates they do shut and open by order and licence of their captaines, which is sent vnto them euery day, written in whited tables, and their sine vnto it. These gates are the force of all the cittie, and thereon is planted all the artilerie they haue; nigh vnto the which gate, is ordinarily the house whereas they are founded or made. At night, when they do shut their gates, they do glew papers vpon the ioinings of them: then they doo seale the papers, with the seale that the gouernour or iudge of that cittie doth weare on his finger, the which is done by himselfe, or by some other in whom he hath great confidence and trust: and they cannot open them againe in the morning vntill such time as it bee seene and acknowledged that it hath not been touched since the night that it was put on. So that if any haue any iourney to ride very early in the morning, he must go forth of the citie ouer night, before the gates be shut, and remaine in the suburbs: for out of the cittie it is not possible to goe vntill the gates be open, which is not till the sunne be vp ordinarily.

They do not vse any castles nor forts, but great bulwarkes and gun bankes, whereas they haue continuall watch, and doo change by quarters according as wee do vse: and the officers with a great number of souldiers do range throughout the city, and bulworkes: and commonly the captaines be naturall of those prouinces, whereas they haue their charge giuen them in consideration that the loue they haue to their countrie, doo binde them to fight to the death for the defence thereof. And for that there should be more quietnesse and rest in the cities, it is not permitted that any do weare weapons, defensiues, nor offensiues, but onely such souldiers as haue the kings pay: neither do they consent[87] they should haue them in their houses, neither vse any in trauaile by sea nor lande. Besides all this, the king hath in the citie of Taybin and Suntiem (whereas hee is resident), and in such cities lying there about, a great number both of horsemen and footemen, alwaies in a readinesse for to go with him into any place, for the safegarde of his person in time of necessitie.

The souldiers of his kingdome are in two sortes and manners, the one sort are such as bee and are naturals of the citie whereas they haue their charge, and these be called in their language Cum: in this place the sonne doth succeed the father, and for lacke of an heire, the king doth prouide one in the dead man's place. Euery one of them hath his name written vpon the post of his doore, and the place appointed whither he shal go when occasion shall serue (enemies being against that cittie or towne). The other sort of souldiers are strangers, and are consorted for yeares or monethes to serue. These be they that ordinarily make their watches, musters, and ioyne companies for the receit of the captaines: these be called in their language Pon.[88] These goe from one place vnto another, whereas they are commanded to go. One captaine and ancient hath charge of a thousand, and a meaner captaine with his ancient a hundreth, that doo depend vpon the other. So that for to knowe the number of people that is in a great campe, it is done with great ease in accounting the ensignes of a thousand men, which are easily knowne. Euery chiefe or petie captaine of these, hath his house vpon the cittie wal, and his name put on it, and there he dwelleth so long as the warres indureth. These captaines euery moneth do exercise their souldiers in marching and putting them in order: sometime[88] with quick speed, and other times more slower, and to giue assalt and retyre as they are taught by the sound of the drum: this they do vse continually in the time of peace, as well as in the time of warre: also how to vse their weapons, which are ordinarie, hargabuses, pikes, targets, faunchers,[89] brushebilles,[90] holbards, dagars, and armour. The horsemen do vse in the warres to carrie foure swords hanging at their saddell bowes, and doo fight with two at once, with great dexteritie and gallant to behold. These do accustome to go into the wars accompanied with many seruants, and familiar friends on foote, all wel armed after the gallantest manner that possibly they may. These footemen be marueillous full of policie, and ingenious in warlike or martiall affaires: and although they haue some valor for to assalt and abide the enemie, yet doo they profite themselues of policies, deuises and instruments of fire, and of fire workes. Thus do they vse as wel by land in their wars as by sea, many bomes[91] of fire, full of old iron, and arrowes made with powder and fire worke, with the which they doo much harm and destroy their enimies. The horsemen do fight with bowes and arrowes, and lances, and with two swordes (as I haue saide before), and some with hargabuses. They cannot gouerne their horses very wel, for that they haue but one peece of iron that is crosse in their mouthes that serueth for a bridle; and for to make them stay, they pull but one raine, and with clapping their hands together and making of a noise before them. They haue very ill Uerie ill horsemen. saddels, so that they be al verie ill horsemen. The like prouision hath the king for the sea: hee hath great fleetes of ships, furnished with captaines and men, that doo scoure and defend the costs of the countrie with great diligence and watchings. The souldiers, as well by land as by sea, are paid with great liberalitie, and those that do aduantage themselues in valor, are very much esteemed, and haue great preferment and rewards. When[89] these Chinos doo take anie prisoner in the wars, they doo not kill him, nor giue him more punishment, but to serue as a souldier in that countrie in the farthest parts from their naturall, the king paying him his wages as other souldiers are paid. These for that they may be knowne doo weare redde bonnets, but in their other apparell they do differ nothing from the Chinos. Likewise such as be condemned by iustice for criminall offences, to serue in any frontier (as is vsed much amongst them), they also weare redde caps or bonnets: and so it is declared in their sentence, that they do condemme them to the red bonnet.

CHAP. VI.

More of the men of war which are in al these fifteene prouinces, and how many there be in euery one of them, as well horsemen as footemen.

In the chapter past you do vnderstande what care these Chinos haue in the time of peace as well as in warre for to defend their citties, and what preparations they haue generrally throughout al the countrie. Now lacketh to let you know particularly the number that euery prouince hath in it selfe, the better to vnderstand the mightinesse therof. They haue in euerie prouince in their chiefe or metropolitan citie, a counsell of warre, with a president and foure counsailers; all the which are such as haue bin brought vp from their youth in the wars, with experience of the vse of armour and weapon: so that vnto them is giuen the charge for the defence of their prouince.

These counsellors doo ordaine captaines, and prouide other officers and all necessaries for the warres, and send them vnto such cities and townes whereas they see it is needfull. And for that in the accomplishing thereof there[90] shalbe no lacke, the treasurer is commanded to deliuer vnto them whatsoeuer they do aske without any delay.

The number of souldiers in all China. The number of the souldiers that euery prouince had in the yeare 1577, at such time as frier Martin de Herrada and his companie entered into China (hauing no wars, but great peace and quietnesse), is as followeth.

The prouince of Paguia, whereas ordinarily the king is resident, hath two millions and one hundred and fiftie thousand footemen, and foure hundred thousand horsemen.

The prouince of Santon hath one hundred and twenty thousand footemen, and fortie thousand horsemen.

The prouince of Foquien hath eight and fiftie thousande and nine hundred footemen, and twentie two thousand foure hundred horsemen.

The prouince of Olam hath three score and sixteene thousand footemen, and twentie fiue thousande fiue hundred horsemen.

The prouince of Cinsay hath eightie thousand three hundred footemen, but of horsemen verie few or none; for that this prouince and the other that followe, are all mountaines, and ful of rockes and stones.

The prouince of Oquiam hath twentie thousand and sixe hundred footemen, and no horsemen, for the reason aforesaide.

The prouince of Susuan foure score and sixe thousande footemen, and foure and thirtie thousande and fiue hundred horsemen.

The prouince of Tolanchia, which is that which doth border vpon the Tartarians, with whom the kings of China haue had wars (as aforesaid), hath two millions and eight hundred thousand footemen, and two hundred and ninety thousand horsemen, and are the most famous and best in all the whole kingdome: for that they are brought vp in the use of armour from their youth, and many times exercised the same in times past, when they had their ordinary war with their borderers the Tartarians.[91]

The prouince of Cansey hath fiftie thousand footemen, and twentie thousand two hundred and fiftie horsemen.

The prouince of Ancheo (there whereas the friers were) hath foure score and sixe thousand footemen, and fortie eight thousand horsemen.

The prouince of Gonan, fortie foure thousand footemen, and fourteene thousand fiue hundred horsemen.

The prouince of Xanton hath fiftie two thousand footemen, and eighteene thousand nine hundred horsemen.

The prouince of Quincheu, hath fortie eight thousand and seuen hundred footemen, and fifteene thousande three hundred horsemen.

The prouince of Chequeam, thirty foure thousand footmen, and thirteene thousand horsemen.

The prouince of Sancii, which is least of them all, hath forty thousand footemen, and sixe thousand horsemen.

All these people aforesaid, euery prouince is bound (by an order set downe in parlement) to haue in a redinesse, the which is an easie thing to be done; the one is for that the king doth pay them roiallie, the other for that they do dwel The souldier is royall paid. in their owne natural countries and houses, wheras they do injoy their patrimonies and goods: leauing it vnto their sonnes. In the time of wars, they are bound to assist the place that hath most necessitie. By this account it plainely appeareth that all these prouinces (which may better be called kingdomes, considering their greatnes) haue fiue millions and eight hundred The number of footemen and horsemen. fortie sixe thousand and fiue hundred footemen, and nine hundred fortie eight thousand three hundred and fiftie horsemen. All the which, if in valor and valientnes might be equalled vnto our nations in Europe, they were sufficient to conquer ye whole world. And although they are more in number and equal in policies, yet in their valientnesse and courage they are far behind. Their horse for the most part are little, but great traueilers: yet they say, within the countrie there are verie great and excellent[92] good horse. I do not here declare the industrie that might (with the fauour of God) be vsed to win and ouercome this people, for that the place serueth not for it; and I haue giuen large notice thereof, vnto whom I am bound. And againe, my profession is more to bee a meanes vnto peace, then to procure any warres; and if that which is my desire might be doone, it is, that with the word of God, which is the sworde that cutteth the hearts of men, wherewith I hope in the Lorde to see it.

CHAP. VII.

Of a law amongst the Chinos, that they cannot make anie wars out of their owne countrie, neither go forth of the same, neither can any stranger come in without licence of the king.

Although in many things that haue bin seene in this kingdome is shewed and declared the sharpe and ripe witts of these men, and with what wisedome and prudence they doo most manifest the same (in my iudgment) is in that which shalbe declared in this chapter. They without all doubt seeme to exceede the Greekes, Carthagenians, and Romanes, of whom the old ancient histories haue signified to vs, and also of those later times; who for to conquere strange countries did separate themselues so farre from their natural, that they lost their owne countries at home. But these of this kingdome being forewarned (as ye prouerbe saith:) Felix quem faciunt aliena pericula cautum. By the hurt of another, etc., they haue found by experience yt to go forth of their owne kingdome to conquer others, is the spoile and losse of much people, and expences of great treasures, besides the trauaile and care which continually they haue to sustaine that which is got, with feare to be lost againe: so[93] that in the meane time whilest they were occupied in strange conquests, their enimies, the Tartarians and other kings borderers vnto them, did trouble and inuade them, doing great damage and harme. And more, considering that they do possesse one of the greatest and best kingdomes of the world, as well for riches as for fertility, by reason whereof, and by the great aboundance of things that the country doth yeeld, many strange nations do profite themselues from them, They haue no neede of other nations. and they haue need of none other nation, for that they haue sufficient of all things necessarie to the mainteining of humane life. In consideration whereof they called a generall court of Parliament, whether came all vizroyes and gouernours and other principall men of all the fifteene prouinces: and there they did communicate, to put remedy in this great inconuenience in the best manner possible. Then after they had wel considered of the same with great care and diligence, taking the iudgment particular of euery one, and in generall by common consent, they found it requisit for their quietnes and profite, and a thing most conuenient for the common wealth to leaue al yt they had got and gained out of their owne kingdome, but specially such countries as were farre off. And from that day forwards not to make any wars in any place: for that from thence did proceed a known damage and a doubtfull profite: and being altogether conformable, they did request the king that was at that present that he would cal home al such people as he had in other kingdomes bordering there about vnder his obedience, perswading him that in so doing, he should remaine a mightie prince, more richer, more in quiet and in more securitie. Then the king perceiuing the request and petition of his kingdome and subiects, and being fully satisfied that this perswasion was requisite to be put in execution: he straight wayes set it a worke, and commanded vpon great penalties, that al his subiects and vassals naturall that were in any strange countries, that in a time limited, they should returne[94] home to their owne country and houses: and likewise to the gouernours of the same countries, that they should in his name abandon and leaue the dominion and possession that he had of them: excepting such as would of their owne good will acknowledge vassalage, and giue him tribute, and remaine friends, as vnto this Straight lawes. day the Lechios[92] and other nations do. This law was then established and is inuiolablie kept to this day: in the which it is first commanded that none whatsoeuer, vpon paine of death, shall make or begin warre in any part without his licence. Also on the said penaltie, that no subiect of his shall nauigate by sea out of the kingdome without the said licence. Also that whatsoeuer will go from one prouince to another within the said kingdome, to traficke in buying and selling, shall giue sureties to returne againe in a certaine time limited, vpon paine to bee disnaturalled of the countrie. Likewise that no stranger whatsoeuer shall come in by sea nor by land, without his express licence, or of the gouernours of such ports or places whereas they shall come or ariue. And this licence must be giuen with great consideration, aduising the king therof. All which lawes haue beene the occasion that this mightie kingdome hath not come to notice and knowledge but of late yeares. All the which that is said, seemeth to be true, for that it is cleerely found in their histories and books of nauigations of old antiquitie: whereas it is plainely seene that they did come with the shipping vnto the Indies, hauing conquered al that is from China, vnto the farthest part thereof. Of all the which they indured possessors in great quietnes, till such time as they ordeined the law of abandoning of their owne good will, as aforesaid. So that at this day there is great memory of them in the Ilands Philippinas and on the cost of Coromande, which is the cost against the kingdome of Norsinga[93] towards the Sea of Cengala;[94] whereas is a towne called vnto this day the soile of the Chinos, for[95] that they did reedifie and make the same. The like notice and memory is there in the kingdom of Calicut, wheras be many trees and fruits, that the naturals of that countrie do say, were brought thither by the Chinos, when that they were lords and gouernours of that countrie. Likewise in those dayes they were of Malaca, Siam, and Chapaa,[95] and other of their borderers. Also it is to be beleeued of ye Ilands of Iapon, for that there are many token vnto the Chinos vnto this day, and the naturals of the country are much after the fashion of the Chinos, and many particular things that do giue vs to vnderstand: and some lawes that are obserued and kept in China. But now in these dayes the gouernors of the sea ports do dispence with the law that forbiddeth ye going out of the kingdome, by certaine gifts which is giuen them by merchants to giue them secret licence, that they may go and trafficke in ilands bordering there about, as vnto the Philippinas, whither come euery yeare many ships laden with merchandise of great riches, of the which is brought many times into Spaine. Likewise they do trauaile vnto other parts and places, wheras they vnderstand they may profite themselues. Yet they do not giue any such licence vntill they haue giuen sureties to returne within one whole yeare.

The desire of gain hath caused them to traueile to Mexico, whither came the yeare past in anno 1585 three merchants of China, with verie curious things, and neuer staied till they came into Spaine and into other kingdomes further off. Likewise the said iudge and gouernours doo giue licence vnto strangers (in the order aforesaid) for to enter into their ports to buy and sel, but first vpon examination and charge, that they should haue a great care not to demand any licence but to the same intent. Then haue they their licence with a time limited, and with condition that they shall not procure to goe about their cities, neither to[96] see the secrets thereof. And this is giuen in writing vpon a whited table, which is set vpon the fore partes of their ships, that when they come to an anker in any port it may be seene of the keepers and guards that they sinke them not, but let them peaceably to enter and to trafficke in buying and selling, paying their ordinarie customes due vnto the king.

In euery port there is a scriuener or notarie, put there by the gouerners, that dooth set downe in memorie the day and houre that any shippe doth enter in, in order that, whether hee be a stranger or natural, to take in his lading and dispatch, according vnto the old custome of those ports, the which is inuiolably kept; which is the occasion that they do lade and dispatch in so short a time, and with so great quietnesse, as though there were but one shippe, although many times you shall see in one port two thousande ships small and great. In this sort, with a bought licence, did the Portugals traficke from the Indies in Canton, a prouince of this kingdome, and in other parts of that kingdome, as they themselues haue declared, and likewise the Chinos.

CHAP. VIII.

Of the kings royall counsell, and the order they haue to know euerie moneth what dooth passe in all the kingdome.

The king hath in the citie of Tabin,[96] whereas he is resident, a royall counsell of twelue counsellers, and a president, chosen men throughout al the kingdome, and such as haue had experience in gouernement many yeares.

For to be one of the counsell, it is the highest and supremest dignitie that a man can come vnto; for that (as aforesaid)[97] in all this kingdome there is neither prince, duke, marquesse, earle, nor lord, that hath any subiectes, but the king only, and the prince his sonne. These counsellers, and the gouernors of these prouinces by them appointed, bee such personages, that they are respected and esteemed for the time of their continuance in the same estimation, as is the other, where as they haue these titles.

Councillors must be expert in sciences. For to be one of this counsell, it is not sufficient that they be expert and learned in the lawes of the countrie, and in morall and naturall philosophie, and commenced in the same, but they must be also expert in astrologie and iudgements. For they say, he that must be of this supreme counsell, by whome is gouerned all these fifteene prouinces: it is requisite that they know all this that is saide, for to prognosticate what shall succeede and happen, the better to prouide for all necessities that shall come. These twelue doo sit in counsell ordinarily in the kinges pallace, for the which there is a hall appointed, maruellous richly trimmed: and in the same thirteene chayres, sixe of them of golde, and sixe of siluer: both the one and the other of great price, wrought with great curiositie: yet the thirteenth is more richer, for that it is of golde and set full of precious stones of great value, and that is placed in the middest of them vnder a canopie or cloth of estate, of cloth of gold: in the which is imbrodered the kinges armes, and is as it is saide, certaine serpentes, wrought with golde wyer: in this chayre the president doth sitte when the king is not in presence: but if hee be there (as seeldome he is) then doth the president sit in the first and highest of the chaires on the right hand, which be of gold: in the which, and in the other of siluer, they bee placed according vnto their antiquitie: in this sort, that if the president do die, then do the most auncient proceede and inherite his roome, and in his chaire doth the fift person rise on the side of the golden chaires: and so from the fourth vnto the fift: and in this order all[98] the rest arise in the chaires of siluer, passing into the other chaires of golde. This may the president doo, preferring euerie one in order (if any doo die) without the consent of the king. And if any of these chaires be voyd, then doth the counsell choose an other by voices: the which is done by vprightnes, and he which hath the most is preferred; but the chiefest in this preferment is merit and sufficiencie. If he that is chosen be absent in any gouernment, then doo they send for him; but if hee be present in the citie, then doo they carrie him before the king, giuing him to vnderstand of their election, in whose power it is to accept or to make it voyde, which neuer doth happen. Then the king himselfe on his owne handes, according vnto their custome, doth make him sweare a solemne oth that he shall doo vpright iustice according vnto the lawes of the countrie, and that he shall likewise doo vprightly in the choosing of viceroyes and gouernours or any other iustices, and not be led with affections nor passions, neyther receiue anie bribes himself nor any other for him: with many other things in this order and effect: and aboue all things hee shall not bee partaker, neyther consent to anye treason at anie time against the king: but rather if that hee doo vnderstande of anie such, directly or indirectly, he shall straight wayes giue the kinge to vnderstande thereof, or his counsell, of all that he dooth knowe or vnderstande, alwaye favouring with his industrie and force the preseruation of peace and life of the king.

This oth of homage being doone, they doo carrie him vnto the chaire which is on the left hande in the hall, and doo giue him the possession with great solemnitie; for the which, certaine dayes after there is great feastes in the citie, as well by them of the counsell as by the citizens and courtiers: during the which time, the marchants do leaue their contractions and trafickes, and handicraft men their occupations.[99]

If any occasion bee requisite to talke with the king, there is none that speaketh with him but the president, and if it so fall out that hee be sicke, then the most auncient and vppermost in the golden chayres dooth talke with him at all times when neede requireth; but when hee talketh with him hee is on his knees, and his eyes inclyned to the grounde, and neuer mooueth although the talke endureth two houres. He is paide with the same money that all viceroyes, gouernours, iustices, and captaines of the kingdome are: when they will talke with the president, it is in the self same order.

In this royall counsell euerie moneth they doo knowe all thinges that doo happen in all the kingdome woorthie to bee aduised of, and this is without falt; for that those which doo gouerne the prouinces haue expresse commandement to sende notice vnto the court of all thinges that doo happen in anye of their prouinces touching warres, the estate of the countrie, the kinges rents, or any other thing: the which is accomplished with so great care, that although it bee a prouince distant fiue hundred leagues from the court, yet the post doth not misse his day appointed. And those which do first come, do tarrie till the last or furthest off doo come, and then vpon the day appointed they do all together giue their relations. Those which are farre off for to be at the court so soone and at the instant as those which are nigh at hand, doo send postes daily, that the one may ouertake the other. They do run post after the vse of Italy and Spain with a horne, but they were woont to haue a coller of belles, the better to be heard: so yt the postmasters when they do heare the horne or bels, do straight waies bridle their horse to be in a readines. Likewise, if their iourney be to passe by water (as many times it hapneth), then ye boat-men do make their barks readie.

Then when the counsell hath taken relation of all the posts in effect, the president incontinent doth giue a straight[100] account thereof vnto the king: then hee, or the counsell by his order (if anie such neede requireth), do put remedie for that that is needfull for the time. And if it be requisite to send any iustice about the same, he is straight wayes appointed, and dispatched and sent in all haste and with great secrecie: and this iustice doth make inquiries in such sort that it is not knowen, no not in the citie where the fault is committed.

And for that, touching this matter, it shall bee spoken of more at large in chapters following, I will conclude with this: that this king will haue such dominion ouer his kingdome and subiectes, that although it be great with so manie prouinces, cities, and townes, yet not one uiceroy, gouernor, nor iustice can put any man vnto death, without his sentence be first confirmed by the kinge and his royall counsell, except it be in the warres actually, for that there in the delaying thereof may growe some perill; therefore they doo permit the captaine generall or his lieftenant, to behead or hang what so euer souldier that shall offende or doo anie ill thing; this may they do without consentment of the king or his counsell, onely with the consentment of the kinges treasorer, or of the generall of the fielde: the which bee both of them graue personages, and they must be both conformable in their iudgementes or else they cannot execute death.

CHAP. IX.

Of such presidents and ministers as the king doth put in euerie prouince, and the order that they haue in their gouernment.

You do vnderstande howe the two prouinces, Paguia and Tolanchia are gouerned by the supreme counsell of the king, and such ministers as they doo send to gouerne. The other thirteene prouinces that do remaine, haue eyther of them a vizroy or gouernor, whom the common people do call[101] Insuanto;[97] who is continually resident, and doth dwell in the metropolitane citie, whereof Euery prouince hath his viceroy. the prouince doth commonly beare the name. And although all the kinges officers and iustices of what sort of administration they are, be generally called by the name of Loytia;[98] yet euerie one hath a speciall and a particular name besides, according vnto his office that he doth execute: of the which and of their proper names I will giue you to vnderstand, for that it doth differ from our purpose. The vizroy, that is in euery prouince principall and supreme magistrate in place of the king, they do call him Comon.[99] The second in dignitie is the gouernour of all the prouince, and he is called Insuanto, who hath verie little less maiestie than the viceroy: then the corregidor or gouernor that is resident in any citie, where as is neither viceroy nor gouernor, is called Tutuan,[100] all of this degree. Of any thing that is of importance, of what citie soeuer they be, they do giue relation thereof vnto the higher gouernor, called Insuanto, and likewise this Insuanto vnto the viceroy or comon, whose charge is to giue the king to vnderstand thereof or his royall counsell, by the postes that we haue spoken of before. The third in dignitie is called Ponchasi;[101] this is the president or counsell, of the kinges reuenewes, who hath vnder him a counsell and many ministers and officers, as sargents and others, which do recouer the rents in euery province. This state dooth giue account of all his office vnto the tutuan, after that he hath paide all kind of wages and charges ordinarie and extraordinarie due to any officer of the kinges in all that prouince.

The fourth degree or dignitie is called Totoc,[102] and this is captaine generall of all souldiers, as well footmen as horsemen.[102] The fift is called Anchasi;[103] Captaine generall. he is president and gouernour ouer iustices both criminall and ciuill: and doth determine with his counsell of matters in difference, whatsoeuer that do appeale vnto him from other meaner iustices. The sixt is called Aytao:[104] this is generall puruier and president of the counsell of warre, whose office is to prouide souldiers when that it is requisite or necessitie demaundeth, and to prouide ships, munitions, and victuals for any fleete that shall passe by sea, as that shall be requisite by land, and for the suppliment of garisons in cities and coastes. To this is giuen the charge to examine such strangers that do come to any prouince, to knowe of whence they are, and wherefore they do come, and of all other thinges, and after beeing knowen, to giue the viceroy to vnderstand thereof, and of all thinges needful.

These sixe offices or charge are of great authoritie, and they that haue the execution thereof are had in great reuerence: euerie one of them hath in societie or counsell tenne, which are men chosen of great experience and diligence, and they do help him in the exhibition and dispatch of matters touching that office. When they are in place of counsell, which is in the pallace of the viceroy (whereas euerie office hath his place appointed, garnished in very good order), their sociates are diuided in two partes, fiue of them do sit on the right hand of the president, and fiue on the left hand; those which do sit on the right hande are the most auncientes and haue the more preheminence, and doo differ from the other that be on the left hande in this only, for that they do weare wastes or girdels imbossed with gold, and yealow hattes: and they on the left hand haue their girdels imbossed with siluer, and weare blewe hats; the which girdels, with gold and siluer, and hats yealow and[103] blewe, there is none that is permitted to weare but onelye the counsellers. Likewise these and the presidents do weare the kinges armes on their breastes and backes imbrodered with golde, without the which they can not goe foorth to anie place where they must be seen, neyther sitte in iustice to determine anie thing whatsoeuer. If they doo, they are not onely disobedient, but are seuerely punished at the time of their visitation.

If the president of any of these counsels doo die, then one of the auncientest of the counsellers dooth succeede him in the office, obseruing in all thinges the order, as I haue saide in the chapter past, of the royall A very good propertie of iustices. counsell. All these iustices generally haue a maruellous morall vertue, and that is, they be all very patient in hearing any complaynt, although it be declared with choller and proude speech. It is the first thing that is taught them in their schooles: they are verye well nourtered, and courteous in their speeches, although it bee with them that they haue condemned by lawe. If that vppon any necessitie they must goe into any part of the prouince to make any information of importance, then is appointed one of the counsell, and hee goeth alone, but he hath with him the authoritie of them all.

Besides these six counsellers or iudges aforesaide, there bee others of lesse dignitie (although greatly respected, as all ministers of iustice bee in this kingdome), and they are called as followeth: Cautoc, this is the chiefe auncient-bearer;[105] Pochim,[106] the seconde treasourer;

Pochinsi, he that keepeth the seale royall; Antzatzi,[107] he is as the maior or bailife of any citie or towne. There be also other three officers, which are called Guytay,[108] Tzia,[109] Toutay,[110] these doo keepe court and haue[104] audience in their houses once a weeke; and when they do open their doores, there is shott off foure peeces of artilerie, to giue all men to vnderstande that they are in place, readie to heare, and to doo iustice. If they do finde any that is culpable or faultie, they doo straight wayes sende them with a sargent vnto the ordinarie iustice of the citie, which is called zompau, with a bill or note, in the which is signified the punishment that he must haue.

Euerie ordinarie iustice hath committed to his charge a thousand souldiers. He can not exceed his limit nor iurisdiction, neyther can anie other haue to doo A very good order. in his charge. Euerie night they doo range their circuit, and doo cause that euery one may be quiet in his house, and to put out their candelles and lightes in time to auoyde fires, which hath happened amongest them verie great, by reason that their houses are so neere one to an other, and all the vpper partes of their houses wrought with tymber, according vnto the vse of Byskaye: and all suche as they doo finde with light after the houre limited, they are punished verie asperly. From these there is no appellation but vnto suche iustices as are sent from the court, and besides them vnto none but vnto the visiters that doo come ordinarily, who doo vndoo and make satisfaction of all griefes or wronges doone by the other, and these are called in their language Gomdim, which is as much to say, a righter of all griefe: this man is respected more than all the rest.

Besides all these there be other particular officers, which be called Tompo:[111] these haue the charge to see the prouision of victualles, and to put a price on them; an other is called Tibuco,[112] he that dooth arest and punish vagabundes and idle persons. Quinche[113] is the cheefe sargent, Chomcan[114] is the[105] keeper of the prison: this is one that they haue in great reuerence, for that he hath a priuilege aboue all the rest: that after hee hath done his dutie vpon his knees at his first entrie, hee may tell his tale on foote, and so can not the rest doo, but kneeling.

When that these gouernours or iustices doo newly come into these prouinces or cities, ordeyned and sent by the supreme counsell, they doo sende two or three dayes before they come themselues their letters patentes and prouisions: the which being seene and obeyed, there goeth foorth to receiue him all the loytias and men of warre with their souldiers and ensignes military, and other officers, making great feastes and pastimes.

Likewise the citizens at this time doo hange their streetes with clothes of silke and other thinges very richly, and trimmed with flowers, bearing him companie vnto his lodging with much musicke and sound of instrumentes.

Aboue all these dignities and offices there is one which is called Quinchay, which is to be vnderstood in their language "the golden seale"; this goeth not from the court, but vpon waightie matters and of great importance touching the quietnesse of all the kingdome. The order they haue in the choyse of these iustices and officers, and of other matters touching good gouernment, shall be declared vnto you in the chapter following.

CHAP. X.

Here is prosecuted the manner how they do choose their gouernors and iustices, and howe they doo execute the same.

All such officers as I haue declared vnto you in the chapter past, the king dooth ordaine them by consent of his[106] counsell, who doo informe themselues with a particular diligence of the qualitie and behauiour of the person that shall be elected. The principall matter that A very good consideration. they doo aduertise themselues is, that the viceroy, gouernour, or counsellor be not a naturall of that countrey that he is prouided for; and that for to preuent the inconuenience that might happen in the executing of good iustice, which many times chaunceth, eyther for the loue of his friendes and kinsfolkes, or else for the hate hee hath to his enimies. All such as are prouided in these offices, after that they do depart from the court whereas the charge is giuen them, til they come to the prouince, citie, or towne, whereas they shall remaine in iustice, they doo spende nothing on their owne horses; for that in all places whereas they doo trauaile or come, the king hath houses appointed, whereas they are receiued and lodged, and serued of all thinges necessarie, as well for horses for themselues as horses for them that come with him; likewise of barkes and boates, if that his iourney be by water, all is of free cost: it is all appointed what they shall haue to eate, which is conformable vnto the qualitie of his person, and the office he hath in charge. And when they do come vnto such houses as are appointed by the king to receiue and cherish them, they of the house do aske him if he will haue his pittance or ordinarie in money or in victualles; who, if he haue any kinsfolkes or friendes in that place that will inuite him, then dooth hee demand it in money, and keepe it to himselfe. These houses are maruelously well prouided of beds, and all other things necessarie; for that the Ponchas, who is president of the kinges reuenewes, hath a particular care to see all these things well furnished, by a commandement from the king and the supreme counsell. When they doo come vnto the citie or towne whereas they take the charge of gouernment, after they haue giuen the intertainment vnto them with feasts and pastime, as is declared in the chapter past, then do they bring him and lodge him in the kings[107] house, and do prouide him of seruants and all thinges necessarie that belongeth vnto him, and ministers needefull for the execution of iustice, who likewise haue their abiding in the same house, as sergeants and notaries, and other ministers of lesse authoritie. The king doth pay them all sufficient wages, for that it is forbidden vpon great penalties to take bribes or any other thing of any clyent. Likewise ye iudges be straightly charged and commanded, and that is one of the chiefest articles that is giuen them from the counsel, not to consent to be visited of any clyents in their houses, neither can they pronounce any sentence but in the place of publike audience, and in the presence of all the officers, and it must be done in such sort that all men that are in the place of audience may heare it, and is doone in this sort following. The iudge doth set himselfe in the seate of iustice, then do the porters put themselues at the entring or doores of the hall, who do name with a lowde and high voice the person that doth enter in to demand iustice, and the effect of that he doth aske. Then the plaintife doth kneele downe somewhat a far off from the iudge, and doth with a loud voice declare his griefe or demand, or else in writing. If it be in writing, then one of the scriueners or notaries doth take the petition and doth read it, the which being vnderstood by ye iudge, he doth straightwaies prouide vpon the same that which is agreeable vnto iustice, and doth firme the petition with his own firme with red inke, and commandeth what is needful to be done. These iudges are straitly charged and commanded by the kinges authoritie, that they must go fasting into ye hal of audience or iudgement hall without drinking of any wine, and they must giue no sentence with wine; and that is such a custome amongst them, that whosoeuer dooth break it is seuerely punished. By way of phisicke they do permit, before they doo go to giue any sentence, to comfort themselues with some conserues or such like. But wine in no manner of wise, although[108] they bee sicke of any infirmitie, and the lacke thereof to be hurtfull unto them: for they esteeme it a lesse euill to leaue of the hearing of any matter, then to giue any sentence after that they haue eaten or dronke. These matters being executed in publike (which is maruelously obserued and kept), it is not possible yt any of the officers should take any bribes, but it must be discouered by one of them; and for that they are vsed with great rigour in their residence, euerie one is afraid of his companion, and are one to an other (in this case) great enemies. The sergeants and notaries and the other officers are maruelous precise in the executing of their office: if that any doo not his duetie in his office, they take him and put a little banner in his hand, and he remaineth with the same, kneeling on his knees till the court of audience be ended. Then do the iudge command the bedelles to giue him so many whippes as hee doth deserue for the neglecting of his office. This same is little esteemed amongest them, for that it is a common thing vsed amongest them. When that anie of these iudges will go abroade into the citie (as seeldome times they doo for the reseruing of their authoritie), they are accompanied with the officers and ministers of iustice, and that in so good order, that the first two doo carrie siluer mases, after the manner as they doo in Rome carrie the mases before the cardinalles. They doo carrie them vpon long roddes, which doth signifie that in the name of the king they are in those offices: then after them followeth other two, and they do carrie ech of them in his hand a long cane and very straight, which doth signifie the vpright iustice that ought to be done and is doone by that iudge that there goeth: then followeth them other two, and they doo trayle ech of them a cane vpon the ground with long red laces, and at the endes tassels, which doth signifie the instrumentes wherewith they do whippe the faultie or malefactors; then followeth them other two with tables, like vnto white targets, in the which is[109] written the name of the iudge, with his title and office. The rest, which be many in number, do accompanie him to do him worship and honor. Those two that we spake of before, that do carrie the mases, do crie out and make a noyse vnto the people apart themselues, and to make roome that the iudge may passe: the which is straightwayes accomplished, for that by experience they know that he that doth neglect the same, is incontinent punished in the streete without remission: and the respect they haue vnto him is such that not one, of what state or degree soeuer he be, that dare mooue himself at such time as he doth passe by, neither crosse the streetes (except it be some superior iudge, vnto whom the inferiors doth the like reuerence). If any man do offend therein, he is then straightwaies punished. In all matters of lawe, as ciuill as criminall, the iudges do nothing but by writing, and do pronounce the sentences, and examine witnesses in publike, before all the rest of the officers, because no subtilty nor falshood shalbe vsed in their demaundes, neither in their writings, to set downe other then the truth. Euerie witnesse is examined by himselfe, and if he do double in his declaration, then do they ioyne together and make their demaunde from one to an other, til by their striuing they may come to a better knowledge of the truth. But when by these meanes they cannot bring it to light, then doo they giue them torments to make them confesse, beleeuing that without it such persons as haue experience and knowledge will tell the truth.

In matters of great importance, and such as doo touche graue personages, the iudge will not trust the scriuener or notarie to write any information; but they with their owne handes will write the declaration of any witnesse, and will consider verie much of that which is declared. This great diligence is the occason that fewe times there is any that doth complaine of any ill iustice doone, the which is a great and notable vertue, and ought to be imitated of all good[110] iustices, for to auoyd many inconueniences which doo happen for the not vsing the same the which these Gentiles haue great care to performe; who, beside the prosecution of right iustice, without respect or exception of any person, do vse certaine preuentions worthie to be suffered.

First these iudges, in al cities and townes of their iurisdiction, do number the households, and do repart them in ten and tenne housholds, and vpon the tenth house they do hang a table or signe whereon is writen the names of those ten housholders, with a commandement, in the which generally they are commanded, and euery one by himselfe particular, yt hauing any knowledge or notice that any of those ten housholders haue committed any trespasse or fault against any of the rest, or against himselfe, that is hurtfull vnto his neighbours or to the commonaltie, to go straight way and giue the iustice to vnderstand thereof, that the fault may be punished, with a mendment vnto the offender, and an example to al other. And vnto him that doth know any such offence and wil not declare it, is allotted the same punishment yt An occasion of amitie betwixt neighbours. the offender should haue, which is the occasion that one neighbour hath a care of an other, and liueth vnder feare, least they should giue occasion to be complained of. And againe, that their enimies may not this way take any aduantage. When that any of these ten neighbours doth remooue into an other streete, or into any other citie or towne to dwell, or will make any long iorney, hee is bound to ring a bell, or play on a coper kettle amongst all the neighbours for the space of ten dayes before he doth remooue or depart, and to aduise them all of his departure, and whether for that if he do owe any thing, or any thing be lent, that they may come and demaund it before their departure, because that none shall loose yt which is theirs. And if it so fall out that any shall depart without vsing this diligence, the iustice doth compell the rest of his neighbours yt are written on the signe to pay his debt, because they did[111] not aduise the iustice or his creditors before his departure. Such as do owe money or debts and will not paye (proouing the debt they doo execute their goods), if they haue none, they put them in prison, and limit a time for him to pay the same. But if it passe, and the debt not paide nor his creditor contented: for the first time they doo whippe them moderately, and do appoint him the second time limited for to pay ye same: if he do then misse, they do whip him more cruelly, and doo appoint him an other time, and so doo prosecute the same till he die with punishments, which is ye occasion yt euery one doth pay that he oweth, or procure amongst his friends to pay, or else giue himselfe for a slaue vnto his creditor, to shun the trouble of the prison and the paine of whippings, which is a thing not to be suffered.

Cruell tormentes. These iudges do vse two maner of torments to make them to confesse the truth, when by fayre meanes they can not, or by pollicie, the which first is procured with great care and diligence: the one is on their feete, and the other on their hands, and is so terrible that it cannot be suffered, but of force they do confesse that which the iudge doth pretende to know; yet doo they execute none of them except first they haue good information, or at the least, semiplena, or else so many indicions that it is a sufficient information for the same. The tormentes on the hands is giuen with two stickes as bigge as two fingers, and a span long, turned round and full of hooles in all places, wherein are put cordes to pull in and out: their fingers of both their hands are put into the cordes, and little and little they do pinch them, till in the end they do breake them at the jointes, with an incredible paine vnto them that doo suffer it, and yt causeth them to giue great shrikes and groanes that will mooue any man to compassion. And if it so come to passe that by this cruell torment they will not confesse, and that the iudge do vnderstand by witnesse and by indicions that hee is faultie and culpable, then dooth he commaund to giue him the torment[112] of the feete, which is a great deale more cruell than that of the handes, and is in this sort: they take two peeces of woode, foure square of foure spannes long and one spanne broade, and are ioyned together with a gume, and hooles boored *A more cruell torment.* thorough, and put thorough them cordes, and in the middest of these bordes they doo put the whole foote, and straine the cordes, and with a mallet they do stryke vpon the cordes, wherewith they do breake all the bones, and cause them to suffer more paine and griefe than with the torment of the handes. At the executing of these torments the supreme iudges are alwaies present, the which seeldome times doth happen: for that such as be culpable will sooner confesse than suffer those torments, desiring rather to die some other death that is not so cruell, than to suffer the paines of this torment.

The prisons that they haue are no lesse cruell and rigorous, as you shall vnderstand in a chapter by it selfe hereafter.

CHAP. XI.

Of the visitors that the king doth send euery yeare to visite the inferior iudges of his prouinces, and of the punishing of such as they do find culpable.

A great care to do true iustice. It is to be woondred at the great and vigilant care that this heathen prince hath, in that his ministers and iudges, as wel viceroyes, gouernors, presidents, as anie other officers, should execute their offices well and vprightly, as they ought to doo: for in the end of three yeares that their gouernment doth indure, they do take of them in residence straight account by the iudges thereof, who bee called Chaenes. Likewise they doo dispatch euerie yeere in great secrecie into euerie prouince, other iudges and visitors, that[113] be called Leachis,[115] the which are persons of great confidence, and prooued by experience of long time to be of good life, good customes, and haue done good seruice in the administring of iustice vprightly. These as they trauaile do inquire in euerie citie and towne that they come in (not being knowen, and in verie secret manner), all griefes and iniustice that is done in that prouince, which is the occasion that euerie one dooth liue (as the prouerbe sayth) with their face discouered. These do carrie from the king so great authoritie in their commissions giuen them, that without returning to the court, if they finde any delict culpable, they may apprehend the iudges and punish them, suspend, and reprieue, and do any thing touching their commission at their owne pleasure, so that it be not to take away the life of any man. This (as it is said) none can do without the consent of the king.

Ceremonies in performing of their oth. And because they should execute their office the better in this visitation, and with iustice and equitie, they do make them to sweare to be loyall, true, and secret. The which oth is executed in this order: they doo giue him to drinke three times of a certaine beuerage which they doo vse, and that is the confirming of their oth. And for that their departure should be with more secrecie, the counsell doth command their secretaries to make their prouisions, leauing in blank a space for his name that shal haue the prouision, and for the name of the prouince whether he shall goe, declaring nothing but that which is their ordinarie, that wheresoeuer the Loytia or iudge (being so dispatched) shall come, that they shall obey him as the king himselfe. But when soeuer it is in secret determined who shall goe, then doth the president of the counsel command the prouision to be[114] sealed, then he himselfe doth write his name in, and the prouince whether he doth goe. And tharewithall hee dooth depart from the court in great secrecie, and vnknowen of any who it is, nor whether he doth go, nor wherefore.

Then when he doth come to the prouince, citie, or town, whether he is sent, he dooth with like secrecie make his inquirie how the viceroy or gouernour doth vse himselfe in his gouernment, and how all other officers do execute their offices, without knowing from whence he came, nor whether he will, neither what he doth pretend. So after that hee hath passed throughout all the prouince, and is fullie certified of all his desire, then doth hee goe vnto the chiefe or metropolitane citie, whereas are resident all those iudges against whom hee hath made his visitation, and there he dooth remaine and abide till such time as the Tutam or viceroy doth make a generall counsell, which is once a month at the least: and at such time as they are in their counsell hall (and peraduenture without thought of any such iudge that should come), then this uisitor doth goe vnto the doore, and sayth vnto the porter, goe and tell them of the councell, that there is a uisitor that must and will come in, to notifie vnto them a commandement from the king: then the viceroy (vnderstanding by these words what he might be) doth commaund the doores to be open, and doth himselfe and the rest that are with him, rise vp from their seates, and doth goe and receiue him as their superior iudge; who doth enter with his prouision open in his handes (which dooth not cause a small feare amongest them all, but in especiall vnto such as their owne conscience doth accuse them): he doth read his prouision in the presence of them all, and at the instant of the conclusion, the viceroy doth arise from his place and dooth vnto him great reuerence and complementes, and so doo all the rest, acknowledgeing their duties.

Then dooth this uisitor place himselfe in the principallest[115] seate of counsell, and maketh his oration as the common vse is amongst them, wherein he doth giue them to vnderstande the cause of his comming, and with what care and diligence he did vse in his visitation to search out the trueth of matters: after which, with well pondred wordes, he doth laude and prayse all such as haue well executed their offices, and according thereunto he doth straight waies place them in their counsels in the higher seates, and promising them to giue the king and his counsell large account of their good seruice, that they might be rewarded according as they do deserue. Likewise he doth sharply reprehende all such as haue neglected their bounden dueties. Then doth he read there before them all the sentence pronounced against them, declaring in summe all such thinges wherein he hath found them culpable, which hath caused him to pronounce that sentence against them, the which, although it be never so rigorous, it is foorthwith executed without any replication or appellation: for from these visitors there is no appellation.

All such as shalbe punished or reprehended, they do first take away from them the ensignes of iustice, which be, as I haue told you, the girdle, bonnet, or narrowe brimd hat:

with the which they can neither punish nor hurt him: and if that any wil absolutely do it, he shall for the same be deprived of his office, and loose his head. So being cleare of these things, then do they execute the rigour of the sentence pronounced against the malefactor. But if there be any doubt in the sentence giuen, doth he straight waies (vppon the same doubt) ordaine nine iudges to sit vpon it, admonishing them (with the present before their eyes) to vse well their offices, wherewith hee doth charge them in the name of the king. Manie times these visitors do carrie power for to reward all such as doo well execute their offices, in giuing them roomes and offices of greater honor: so that the present and knowen reward which is done vnto the good, and[116] the rigorous punishment for the malefactors, is the occasion that this mighty kingdome is one of the best ruled and gouerned of any that is at this time knowen in all the world: waying the gouernement of the one (as in many places of this historie it is expressed) and ioyne it vnto the long and great experience which we haue had in the other, and then you will say as I say. Many times these visitors do visite the colleges and schooles, such as the king hath ordained of his owne cost in euerie prouince (as in the processe of this booke you shall vnderstand), and do examine the schoollers of the same, animating them to promotion all such as doo profite themselues in their studies, and doo whip and put in prison, yea and thrust them out of the schooles all such as are to the contrarie. Of all the which and of their commencing and rewardes, which is given vnto such as they do find sufficient, shall be at large declared vnto you in a particular chapter for the same.

CHAP. XII.

Of their prisons they doo vse, and the order they haue in the executing of iustice vpon the culpable.

Euen as the iudges and ministers are seuere and cruell in punishing, euen so are they in putting them in prisons, the which are as terrible and as cruell, with the which they doo keepe in peace and iustice this mightie kingdome: and as there is much people, so haue they manie prisons and verie great. There are in Thirteene prisons in euery great cittie. euery principal citie throughout al these prouinces thirteene prisons, inclosed and compassed about with high wals, and of so great largenesse within, that besides the lodgings of the keeper and his officers, and for a garison of souldiours that are there continually, there are[117] fish ponds, gardeines, and courts, whereas the prisoners do walke and recreate themselues all the day, such as are in for small matters. Likewise there are Victualing houses in the prisons and shops. victualling houses and shops, whereas is solde all manner of such things as the prisoners doo make for to sustaine themselues: which if they did not vse, their whole substance were not sufficient for their maintenance, the time is so long that they be there, although it be for a small matter: the occasion is for that the iudges take deliberation in their sentences: and againe, their cities are great and ful of other matters. Likewise they are slowe in the execution of any sentence. So that many times it doth fall out, that men being condemned to die, doo remaine so long in prison after their condemnation, that they die with pure age, or some other sicknesse or infirmitie, or by the crueltie of the straight and asper prison. Of these thirteene prisons aforesaide, alwayes foure of them are occupied with prisoners condemned vnto death, and in euerie one of them there is a captaine ouer one hundred souldiers which are reparted, and dooth keepe watch and warde day and night:

euery one of these condemned prisoners hath a bord tied about his necke that hangeth downe vnto his knees, a third of a yarde brode; it is made white with a certain whiting, and written vpon it the occasion wherefore he was condemned to die. The keeper of the prison hath a booke, wherein is written all the names of them that are condemned, and the occasion wherfore: for to be accountable of them at all times when they shalbe demaunded of him by the iudges or vizroies. They are shakled and manakled, and put in wards that do answere into the court, whereas the officers of the prison do make them to lie with their face downewarde vpon a floore made of bords for the same purpose, and do drawe ouer them iron chaines, drawne through great iron rings that are placed betwixt prisoner and prisoner, wherewith they are so strait crushed that they cannot mooue nor turne them from one side to another: also[118] they doo lay on them a certaine couering of timber, wherein remaineth no more space of hollownesse then their bodies doth make: thus are they vsed that are condemned to death. This prison is so painefull and grievous, that many doo dispaire and kill themselues because they cannot suffer it. In the day time they do take them forth and take off their manacles, that they may worke for to sustaine themselues; all such as haue nothing to maintaine themselues, nor any other that will help them, them the king doth giue a pittance of rice to sustaine them. Likewise they do worke what they may to better the same.

There is neuer no execution done vpon such as are condemned to die, but at the comming of the visiters or iudges of residence, whom they do call Chenes and Leuchis,[116] the which doe make their visitation in secret (as you doo vnderstande in the chapter where I spake of them). These doo visite the prisoners and demaund a note of the names of all them that are condemned, and the cause wherefore: and although that some of their sentences are confirmed by the king and his counsell, yet they will see them againe in the presence of these iudges that did condemne them, or such as did gouerne in their absence, for to be informed of them the faults of euerie one: whereby he may see and vnderstand whether his sentence of condemnation bee done with iustice or not. This diligence being done, they doo choose out among them fiftie condemned men, such whose faults are most odious, and commande the iayler to put all things in order for to doo execution on them: the which being done, they do examine them a new, and looke vpon the causes and faults, to see if by any meanes they can saue them. And if they do finde in any of them any iot of discharge, they do apart them from the rest, and straightwayes command three pieces of ordinance to be shot off, which is to giue warning to bring forth them that shalbe executed.[119] Then againe, when they doo bring them forth, they doo a new enter into counsell, to see if they can saue any of them: and when not, they command other three peeces of ordinance to be shot off, to cause them to be brought out into the fielde, and yet before they do breake vp their counsell, they doo turne and see once againe all their faults, to see if that by any meanes possible there might bee some remedie to saue them. If they do finde any, or any suspect of indicion, they do returne out of the fielde that person, and sende him againe to the prison. Some doo returne with an euill will, for that they had rather die at once, then for to suffer the straightnes and crueltie of the prison. In the meane time while they are perusing their causes, and concluding the same, they do cause these condemned prisoners to sit vpon heaps of ashes, and do giue them to eate. So when all yt these diligences are concluded, and they can find no remedy to saue any of them according vnto iustice, they doo commande three peeces of artilery more bee shot off, then do they execute iustice according vnto their sentence giuen them.

The deathes that they do execute is hanging, setting vppon stakes, quartering, and burning: but there is none that is burned, but such as are traitors to the king. When the last three of artilerie is shot off, then the belles do ring, and a great rumor is in the cittie, for that this execution is done but seldome. The day of execution all their shops are shut in, and there is none that doth worke vntill sun be set, which is after that the executed men are buried, the which is done with the companie of much people. The next day after this is done, the visitors do make the second visitation, which is of the theeues (a thing verie much abhorred amongst them): and such as they doo finde culpable, hee is whipped throughout the common streetes with great shame, with a borde hanging about his necke (as aforesaide), whereon is written his fault: and therewith they are carried throughout[120] the streetes three or foure dayes. They do beate them on the calues of their legges, with a broade and thicke cane of foure fingers broad, and as thicke as a mans finger, the which they do lay in water before, the more for to torment them: they are bound with their hands behind them, and their faces downewards to the earth: two hangmen do execute this whipping of them, the one at one legge and the other at the other, and it is done with so great crueltie, that after they haue giuen sixe blowes, they cannot stande vppon their feete, and many times it chanceth that with fiftie blowes they die. The most part of these theeues do die in the punishments, and many times there is whipped togither of theeues two hundred. So that with these and others that are punished in the prisons (is of a verie truth) that there do die euerie yeare in one of these principall cities of the prouince more than sixe thousande persons. At these punishments the iudges are alwaies in presence, and for that they should not be mooued to compassion, in the

meanetime that execution is done, they do occupie
themselues in banquettings or other
pastimes. Adulteries are death, and such as do consent to be
coockoldes (which is neuer founde but amongst them of the
basest sort), are punished with exemplar punishments
ordained for the same.

Adulterie is death. (marginal note)

CHAP. XIII.

Of the characters and letters that the Chinos do vse, and of the colleges and scholes that are in this kingdome, and of other curious things.

It is not from our purpose (now after that we haue told you of the gouernement of this mightie kingdome) to giue you to vnderstand how that there be great and famous philosophers, as well naturall as morall, and other things of great[121] pollicie and curiosity: to tel you now of their characters, and the manner they haue in writing, and then of the colledges and schooles. Now vnto the first. You shall finde verie fewe in this kingdome but can both write and reade, yet haue they not the alphabet of letters as we haue, but all that they doe write is by figures, and they are long in learning of it, and with great difficultie, for that almost every word hath his character. They do signifie the heauen, which they do call Guant, by one character alone, which is this :[117] the king, whom they doo call Bontay,[118] by this , and by consequent the earth, the sea, and the rest of Sixe thousand characters in writing. the elements. They do vse more than six thousand characters different the one from the other, and they doo write them verie swiftly (as it hath beene seene many times at the Philippinas, by manie Chinos that are there, and come thither daily); it is a kinde of language that is better vnderstood in writing then in speaking (as the Hebrue toonge), by reason of the certaine distinction of points that is in euery character differing one from the other, which in speaking cannot be distinguished so easilie. Their order of writing is cleane contrarie vnto ours, for that they doo beginne their lines from aboue downewards, but in verie good order: likewise they begin their lines at the right hande and write towards[122] the left, contrarie vnto vs. They keepe the verie same order in their printing, as you shall vnderstande, and as may be seene this day at Rome in the librarie of the sacred pallace. And likewise in that which King Philip hath caused to be erected in the monasterie of Saint Laurence the royall, and also in other places; in this order as I haue saide, and of their characters to the which I referre me, it is an admirable thing to consider how that in that kingdome they doo speake manie languages, the one differing from the other: yet generallie in writing they doo vnderstand one the other, and in speaking not. The occasion is, for yt one figure or character vnto them all doth signifie one thing, although in the pronouncing there is difference in the vowels. The character that doth signifie a citie is this ,[119] and in their language some doo call it Leombi, and others Fu, yet both the one and the other doo vnderstande it to bee citie; the like is in all other names. And in this order doo communicate with them the Japones, Lechios, those of Samatra, and those of the kingdome of Quachinchina and other borderers vnto them: whereas in their speech or language, there is no more vnderstanding then is betwixt Greekes and Tuskanes.

The king hath in euerie citie colleges or schooles at his owne cost, in the which they doo learne to write, read, and count, as well as to studie naturall or morall philosophie, astrologie, lawes of the countrie, or any other curious science. They that doo teach in these schooles be such persons as excell in euerie facultie, such as may be found none better, but speciallie in writing and reading: for that there is none, although he be neuer so poore, but dooth learne to write and read, because amongst them he is accounted infamous that cannot doo both. Unto higher studies come a great[123] number of students, and doo trauaile all they may possiblie to profite, for that it is the best course and surest way to obtaine the name of a Loytia, or gentleman, or other dignitie: as more plainelie shall bee showed you in the chapter following, where the order howe they doo giue them the title Loytia shall bee spoken off, and is amongst vs after the fashion of proceeding or commencing doctor.

Unto the colleges, as well maiors as minors, the king dooth sende euerie yeere uisiters, for to see and vnderstande howe the studentes doo profite, and what the masters bee, with other matters touching their good gouernement. In their visitation they doo honour in wordes those whome they finde of abilitie, animating them to perseuer in the same: and doo put in prison and punish such as they knowe to haue abilitie, and doo not profite themselues thereof; and such as haue none, nor will not learne, they put out of the colleges, that others may occupie their places that better will imploy themselues. They haue great Paper made of the filme of canes. abundance of paper, the which is made of the filme of canes, and with great facilitie: it is verie good cheape: their printed bookes are made thereof: the most part of it can be written but on the one side, for that it is so thinne: they doo not write with pennes as wee doo, made of quilles, but with pennes made Pens made of canes. of canes, and at the end like a fine brush, like vnto a painters pensill: and although this bee their order, yet haue they amongst them excellent scriueners, that grow thereby to bee verie rich. When they write letters vnto anie principall person, they gilde the margent of the paper, and limbe it, and they put the letter written into a purse made of the same paper all guilt and painted, the which they shut and seale, so that the letter is onely contained therein.

This they doo vse verie much, that although one go to visite another in person, yet they doo carrie a letter written in their sleeues, and possible there shall not bee written in the same tenne letters, and that signifieth that they doo come[124] to kisse their handes; these things are to bee solde at the bookebinders of all sortes, as well for principall persons and men of authoritie, as for others of meaner estate for to desire, reprehend, or discommende: and to conclude, for all thinges that they will desire or haue neede of, yea if it bee to defie anie bodie, so that the buyer hath no more to doo but to close it vp and seale it to sende it whither his pleasure is. These and manie other curiosities they do vse, as you haue heard and shall heare in the discourse of this small hystorie, or at the least somewhat touched, for that the breuitie that I doo pretend and will vse, will not permit that I shoulde enter so farre for to declare at large, but to be briefe in that I shall declare.

CHAP. XIV.

Of the examination of such whome they preferre to the degree of Loytia, which is with vs the degree of a doctor: and howe they doo commence them, and howe they doo beare him companie.

These uisitours of whome wee haue spoken, the king and his counsaill doo sende them to visite his prouinces; and amongest the greatest things that are giuen them in charge, is the visitation of the colledges and schooles which the king hath in all the principall citties, as is saide; the which visitour hath a particular authoritie for to commence or graduate such students as haue finished their course, and are of abilitie and sufficiencie to perfourme the same. They doo make them gentlemen, if they bee capable of anie charge of iustice or gouernment. And for that the vse of their ceremonies is a thing woorthie to bee knowne, I will here declare the same order which Frier Martin de Herrada, and his companions, did see in the citie of Aucheo,[120] at the time of their commencement.[125]
 At such time as the visitor hath concluded the visitation of his prouince, and hath punished the malifactors, and rewarded the good: in the metropolitane cities, hee doth straight wayes cause proclamation to bee made that all students and scholers that doo finde themselues sufficient, and haue a corage to be examined to take the degree of Loytia, the which, although amongst them is vnderstoode to bee made a gentleman, yet amongst vs is a doctour.

The day appointed being come, they are all presented before the visitour, who taketh all their names in a scrowle, and appointeth another day for their examination. This day, for honour of the feast, the visitor dooth inuite all the learned Loytias that are in the citie, who ioyntly with him do make the examination with great rigour, alwayes putting forwardes and preferring those that are skilfull in the lawes of the countrey, by which they do gouerne all other faculties whatsoeuer, and that they be therewithall good, and vertuous. And all those that they doo finde with these properties, they do write their names in an other scrowle, and doo appoint the day of commencement, the which is done with great ceremonies and much people, in whose presence the visitor, in the name of the king, doth giue vnto them the ensignes of degree and dignitie to be a Loytia; that is, a waste or girdle bossed with gold or siluer, and a hat with certaine thinges on it, as shall be shewed you in the chapter following; which is a signe and token that doth make the difference from the vulgar people, without the which none can shewe himselfe in publike.

And although al be called Loytias, I meane those that come to it by letters or learning, and others by the warres, and others by a gift of the king, yet they differ the one from the other in estimation. For that those of the royall counsell, viceroyes, gouernors, and visitors, are made Loytias by disputation in learning; and the generall captaines, maiors, bailifes, and testators, are a gift of the kinges in recompence[126] of some good seruice that they haue done. These haue no more preheminence, but onely that they haue the benefite of their priuileges, and haue the dignitie of that vocation, but these are neuer preferred to greater honours, as the other Loytias are, of these you have in euery citie very many.

There be others likewise of great estimation, and are put in the second degree, and are those that are made by desert in the warres, and are elect and chosen by the generals by authoritie of the king, for some act or worthie deede done in the wars, by force of armes or such like, approued by witnesse of great credite; vnto whom, besides the title and honour giuen vnto them, they doo giue them great liuings, for that no valiant or worthie deede but is had in Any good thing gratified. estimation, and gratified with great liberalitie, which is the occasion that those which are meane souldiers, are animated to imitate those that be most principall and valiant. According vnto my promise I will here, with as much breuitie as may bee, declare vnto you the order of their commencements, and how they do accompanie them after that they are made Loytias, for that it is a thing worth the hearing.

The day appointed being come for to commence or giue degrees, all the Loytias, with the visitor, doo enter into the royall hall whereas they were examined, al richly apparelled, and being assembled, then do enter in al those that shal receiue degrees, galantly apparelled without any upper garment, and before euerie one of them, go the padrines,[121] and after them the graduates with garments very finely made, riding on gennets very sumptuously couered with cloth of gold and silke, that do carie the ensignes that shalbe giuen vnto him, the which hee dooth demande of the visitor, kneeling vpon his knees with great humilitie. Who first sweare them, that in all offices committed vnto them, they shall with all care and diligence doo iustice equallie vnto all men, and that they shall not receiue any bribes or presents whatsoeuer: that[127] they shall be true and loyall vnto the king, and that they shall not conspire in any confederacie or treason against him, and manie other things: which ceremonies he standeth long about.

This oth being taken, the visitor who presenteth the kings person, dooth put on them the ensignes aforesaide, with the facultie belonging thereunto, and then hee and all the Loytias imbrace them presently. This doone, they depart out of the hal in verie decent order, at which instant all the belles in the citie are rong, and great store of ordinance and artilerie discharged, which continueth a good space. Then they carrie these newe Loytias throughout the citie, accompanied with a multitude of people in manner following.

There go first before them many souldiers, marching in good order, with drommes and trumpets and other musicall instruments verie melodious: after them are borne many maces, then follow all the Loytias, some on horsebacke and some are carried in litter chaires, in most gallant order, after which follow the Padrines. Then the new commenced Loytias, without any upper garment as before is saide, all mounted vppon white horses verie richly couered with cloth of golde; hauing euerie one of them a tippet of taffeta vpon his shoulder, and on his head a hat with two small tippets hanging downe behinde, much after the fashion of those that hang on the bishops miter; this is permitted unto none but vnto those of their orders abouesaide: vpon their hats they haue two branches of golde, or of siluer and guilt, made like vnto a bunch of fethers: before euerie one of them are carried six frames, couered with satten, and euerie one is carried by foure men: in these frames are written in letters of golde their disputation, facultie, and title giuen them for the same, and their armes, with manie other things which I omit for breuitie sake, because this marching and passing holdeth eight houres togither. The citizens there keepe this day festiuall, and do ordeine manie dances and sportes. And the better sort doo celebrate three or foure daies after,[128] banquetting the newe made Loytia, and giuing him ioy of his newe preferment, euerie man seeking his good will and fauour. From this day forwards hee is of abilitie to take vppon him any office and gouernement whatsoeuer: and therefore straight wayes he goeth vnto the court to procure the same, and carrieth with him the ensignes of his commencement, and is apparelled so that he may be knowne, wherefore they doo him great honour in the way as hee goeth, and lodge him in such houses as the king hath appointed in euerie towne for such as they be. When he commeth to the court, hee goeth and dooth his duetie vnto the president and vnto the rest of the royall counsell, who euerie one a part, doo giue him ioy of his new dignitie, and with many words of great curtesie and praise promise him, as occasion shall serve, to prouide him a place, as they by their examination doo vnderstande his abilitie, and, againe, as they see his discreete dealing and care in such matters as they do giue him in charge, so will they preferre him to better dignitie and honour. So the next day following they register him in their booke of memorie, which is alwayes in the counsell chamber; and they remaine there waiting and seruing them vntill they haue prouided them of some gouernment, which is not long after, for that the kingdome is great, with manie prouinces and citties, as by this historie you shal vnderstand.

CHAP. XV.

How that with them they haue had the vse of Artilery long time before vs in these parts of Europe.

Amongst many things worthie to bee considered, which haue beene and shalbe declared in this historie, and amongst[129] manie other which of purpose I omit, because I would not be tedious vnto the reader, no one thing did cause so much admiracion vnto the Portugals, when that they did first traficke in Canton, neither vnto our Spaniards, who long time after went vnto the Philippinas, as to finde in this kingdome artilerie. And wee finde by good account taken out of their histories, that they had the vse thereof long time before vs in Europe. It is said that the first beginning was in the yeare 1330, by the industrie of an Almane,[122] yet howe he was called there is no historie that dooth make mention: but the Chinos saie, and it is euidently seene, that this Almaine dooth not deserue the name of the first inuenter, but of the discouerer, for that they were the first inuentors, and from them hath the vse thereof beene transported vnto other kingdomes, where it is now vsed. The Chinos saie that their first king, called Vitey, did first inuent the same, and that he was taught the matter how to make them by a spirite that came out of the earth, for to defende himselfe and his kingdome from the Tartares, that did much molest him with warres: for, according vnto the tokens giuen him, (as it dooth appear in their histories,) and the industrie for the same, it appeareth that it was some spirit, enimie vnto mankind, onely for to destroy them, as in these daies the experience thereof is apparent vnto vs. All the which carieth a similitude of the trueth, for that this king was a great sorcerer and inchanter, as you may well vnderstand by the herbe that he had growing in ye court of his pallace, whereof before I haue told you. And if this be not credible,

The first inuenting of armor.

because so many yeres are past since this kings raigne, yet it is of truth, yt when these Chinos went to the kingdom of Pergu,[123] Artilerie 1300 years before us. and to cōquest ye east Indies more then 1500 yeares since, they caried with them ye like instruments of warre, which did serue them in their conquest: the which conquest being ended, they left behind them certaine peeces of artilerie,[130] which were found afterwards by the Portugals, whereon were grauen the armes of China, and in what yeare they were made, agreeing iust with the time of the conquest.

Such artilerie as the frier Gerrarda and his companions did see at their being there, they say it was of antiquitie, and very ill wrought, and was for the most part peeces to shoote stones, or murderers: but it was giuen them to vnderstande that in other prouinces of the kingdome, there be that bee verie curiouslie wrought and faire, which may bee of such which the Captaine Artreda did see: who in a letter that hee wrote vnto King Phillip, giuing him to vnderstande of the secreats of this countrie, amongst which hee saide, the Chinos doo vse all armour as wee doo, and the artilerie which they haue is excellent good. I am of that opinion, for that I haue seene vessels there of huge greatnesse, and better made then ours, and more stronger.

In euerie citie they haue certaine houses, where they make their ordinance and artilerie continuallie: they doo not plant them on castles (for that they haue not the vse of them in all the kingdome), but vppon the gates of their cities, which hath mightie great and thicke walles, and deepe ditches, which they doo fill with water out of the next riuer, at all times when neede requireth, which they account the greatest strength in all the kingdome. At euerie gate of the citie there is a captaine with manie souldiours, that keepeth watch and warde, night and daie, to suffer no stranger to enter in without especiall lycence of the gouernour of the citie or towne. By this that I haue alredie saide, as seemeth vnto me, is apparantlie shewed and declared the antiquity of artilerie in this kingdome: and howe that they were the first inuentors thereof. Likewise it dooth plainely appeere that there was the first inuention of printing, a thing as strange as the other, whose antiquitie in that kingdome shall be shewed in the chapter following.[131]

CHAP. XVI.

Of the antiquitie and manner of printing bookes, vsed in this Kingdome, long before the vse in our Europe.

The admirable inuention, and the subtill ingenie of printing is such, that for lacke of the vse thereof, should haue beene forgotten the worthinesse of manie excellent men, and of their deedes doone in the happie daies and times long past: and manie in these our daies woulde not trouble themselues so much as they doo, in learning to get honour and promotion, or in feates of warres, if that their fame should no longer continue in writing then their liues on the earth. Leauing apart the woonderfull effectes of this subtile inuention, least speaking thereof I should be ouer tedious, I will heere onlie goe about to prooue that which this chapter dooth propounde, with some ensamples, whereof manie are found in their histories, and likewise in ours. It doth plainlie appeare by the vulgar opinion, that the inuention of printing did beginne in Europe in the yeare 1458, the which was attributed vnto Toscan,[124] called John Cutembergo: and it was saide of trueth, that the first mould wherewith they doo print was made in Maguncia, from whence an Almaine called Conrado[125] did bring the same inuention into Italie. And the first booke that was printed, was that which saint Austine[132] did write, intituled De ciuitate Dei: wherein manie authors agree. But the Chinos doo affirme, that the first beginning was in their countrie, and the inuentour was a man whome they reuerence for a saint: whereby it is euident that manie yeares after that they had the vse thereof, it was brought into Almaine[126] by the way of Ruscia and Moscouia, from whence, as it is certaine, they may come by lande, and that some merchants that came from thence into this kingdome, by the Redde Sea, and from Arabia Felix, might bring some books, from whence this John Cutembergo, whom the histories dooth make authour, had his first foundation. The which beeing of a trueth, as they haue authoritie for the same, it dooth plainlie appeare that this inuention came from them vnto vs: and for the better credite hereof, at this day there are found amongst them many bookes printed 500 yeares before the inuention began in Almaine: of the which I haue one, and I haue seene others, as well in Spaine and in Italie as in the Indies. The frier Herrada and his companions, when they came from the China vnto the Philippinas, did bring with them manie printed bookes of diuers matters, which they did buy in the citie of Ancheo, the which were printed in diuers places of the kingdome.[127] Yet the most part[133] of them were printed in the prouince of Ochian,[128] whereas is the best print: and as they did report, they woulde haue brought a great number more, if that the vizroy had not disturbed them, for they haue great libraries, and very good cheape; but hee suspected that those bookes might be a meane to giue them to vnderstande the secrets of their kingdome, the which they doo indeuour to keepe close from strangers. The vizroy vsed a policie, and sent them word, how that he was certified that they went about buying of bookes for to carry them into their countrie, and howe they shoulde not spende their money on them, for hee would giue them for nothing so manie bookes as they woulde haue, which afterward hee did not performe, possible for the reason aforesaide, or else he did forget his promise.

At such time as this commandement came vnto them, they[134] had bought a good number, out of the which are taken the most things that wee haue put in this small historie, for to giue a briefe notice of them and of that kingdome, till such time as by a true certificate the experience of manie shall cause more credite thereunto: for that vnto this day, by reason of the small notice wee haue, we cannot with so great authoritie make it so credible as wee hope that time hereafter will doo. The which hath moued mee, yea and constrained me, to leaue to intreat of manie things, which in those parts are to bee credited, yea and are most true: and for the same I haue beene blamed and reprehended by such as haue had perfite notice thereof.

And nowe for that I will not go from my purpose, you shall vnderstand in the chapter following, whereof these bookes that they brought doo intreat, that the better you giue credite vnto the curiositie and policie of that kingdome, as in manie places I haue declared, and hereafter will declare.

CHAP. XVII.

The substance and manner of those bookes that Frier Herrada and his companions brought from China.

They brought with them a great number of bookes, as wee haue said, that did intreate of diuers matters, as you shall perceiue in the sequell.

Of the description of all the whole kingdome of China, and the placing of the 15 prouinces, and the length and bredth of euery one of them, and of other kingdomes bordering vppon them.

Of all tributes and rentes belonging vnto the king, and of all the orders of his royall pallace, and of his ordinarie pensions that hee giueth, and the names of all officers in his house, and how far euery office doth extend.[135]

How many tributaries euerie prouince hath, and the number of such as are free from tribute, and the order and time, how and when they are to be recouered.

For the making of ships of all sorts, and the order of nauigation, with the altitudes of euery port, and the quantitie of euery one in particular.

Of the antiquitie of this kingdome of China, and of the beginning of the world, and in what time and for whome it beganne.

Of the kings that have raigned in this kingdome, and the order of their succession and government, with their liues and customes.

Of the ceremonies they vse in doing sacrifice vnto their idols (which they hold as gods), and the names of them: of their beginnings, and at what time they shoulde make their sacrifices.

Their opinions of the immortalitie of the soule, of the heauen, of hell, of the manner of their funerals, and of their mourning apparel that euery one is bounde to weare, according as he is alianced vnto the dead.

Of the lawes of the kingdome, and when and by whome they were made; and the punishment executed on those which violate the same, with manie other matters touching their good government and policie.

Manie herbals, or bookes of herbes, for phisitions, shewing how they should be applied to heale infirmities.

Many other bookes of phisicke and medicine, compiled by authors of that kingdome, of antiquitie and of late daies, containing in them the maner how to vse the sicke, and to heale them of their sicknes, and to make preseruatiues against all sicknesses and infirmities.

Of the properties of stones and mettals, and of things natural that haue vertue of themselues; and wherefore pearles, gold, and silver, and other metals, may serue for the vtility of man, comparing with the one and the other the vtilitie of euerie thing.[136]

Of the nomber, and moouings of the heauens: of the planets and stars, and of their operations and particular influences.

Of such kingdomes and nations as they haue notice off, and of particular things that are in them.

Of the life and behauiour of such men, whom they holde for saints, where they lead their liues, and where they died and were buried.

The order howe to play at the tables, and at the chests, and how to make sports of legerdemaine and puppets.

Of musicke and songs, and who were the inuentors thereof.

Of the mathematicall sciences, and of arithmeticke, and rules how to use the same.

Of the effectes that the children doo make in their mothers wombs, and how they are euery moneth sustained, and of the good and bad times of their birth.

Of architecture, and all manner of buildings, with the bredth and length that euerie edifice ought to haue for his proportion.

Of the properties of good and bad ground, and tokens how to know them, and what seede they will beare euery yeare.

Of astrologie naturall, and judiciarie, and rules to learne the same, and to cast figures to make coniectures.

Of chiromancia and phisiognomia, and other signes and tokens, and what euery one doth signifie.

The order how to write letters, and how to give euerie one his title, according to the dignitie of his person.

How to bring vp horses, and to teach them to runne and trauaile.

How to deuine vpon dreames, and cast lottes when they beginne any iourney, or take any thing in handes, whose ende is doubtfull.

Of apparell worne in all the kingdome, beginning with the king, and of the ensignes or coates of armes of such as doo gouerne.[137]

How to make armour and instruments of warre, and howe to firme a squadron.

These bookes, and many others that the fryers brought, out of the which (as afore saide) haue been taken all such thinges as haue beene and shall be declared in this historie, interpreted by persons naturally borne in China, and brought vp in Philippinas with the Spaniards that dwell there, who affirme that they haue seene great libraries in cities where they abode, but especially in Ancheo and Chincheo.

CHAP. XVIII.

The order that these Chinos obserue in making bankets, and in celebrating their festiuall daies.

For that in some parts of this historie wee haue touched the bankets that the Chinos do make, it shall not bee amisse to declare here the order they vse therein, for that they are curious, and differ verie much from our order and vse in their banquetting, the which we haue perceiued as well by their feeding as by many other thinges.

Amongest these Chinos, more than amongest any other people of the world, are vsed bankets and feastes, for they are rich and without care, and also without the light of heauen, albeit they do confesse and beleeue the immortalitie of the soule, and the rewarde or punishment in an other worlde, according vnto their workes in this life (as we haue saide). All that euer they can, they doo giue themselues vnto the contentment of the flesh, and vnto all maner pastimes, wherein they liue most delicately, and in verie good order. Their custome is, although they haue a hundred guestes, yet euerie one must sit and eate at a table by himselfe. Their tables be verie fine, gilt and painted full of birdes and[138] beastes, and other varieties verie pleasant vnto the eye. They do not vse to put table clothes on them, but onely a forefront of damaske, or some other silke, on euerie one of them, which hangeth downe to the ground; and on the foure corners they doo sette manie little baskettes curiously wrought with golde and siluer wyre, full of flowers and knackes of sugar, made with great curiositie, as elefantes, grayhoundes, hares, and all other kinde of beastes and foules, gylt and painted: in the middest of the table they doo sette the victualles in maruelous good order, as flesh of diuerse sortes, fowle, and fishes: of the which they make diuers manners of brothes passing well dressed, and are serued in fine earthen dishes of great curiositie, and of siluer (although these they vse verie seeldome, except for the viceroyes): they haue no neede of table clothes nor napkins, for they eate so delicately, that they doo not touch the meate with their handes, but with little forkes of golde or siluer, with the which they eate so cleanly, that although it be verie small that they eate, yet will they let nothing fall: they drinke often, but a little at a time, and therefore they vse verie little cuppes.

At these bankettes and feastes, there are present alwayes women gesters, who doo play and sing, vsing manie prettie gesters to cause delight, and make mirth to the gestes: besides these they haue diuerse sortes of men with other instruments, as tomblers and players, who doo represent their comedies verie perfectly and naturally: in these bankets they spende the greatest part of the day, by reason of so manie diuersities of meates that they serue in. They passe manie times a hundreth sundrie dishes, when that the estate of the person that is inuited, or of him that maketh the banket, dooth require. As may shew the report of the Augustine fryers, in the beginning of the second part of this historie: where one doth tell of bankets that were made him by the Insuanto, a gouernor of the prouince of Chincheo,[139] and the uiceroy of Ancheo, and of the gallant deuices they had to driue away the time so long as the banket lasted. Unto euerie one of their guestes they doo set a table, euerie table standing one along by an other, making a difference of the number of them, according vnto the qualitie of the persons: vpon the first table (where sitteth he that is inuited) they set the victualles readie dressed, sweete meates, or march-panes,[129] which is the last seruice: and on the rest, although they be twentie, they set great store of diuerse kindes of meates, all rawe, as capons, ducks, teales, hennes, peeces of salt and martlemas biefe, gammons of bacon, and many other thinges. All these doo remaine vppon the tables till the banket be ended, and the guestes departed: then doo the seruantes of him that made the banket take all these rawe meates, and carrie them before their guestes till they come vnto their houses or lodges, where they doo leaue it with great ceremonies. When they doo make any banket to a viceroy or to any embassadour, it is with so great cost and sumptuousness, that they spend a great substance therein. These bankets do commonly indure twentie daies together, continuing vntill the last day as royally and as plentifully as the first day.

They do celebrate all their festiuall dayes in the night, which is ordinarily their newe moones; and they doo solemnize them with much musicke and newe inuentions. But more particularly they doo celebrate the first day of the yeare, which is, after their account, the first day of the moneth of March: on this day they apparell themselues verie costlye and sumptuouslie, both men and women, and doo adorne themselues with all their iewelles and newe toyes, and doo hang their houses and doores with carpettes and clothes of silke and cloth of golde, and dresse them vppe trimme with roses and other flowers, for at that time there is great store in that country: likewise they doo sette at all[140] their doores great trees, on the which they doo hang manye lightes, and all the triumphall arches that bee in the streetes (which bee verye manie, as wee haue sayde) are decked with bowes this day: wherein they put manie lightes, and set full of canapies of cloth of gold, damaske, and manie other sundrie sorts of silkes.

Their priestes doo assist them in these feastes very richly apparelled, and doo offer sacrifice vpon their altars vnto the heauen, and vnto their idolles, and they sing many songes.

This day dooth all people generally sport themselues with great singing and sounding of instruments, in the which they are very cunning. Such instruments as the Augustine fryers did see, were lutes, gytternes, vyalles, rebbukes, wayghtes, virginalles, harpes, and flutes, and other instrumentes which wee doo vse, although they doo differ something in the fashion of them, but yet easie to be knowen. They do tune their voyces vnto their instrumentes with great admiration: they haue all commonly very good voyces. In these feasts they do make many representations of great pastime according vnto nature, with vestiments that they haue for the purpose. All the dayes that these feastes do indure, their tables be full of diuerse sorts of meates, as well of fish as of flesh, and of all sortes of fruites, and excellent good wine, the which they make of the palme tree, with certaine mixtures, which maketh it have an excellent good taste. All the day, they and their priestes do eate and drinke so much till they can no more. They haue it for a thing most certaine amongest them, that looke how they are in disposition that day, so shall they passe the whole yeare, eyther sorrowfull or merrie. I omit the feastes which they make at marriages, and at any good successe, though they be in great number and very sumptuous, because I would not be tedious: in all things they couett to auoyde melancholy.[141]

CHAP. XIX.

How they salute one another in this countrie, and of some part of their ceremonies.

There is no nation in all the worlde, be it neuer so barbarous, that hath been found out vntill this day, without a manner of courtesie, or some ceremony of salutation in their meetinges and visitinges, or when they do assemble in any particular businesse: whereof wee haue large notice by auncient histories, and sufficient experience in that wee haue seene and vnderstoode in these kingdomes and prouinces which in our dayes hath beene discouered: although herein (as I am fully perswaded) those of this kingdome do exceede all nations of the world (as is affirmed by them that haue had the experience), for they haue so many ceremonies and vsages of courtesie and ciuilitie amongest them, that they haue bookes to teach them only how they should behaue themselues in making difference of persons. Of all the which, such as shall seeme expedient to giue notice of, I will declare in this chapter, using therein the breuitie that this historie requireth.

They esteeme it a great discourtesie, not to salute one an other when they see or meete one an other, although the acquaintance betwixt them be but small.

The salutation that the common people do vse is, when they do meete the one with the other, to shut the left hande, and to couer it with the right, ioyning therewith their breastes together, with much bowing their heades downewardes, signifying that loue and amitie is as firme betweene them as their handes are fast, and that their friendshippe is not alonely in the ceremonie, but also in the heart: the which they giue to vnderstande by woordes at the same time. But amongest courtyers and gentlemen they vse an other manner[142] of courtesie, which seemeth vnto them of much more curiositie, that is: at such time as they doo meete, they make a little staye, then they caste abroad their armes, and claspe their fingers together, remayning in compasse, humbling themselues manie times, and contending one with an other about their parting for to prosecute his waye; and the higher estate they are of, the more is their contention. When that anie meane person doth meete with a principall man, who for dignitie or for any other occasion dooth acknowledge superioritie, straight wayes hee dooth stay with great silence, declining his head, till such time as he is past by, although the most part of them dooth it more for feare than for courtesie: for that experience hath taught them, that he that dooth it not, is straight wayes punished and whipped cruelly.

When that any of these commeth to speake with any Loytia, at the entering in at the hall whereas he is, hee kneeleth downe, declyning his head and looking vpon the ground: and on this sort he goeth vpon his knees till hee come into the middest of the hall, and there he stayeth and declareth his petition by worde of mouth, with an humble and meeke voyce, or else presenteth it by writing: and hauing receiued answere, hee dooth returne on his knees backwardes, without turning his backe to the Loytia, vntill hee bee quite out of the hall. And if they which doo meete or visite one an other be equall in dignity, they shew great courtesie on both sides, contending who shall surpasse in courtesie and wordes: wherein they are verie ceremonious. When one doth goe to visite an other, he that is visited, after the visitation done, doth bring the other vnto the streete doore. This custome is vsed most amongest the common people, being equal in degree, or differing little. Likewise they vse one thing verie strange, and neuer heard of amongest other nations, that is: if that one doo come out of A strange kind of courtesie. the countrie, to visite an other that is in the citie or towne (although he be a nigh kinsman, and long time acquainted), if that[143] knocking at the doore or in the streete hee doo meete with him whome he dooth come to visite (hee being not well apparelled), although he speake vnto him, yet will hee not make any aunswere, nor any resemblance that euer he sawe or knewe him before: but straightwayes returneth home to his house in all haste possible, and doth apparell him selfe with the best apparell that he hath, and then he goeth foorth and receiueth his guest and friend, dissembling as though he had not before meete nor scene him.

This ceremonie amongest them is infalliblie kept, for that it is amongest them an auncient tradition, and founded vppon their religion. They giue great intertainement vnto their guestes, and make them straightwayes a beuer[130] or collation with manie sortes of conserues and fruites, and good wine, and an other kinde of drinke, that is generally vsed thorough out the whole kingdome, and is made of diuerse physicall hearbes, good to comfort the heart, the which they warme when they drinke thereof.

These ceremonies they vse when that one neighbour dooth visite an other. But when that one of the towne dooth meete with a stranger that hee dooth knowe, and hath beene in the towne certaine dayes, and he not seene him, then hee of the towne dooth aske of the other if that hee hath eaten any thing: if he aunswere no, he dooth by and by, without any delay, carrie him to the next victualling house, whereas hee dooth banket him deliciously: for in euerie towne there is good opportunitie for the same, by reason that in the market places and streetes, and in the suburbes, there is great store of victualling houses, that doo keepe tabling verie orderly, and for little cost: for there (as we haue sayde) all kinde of victualles are verie good cheape. But if the stranger dooth aunswere that he hath eaten, then dooth the citizen or townesman carrie him to an other kinde of victualing houses,[144] where are to be had al sortes of conserues and iunkettes, fruites and marchpanes, and there dooth hee make him a banket with great love and good will. Of the women as well strangers as towneborne, or of what degree soeuer, they haue great respect, but especially of the married women: vnto whome if any man giue an ill or dishonest woorde, he is accounted infamous: and likewise if he doo not offer to them courtesie, and giue them place or way when they passe the streetes, which is seeldome seene. But when they doo passe they behaue themselues so discreetly that they giue no occasion that anye shoulde misuse them: towardes strangers they vse verye great courtesie: but especially the principallest: as you shall perceiue in the relation of the seconde part of this historie, where it shall be declared by experience.

CHAP. XX.

Of the great closenesse that the women of this kingdome do liue in, and with what condition they permit common women.

The principall intent that this king and his gouernors haue, as is gathered by their lawes, is to preserue their common weale from vices; for the which he dooth set downe great penalties, and executeth the same without any remission; and least any should offend they vse great vigilancie, and do iudge that the libertie and dishonestie of the women is most preiudiciale thereunto, and is the occasion that their common wealth falleth to decay, being neuer so well gouerned: therefore they haue ordained many preseruatiues and remedies by their lawes and customes to preuent the same, which is the only occasion (that although it is so long since this kingdome first began, and againe, being so great as you may vnderstande), yet in this one point there is lesse[145] inconuenience or preiudice than in any other countrey of lesse antiquitie and fewer people. So that a dishonest woman is knowen by name, although it be in a great citie, the which is seldome seene, and a rare thing. And the best way they haue to preuent this is, that all people that haue daughters are commaunded by expresse order, that they shall bring them vp (after they haue the vse of reason) in their owne houses very close, and not be seene, but alwayes to doo something to auoide idlenesse, for that it is the mother of all vices, whereby it may take no roote in them. This lawe dooth comprehende married women, and is kept in such sort that the wiues of the viceroyes and gouernours do obserue it, yea they say that the queenes themselues doo obserue it, and that they are alwayes spinning golde, silke, or flaxe, or doing some other exercise with their handes, esteeming all idle persons woorthie to be hated and contemned: so that the children being brought vp in this manner, seeing the good example of their mothers, is the occasion that this vertuous exercise, worthie to be imitated, is conuerted vnto a dayly and perpetuall custome, in such sort, that they think it a perpetuall torment to commaunde them to be idle. These ordinarie and voluntarie exercises haue the women of this kingdome in such sort, that it is newes and a strange thing to meete a woman in the streetes of any citie or towne, neither at the windowes, which is a signe that they liue honest. If it so fall out that of force they must go abroad, as to the buriall of parents and kinsfolkes, or to visite any one being sicke, or vpon any like occasion, then are they carried in litter chaires where they are seene of none, as we told you before: but other superfluous visitations or meetings of gossips are not there vsed. Albeit tendering the conseruation of this honest crewe, and to eschewe greater euils in the common wealth, they permit common women as a necessarie thing: yet they do allow them in such sort, that their euill example may not be hurtfull vnto the honest state[146] of them which liue chast. And therefore they do build for them houses out of the cities and townes in the suburbes, giuing them straight commandement there to remaine in the said houses, and not to straggle and go abroad at all. And whilst they liue there they are prohibited, vppon paine of death, to enter into the gates of the citie or any part thereof.

Such women as doo vse this facultie are nothing esteemed amongst them, for they are for the most part of the basest sort, as strangers, slaues, or such as haue beene bought of their mothers being yoonge, which is a kinde of perpetuall bondage, yea a great crueltie which is vsed amongst them there, and yet suffered amongst them. You shall vnderstande, that such as are poore widowes and driuen by necessitie, cannot sustaine themselues, may for the supplying of their want, sell their children and binde them to perpetuall seruitude, the which is permitted in such sort, that there are amongst them rich merchants that deale in no other thing: and all the maiden children that they buy so bee brought vp with great care, and taught to plaie and sing, and other things appertaining vnto pleasure. Then after, when they are of yeares, they carrie them vnto the houses aforesaid ordained for common women. The first day that they doo dedicate her to this ill office, before shee is put into this common house, they carrie her before a iudge, which the king hath ordained for euerie house appertaining to any cittie or towne appointed to bee their keeper, and see that there bee no euill rule kept amongst them: and this iudge dooth place her in the house himselfe, and from that day forwards her master hath no more to doo with her, but to go euerie moneth vnto the iudge to recouer his tribute, which is a certaine summe set downe by the iudge, by agreement made betweene them both, and hee appointeth besides this the time when hee shall be paide for her, and for that was spent in her bringing vp and teaching.

These women be very much haunted, and passe away the[147] time maruellous pleasantly by reason of their singing and playing, which they doo with great cunning: and according vnto the report of the Chinos, they apparell themselues with great curiositie, and paint themselues. They haue amongst them many blinde women, that are free and not bonde: these are trimmed, dressed, and painted by others that haue their sight; and such as haue spent all their youth in these houses, can not goe foorth so long as they liue, as is commaunded by a lawe publike, least by their dishonest demeanure they should be an occasion of some harme and an euill example to others. Whatsoeuer profite dooth remaine vnto these women when they haue payed their maister, they giue vnto the iudge their superiour, who doth keepe it faithfully and carefully, and giueth a good account thereof euerie yeare vnto the uisitors. And afterwardes when these women waxe olde, it is repaied vnto them againe by order of the said iudge. But it is bestowed in such sort, that they shall not lacke, neither haue vrgent necessitie. But if it so fall out that they should lacke, they will giue them a stipend to maintaine them, onely for to dresse and trimme the blinde women, or else they will put them into the kinges hospitall, a place ordeyned for such as cannot helpe themselues.

The men children which they buy, and are solde to supplie their necessitie, in the order aforesaide, of the women, they put to learne some occupation, and after that they are expert therein, they doo serue a master in the same trade for a certaine time; the which being expired, their masters are not only bound to giue them their libertie, but also to provide them of wiues and to marrie them, prouiding also for them houses and necessaries wherewith they may get their liuing. Which, if they doo not of their owne free will, they are compelled by iustice to doo, whether they will or no. And they for a token of greatefulnesse must come vnto their masters the first day of the yeare, and other dayes appointed, and bring them some present. The children of[148] these be all free, and subiect to no bondage for the benefite doone vnto their father for their bringing vp.

CHAP. XXI.

The fashion of their ships, as well of those that passe the seas, as of those that doo roade riuers, which are manie and great: and howe they doo prouide themselues of fish for all the yeare.

There is in this kingdome a great number of shippes and barkes, with the which they sayle all a long their coastes, and vnto ilandes neere hande, and into their riuers, the which doo runne cleane through the most part of all their prouinces: and there dwelleth so much people vpon these riuers in shippes and barkes, that it seemeth to be some great citie; there is so many of them that they do esteeme that there is almost as many people that dwell vpon the water as vpon the lande.

They make them slightly and with small cost, for they haue in all partes of this countrie great aboundance of tymber, iron, and other thinges necessarie for this vse: but in especiall a kinde of glew, wherewith they doo dawbe and trimme their shippes, that is much more tougher and stronger then the pitch which wee vse, which after it is layde on, sticketh fast and maketh their shipping as harde as stones; the aboundance whereof, and the great number of ship-wrightes, and againe for that there is not on the lande roome enough for the people to inhabite, being so many in number, causeth them to build so great a number of shippes and barkes. They vse their shippes and barkes of many fashions, euery one hath his proper name. Such ships as they haue to saile long voiages be called Iuncos, but for the warre they make huge and mightie vessels, with high castles, both on[149] the prowe and sterne, much after the fashion of them that come out of the Easterne Seas, and vnto those with which the Portingales sayle into the East India. They haue these in so great number, yt a generall may ioine together in 4 dayes an armie of more than 600. Those which they do commonly vse for burden and to lade, are much after ye same fashion and greatnes, and smal difference there is betweene them, but that they are lower both before and at the sterne. There is an other sort of lesser vessels, and are much like vnto pinases, and haue foure great ores on ech side, whereat row sixe men at euery ore and foure at the least. These are excellent good to rowe in and out ouer their bard hauens, or into any place where is litle water: they do call them Bancoens. There is an other sort that is more brode than these, which they call Lanteas, and carie eight ores on a side, with sixe men at euerie ore. Of these two last sorts of vessels pirates and rouers at the sea do commonly vse (for in those seas there be very many), for that they be very nimble to fly and to giue assalt as occasion doth serue. They haue an other sort of vessels yt are long, like vnto a galley, but more square, being very brode and neede little water: they do vse them likewise to transport merchandise from one place to an other: they are swift and run vp the riuers with smal force of the armes. Many other sorts of barks they haue, besides the aforesaid, some with galleries and windows painted and gylt, but chiefely those which the uiceroyes and gouernours doo make for their recreation. Of those sortes of shipping afore sayd, which they call Iuncos, the king hath in al his prouinces great armies, and in them souldiers with their captaines to defend the coastes, that as well all ships of their owne countrie, as those that doo come from other places to traficke with them, may goe and come in safetie, and not bee spoyled and robbed of the roauers that be there abouts. In the riuers there are pynases well equipped appointed for the same purpose. And the king doth out of his[150] rentes pay all these ordinarie souldiers, and that with great liberalitie.

The pitch wherewith they doo trimme their shippes (as we haue sayde) is founde in that kingdome in great aboundance; it is called in their language Iapez, and is made of lyme, oyle of fish, and a paste which they call Vname:[131] it is verie strong and suffereth no wormes, which is the occasion that one of their shippes dooth twise out last one of ours: yet dooth it hinder much their sayling. The pumpes which they haue in their shippes are much differing from ours, and are farre better: thay make them of many peeces, with a wheele to draw water, which wheele is set along the shippes sides within, wherewith they do easily clense their shippes, for that one man alone going in the wheele, doth in a quarter of an houre cleanse a great shippe, although she leake verie much.

Many men be borne and brought vp in these shippes and barkes (as is aforesayde), and neuer in all their liues haue beene on lande, and doo knowe none other occupation wherewith to liue, but that which they doo inherite of their fathers, which is, to goe in one of these shippes or barkes, carrying and recarrying of merchandise from place to place, or to ferrie people ouer the riuers. They haue in them their wiues and their children, and haue like neighborhood amongst them on the riuers as in their cities and townes, of whom they stand in little need, for they do bring vp within their ships all things necessarie for their sustenance, as hens, duckes, pigeons, and other foules good to be eaten: and if they do lacke any thing, they haue it in victualing houses and shops, which they haue amongst them on the same riuers in great abundance: and of other superfluous thinges such as may bee founde in a citie, they are well furnished: as of[151] many sorts of silkes, amber, and muske, and other things more curious then needefull. They haue also in their shippes, pots with little orange trees and other fruits, and gardins with flowers, and other herbes for their recreation, and in the wide shippes pooles of water, wherein they haue great store of fish aliue, and yet doo dayly fishe for more with nettes. This kingdome is the best prouided of fish of any that is knowen, by reason of the great number of these barkes, as also because they haue many fisher men at sea and in the riuers, that continually fish with nettes and other engines for the same purpose: and doo carrie the same fishe (in infinite number) aliue into their pooles fiue hundreth leagues vp into the lande by the riuers, which they doo with great ease in shifting the water euerie day, and doo feede them with thinges fit for the nature of the fish.

The chiefe and principallest time of fishing in this countrie, is in three monethes of the yeare, which is Februarie, March, and Aprill, at such times as are the spring tides, which do bring the fish out of the mayne sea into the riuers, and there they do spawne and leaue their young: then these fisher men, who doo liue by that facultie, doo take them and put them into their pondes, and feede and nourish them in the ships till they come to bignesse to be solde.

Unto these fishermen repayre many barkes from diuerse partes of the countrie to buye their fishe, and doo bringe with them wicker baskets lyned with a certaine thicke paper for that purpose, and annoynted with oyle, so that the water can not goe out: wherein they doo put their fish, and do shift them euerie day, and feede them as aforesaide. All people doo buye of this fish, although they bee verie small and leane, and doo put them in their pondes which euerie one hath in his house (as common vse in all that countrie is), whereas in a small time they waxe great, fitte to be eaten. They doo feede them with a paste made of cowes doung, buffes doung, and pigins doong.[152]

Likewise they doo throwe of these small fishes into the mootes of their cities, which is the occasion that they are so full of fish. But all that breede in them do appertaine vnto the gouernors or iudges of the cities, so that none without their expresse commandement dare fish for them. These gouernors and iudges doo vse much to recreate themselues vppon the riuers, and haue for the same purpose barkes made close, and chambers in them verie curiously wrought, with windowes and galleries likewise hanged with rich clothes, and many other thinges for their contentment and pleasure.

CHAP. XXII.

A curious order that these Chinos haue to bring vp ducks in great abundance, and with small cost: and of a pleasant and ingenious order of fishing which they vse.

The great number of people that is in this countrie, and not permitting any idle people to liue therein, is the occasion that it doth stirre vp the wits of poore men (being constrained thereunto by necessitie, the inuenter of manye thinges) to seeke new inuentions to get their liuing, to relieue and supply their necessities. So that many of this kingdome, seeing the whole countrie so throughly inhabited and tilled, that there is not one foote without an owner, they do take them vnto the riuers (which are verie great), and there they do make their dwellinges in ships and barkes (as is aforesaide), where they have their whole families vnder borde to defende them from the sunne and rayne, and inclinations of the heauens. There they do vse the occupation that they do knowe, or that which they did inherite of their father, and many misteries to liue by, verie strange: whereof the most principall[153] is to bring vp in some of their barkes so great quantitie of duckes, that they sustaine a great part of the countrey therewith; and the vse thereof is as followeth.

They haue cages made of canes so bigge as the vpper most holde of the barke, in the which may be foure thousand duckes at once. They haue in certaine places of these cages made nestes, where these duckes do almost euery day laye egges, the which they take: and if it be in the sommer, they doo put them in buffes doong, or in the doong of those duckes, which is verie warme, where they leaue them so many dayes as experience hath taught them that they will come foorth. Then they doo take them out of the doong, and do breake them one by one, and take a little ducklin, the which they do with so great cunning that almost none of them doth perish, which is yt which causeth great admiration vnto some that go to see it: although they bee but few, for that it is an aunceint custome vsed for long time in that countrie. And for to haue the fruition of this benefite all the yeare, in the winter they must vse an artificiall helpe: to giue a little warmenes vnto the doong for the bringing forth of their egs, they do vse then an other inuention as ingenious as the first, and that is this: they take a great number of canes tied one by another, whereon they do laye the doong, then vppon that they doo lay their egges, and do couer them verie well with the same: this being done, they put vnder the canes straw, or some other like thing, and set it on fire, but in such sort that it dooth not burne, but keepeth a naturall heat all the time, till they thinke that they are readie to be taken out. Then doo they take and breake them, as aforesaide, so that their pultrie dooth increase in such number as though they were antes. Then doo they put them into an other cage for the same purpose, wheras be old duckes brought vp for no other purpose but to couer the little ones vnder their winges and keepe them warme: and there they doo feede them euery day, till such time as[154] they can feede themselues, and go abroad into the fieldes to profit themselues in the companie of the olde duckes. Many times they haue in number aboue twentie thousand, yet do they maintain them with a small cost, and it is in this order: euery morning they do giue them a small quantitie of boyled rice, then do they open a doore of the cage, which is towardes the riuer, and doo put a bridge of canes that doth reach vnto the water: then doo they come foorth with so great haste one vpon an other, that it is a pastime to see them. All the day after they do passe the time vpon the water, and in the fieldes of rice vpon the land, wheras they do feede: the owners of the rice doo giue vnto the owners of the duckes somewhat to let their duckes go into their fields, for that they do destroy all the grasse and other weeds in it, and hurt nothing of the rice.

When that the euening draweth on, then they of the barke do make a sound with a taber or such like, ye which being heard of his duckes, they throwe themselues with great speede into the water, and swimme straight vnto their owne barke, whereas their bridge is readie put for them; and euerie flocke doth know his owne barke by the sounde, without missing at any time, although there be many flockes together. For euerie barke doth vse a different sound the one from the other, to the which the duckes are vsed, and their ears full thereof, so that they neuer fayle their owne barke.

This manner of liuing is greatly vsed in all that countrie, and verie profitable, for that it is a victuall most vsed amongst them, and is esteemed as a thing of great sustentation and of small price, by reason that at al times there is breeding of them and of small cost.

Likewise in this country they do vse a kinde of fishing, that is of no lesse industrie then the bringing vppe of these duckes, and a thing to be scene. The king hath in euerie citie founded vppon the riuers, houses wherein euerie yeare[155] is brought vp many cormorantes or sea rauens, with whome they doo fishe in those monethes that the fish dooth spawne, and that is in this maner following. They take the cormorantes out of their cages, and carrie them vnto the riuer side, whereas they haue many barkes ordeyned for their fishing, and they are halfe full of water. Then they take their cormorantes, and with a corde they do binde their mawes, in such sort that no fish can fall into it: then they do cast them into the riuer to fish, the which they do with such good will and couetousnesse, that it is a woonder to see; they throwe themselues into the water with great swiftnesse, and diue, whereas they do fill their throate with fish. Then they come foorth, and with the like hast they go vnto the barkes that are halfe ful of water, and the fish which they have taken they put in that water, which is put there for that purpose, that the fish may not die; the which being done, they returne againe vnto their fishing as they did before.

In this order they do indure their fishing foure houres together, in such sort that the one doth not trouble the other; and when yt their boates with water are ful of fish, then do they vnbind them, and turne them againe into the riuer for to fish for themselues, for they haue neede thereof, for that alwayes the day before that they will fish they keepe them from their ordinarie victualles, which is a litle millio, that they may ye better do their office. So after a while that they haue filled their bellies and recreated themselues, they take them out of the water and carrie them vnto the ordinarie places, whereas they are kept; and euerie third day during the time of this fishing, they do take them forth for the same exercise, which for them is so great pastime, that they would it should indure all the yeare.

In these three monethes they do take so much fish, that they do prouide the whole kingdome for all the yeare; as in the chapter past it hath beene tolde you, which is the occasion that they are as well prouided of fish as of any other[156] thing: so that, if they please, they may eate euerie day fresh fish, although they are farre from the sea.

CHAP. XXIII.

Of the curtesie that the king of this mightie kingdome doth vnto the ambassadors that come to him from anie other king, prince, or comonaltie.

We should in the chapter following intreate of the ambassage that king Philip of Spaine, with the Christian zeale that he had, to sende vnto the king of this kingdome, who being mooued by certaine causes and reasons, did referre it till a better occasion, and we do beleeue that it will be offered shortly. Therefore now it shall not be from our purpose to declare in this chapter the honour and curtesie that this king doth vnto the ambassadours of kings, princes, or any other prouince, that doth come vnto him, in what sort soeuer it be; and for that it is of great curiositie, it shall be necessarie to declare it with the circumstance wherewith it is done.

All such as doo enter into this kingdome, with the title of ambassadour, be it from a king that is a friend or enemie, they are respected, intreated, and made of, with so great care and diligence, as though they came themselues in person that doo send them. Unto whome, besides the obseruing the law of nations, which is obserued and kept among all kings in the worlde, in especiall that their persons shall not receiue neither incurre any danger, although their ambassage bringeth discontent or harme vnto the king; besides all the which, there is granted vnto them great and particular priuiledges. When that he doth enter into the kingdome, by any of the prouinces whatsoeuer, the iudge or gouernor of the first towne dooth in person go forth to meete and receiue him, and giue him his welcome, with great complement of words[157] and ceremonies. All the loytias, captaines, souldiers, and the inhabitants of the towne, doo accompanie the iudge or gouernour, when that

they go to receiue him. But at his disembarking to come a
shore, they will not suffer him to set his feete vppon the
ground (although it be but a little way that he should go),
but hath at the waters side in a readinesse eight men, with a
chaire made of yuorie, or of some other pretious thing, with
the curteines of ueluet, damaske, or cloth of golde: which
for the like oportunitie, they haue in euerie cittie or
principall towne appointed by the king, wherein they do
carrie him to his lodging. Likewise they haue in euerie citie
and great towne throughout all the kingdome, a principall
house, and sufficient for to lodge such like personages. It is
also vsed to lodge such iudges as are sent by the king to
execute his commandement, when they passe by anie of
such cities or townes. There is in euery one of these houses
a lieutenant, and he hath in it maruellous and excellent
household stuffe, as hangings, beddes, seruants, and all
other necessaries, not only to lodge one ambassador, but
many, if they should there meete, and not one to disturbe
another. So as aforesaide, they doo beare him company
(either on horsebacke, or in a chaire, which is the ordinarie
carriage amongst them) till hee come vnto this house,
whereas they do leave him with much curtesie and many
ceremonies, alonelie with them that waite vppon him and
serue him. And also a captaine with a thousand or two
thousande souldiers for to garde him continuallie, and to
beare him companie till hee returne againe out of the
kingdome.

Then the next day following, the iudge or gouernour that
did receiue him dooth go and visite him. And after that they
haue demanded of him such ordinarie thinges as is vsed in
such like visitations, then doo they learne of his estate, and
of the prince that hath sent him, and in summe, the effect of
his comming and ambassage: then doo they straightways at
the houre dispatch a post vnto the gouernour or[158] vizroy
of the prouince, who is alwayes resident in the chiefe or

metropolitan citie thereof, and hee at the same instant dooth dispatch another post with that message vnto the king and his counsel. And he dooth sende order vnto the ambassador, either to stay, or a safe conduct for him to go vnto the place whereas hee is. Likewise hee sendeth order vnto the iudge, how hee shall intreate that ambassador, which is giuen according vnto the relation sent him, wherein he did vnderstande the state of the king and prince that sent him. Likewise the number of souldiers yt shall beare him companie, and of all other thinges needefull for him in his iourney: all the which is set downe in order, and in particular, as what they shall giue euery man to eate for him and his seruants, and in what townes, and howe hee shall be lodged. His safe conduct is brought him, written vppon a whited table (after the fashion as we haue tolde you heere before in manie places), and is with great letters, wherein is contained from what king that ambassador is sent. This table is borne always before him, wheresoeuer hee dooth go. But that pasport, which is sent him afterwards from the royall councell, with facultie, that hee may go vnto the court, is after another sort: for that it is written in parchment and gallantlie lymned, and with the kings seale of golde hanging at it, which is neuer giuen but at such like occasion, or for some prouision giuen to a vizroy.

Looke what is spent vppon this ambassadour in all his iourney, and vppon them that doo beare him companie for all necessaries, is vppon the kings cost and charges, and is paide by the kinges treasurers in euerie place whereas they doo go. Generallie in all partes, they doo make him great feastes and banquets, with pastimes and presents, that day that hee dooth enter into the cittie of Taibin or Paquin, whereas the king is.

There goeth foorth to meete him without the citie, all the gentlemen of the court, with the royall councel and president,[159] who, according vnto the saying of the Chinos, goeth forth with little lesse maiestie and companie than the king: who, if the ambassadour be from a king that is mightie, they giue him the right hand, if not they giue him the left hand: and in this sort they go, ether talking with himselfe, or, by interpreters, demaunding of him of his health, and of his trauail in comming, and other thinges, till hee come into the court of the pallace, whereas he is lodged; and there they doo leaue him, with some to beare him companie, and hee dooth returne vnto his house with all this company aforesaid. But when they do depart from him, they doo giue him power in the name of the king, to make a certaine number of loytias, and to set at libertie a certaine number of prisoners, such as are condemned to die, and other good deeds particular.

Those that doo enter in this kingdome with the title of an ambassador, they cannot do him any griefe, for anie delight or euill that he doth, although they can make good proofe thereof. And for that it is of a truth, you shall vnderstande the proofe by experience. There was sent vnto this king, one Bartholomew Perez, a Portugall, and his company, by order of the vizroy of the India, with an ambassage from the king Don Manuel of Portugall, and they were accused before the vizroy of the prouince of Canton, by the ambassadors of the king of Malaca, that were there present, who were bounde vnto the court to treat of matters of their king; they did testifie that the ambassage that the Portugall did bring was false, and they were spies sent from the vizroy of the India for to view the fortresses of the citie, that they might come afterwards and take it, as they had done in many places of the India: they perseuering still in the euill and mischieuous intent, did will the vizroy to apprehend them, and to punish them as such spies did deserue, offering themselues to giue good information for the same.

Who, after that he had well considered thereof, and consulted[160] with the loytias of the citie, and with his counsailors, they commanded that they should be apprehended and put in straite prison, whereas their declarations were taken with great care, deceit, and pollicie: and by reason that in them they found contrarieties: some for feare confessed much more then that which was demanded, and other saide that it was of truth; so that by their confessions, according vnto the lawes of the countrie, they were condemned to die, and sent their iudgment vnto the roiall councell for to confirme the same, with intent and great desire for to execute the same. The which being seene by the roiall councell, and considering with what title they entred into that kingdome, did not onely make voide the sentence and would not confirme the same, but did send commandement vnto the vizroy to set them at libertie, and to returne freely back againe vnto the India from whence they came, and that hee shoulde furnish them with all things necessarie in aboundance, til they were entred into the same, although in this time the ambassadors of the king of Malaca, who were in the court, did still perseuer in their malicious intent.

In which commandement, although it were true all that which the foresaide ambassadors did testifie, and that they for feare of death did confesse it, yet it is sufficient that they entred into his kingdom with the title of ambassador, whereby they should receiue any harme. But now let vs returne to our purpose. So after this ambassador hath refreshed himselfe of his iourny, and receiued many banquets and orations of the gentlemen of the court: vpon a day appointed he goeth to speake with the king, accompanied with all the gentlemen of the court, and with the president of the councell, who doth giue him audience in one of the three rich hals aforesaide, at all times as his businesse doth require. So when that all his busines is dispatched and gratified with many gifts, he returneth backe againe from whence he came; and looke with what curtesie they did receiue him at his comming, the like they doo vnto him at his returne.[161]

But if an ambassador doo come from any common wealth of the said kingdome, they do not giue him the intertainement abouesaid, but cleane contrarie thereunto, for that he dooth enter into the citie, accompanied onely with the iustice, whose charge it is to lodge him in such houses as the king hath ordeined to the same effect, and to giue him all that is necessarie, takeing of him the summe and effect wherefore he doth come: and he doth giue relation thereof vnto the president of the councell, and the president doth giue the king to vnderstand therof: then doo they appoint the day of audience, with this condition, that when he dooth go thither, hee must go on foote, or else on horse back without a bridle, with onely a halter on his horse head, in token of humility, and acknowledging to be a subject. The day of his audience, he commeth forth obseruing the order and condition aforesaid, accompanyed with the iustice. And when hee doth come into a great place, which is right against the pallace of the king, he staieth there till an officer of the king doth come vnto him (who is master of the ceremonies), and hee dooth cause him to proceede forwards, and dooth shew him the place whereas hee must first kneele downe, with his handes ioyned togither in token of adoration or worship: and all the time of this ceremonie, his eis must bee fixed on that part where as they say the king is. In this sort hee goeth onwards his way, making in it other fine adorations like vnto the first, vntill such time as he do come into the first hall of the pallace, which is at the staires heade, whereas the president is set with great majestie, and doth represent the kings person: who after that hee hath hearde the effect of his ambassage, dooth sende them away without answering one word at that time; but after that hee hath giuen the king to vnderstande, hee dooth sende him answere by that iustice, who hath the charge to lodge him, and to prouide him of all things necessarie for the time that hee is in the court.[162]

CHAP. XXIV.

Of the ambassage that the king of Spaine did send vnto the king of this kingdome, and the occasions that did mooue him therevnto, as also wherefore it was declared.

For to conclude this small historie, in the which I haue declared, in summe, all such things as I haue vnderstoode of this kingdome of China vnto this, I meane such as I might wel set forth, leauing a great number more, of the which I haue particular note: some for that they are vnknowne, and others for that they will cause admyration because they haue not beene seene. And according vnto the counsell of the wise, they should not be intreated of, vntill that time that experience dooth make them more credible. And againe, I doo hold it for a lesse euill, to be reprehended for breuitie (as some haue beene), then to bee prolix and tedious in the declaring, although it bee hurtfull vnto this worke, from the which I doo take away much that I might put in. Nowe letting all passe, I will in this last chapter declare of the letter present, and ambassage, wherewith the king of Spaine did sende mee in the yeare of our Lorde one thousande one hundred and foure-score: for that in company of other religious men of my order, I should passe from his mightie kingdome of Mexico to China, and to present it vnto the king of that countrie in his name: of all the which I will declare that which I doo vnderstande and know, not exceeding the limits of fidelitie, by reason that the ambassage was not ended, nor no conclusion in effect of that which was pretended, but doo hope in the deuine maiestie, and with the care and diligence that is put therein by the king of Spaine, shortlie to haue a conclusion of that they desire, for the which the letter and the rest was sent.

Beeing considered of by the Spaniards (such as were[163] dwellers in the Ilands Phillippinas, which by another name are called the Ilands of the Ponent or West) the thinges of great valour and riches, as of golde and silkes and many other thinges which is brought from the kingdome of China, and out of their ports, and how those which brought it did sel it for a small quantitie in respect as they did esteeme it, and being certified by the saide Chinos of many other things which were in the firme land, wherof some of them haue beene made mention in this historie: being mooued with the conuerting of these soules, and with the profite that might come of trafike that they might haue with the Chinos, it was concluded by the gouernour and principals of the citie of Manila, with the iudgement of the prouinciall of the order of Saint Augustine, and of many other religious men that were both graue and wise, such as were the first, that in those parts did preach the Gospell, and did baptize a great number of the dwellers therein, and did many other thinges, of the which I might say much, if it were to my purpose, and that my part were not therein: so that I say it was concluded amongst them to sende vnto the Catholike king graue personages, vnto whome intire credite might be giuen, for to giue relation what they vnderstoode of that kingdome, and also of the euident necessitie (that all those ilands that were his) had for their conseruation to holde to friendes the Chinos their borderers, whereof might growe vnto them great benefites and profites: and likewise to request him (if it were his pleasure) to sende an ambassador to the king of that kingdome, the better to confirme their friendship, and to carrie with him some things which he vsed in his countrie, which would be maruellous well esteemed of the Chinos, and be a way vnto the preaching of the Gospel, and bee a beginning that a farther contraction may growe betwixt the Christians and Chinos, of the which shall follow the aforesaid profite vnto other countries, by the great quantitie of things, as well of riches as of other curiosities that shalbe brought from[164] thence. After they had well considered with great deliberation, who should be the person that they shoulde send vpon so long a iourney, for to request his maiestie of the aforesaid: in the ende they did agree vppon for to desire the prouinciall of the Augustine friers, who was called Frier Dilho de Herrera, a man of great learning and of great experience touching matters of those ilands, for that hee was one of the first discouerers of them: they requested him for the loue of God and the good seruice to his maiestie, and the benefite that might come thereby vnto these ilands, that he would take vpon him to go with this petition, for they were fully perswaded for that he had trauailed so manie places of those ilands, as also for his office and vocation, there was none that better coulde put in effect their desire, and perswade with his maiestie the great importance of that ambassage: and manie other things necessarie touching the gouernement of those ilands. This determination was liked well of them all, and that they had chosen well in sending of the prouinciall, who incontinent departed from the ilands in a shippe that was prepared for Noua Hispania, which was in the yeare of Christ 1573. At his imbarking, hee was accompanied with the gouernour, and all those of that citie, of whom hee was maruellouslie well beloued for his holinesse and good condition. Desiring him with all diligence to procure to returne, with as much breuitie as was possible, vnto those ilands, whereas they so much loued him, and had neede of his presence.

He did promise them to make all the speede possible, and in paiment of the trauel that he did take vpon him, for the benefite and profite, he requested them al that they would pray vnto God to giue a good voyage: they promised him to doo it, the which they did performe with particular care. Then did the master command to weigh ankers, and to set saile, which was in the moneth of Nouember the same yeare: and with reasonable wether they arriued at the new Spaine,[165] and came vnto the cittie of Mexico, and from thence they went and embarked themselues in the North Seas; who with prosperous winds the 13 day of August, the yeare following, they ariued in San Lucar Debarameda, in Spaine, and caried me in his company. From thence, the day following, we departed from Syuel, from whence wee departed forthwith toward Madrid, whereas his maiestie was at that present, and we came thither the fifteenth day of September in anno 1574, the same weeke that they had newes of the losse of the Goleta.[132] Wee went straightwayes to kisse the kings hands, and caried the letters which we brought from his gouernor and citie: by whom both we and the letters were receiued with his accustomed benignitie, and did heare the petition with great satisfaction, for that the desire was holy and profitable, and told vs that he would command his counsell to vnderstand in the same with a particular consideration, and with so much breuitie as the thing required: and gaue vs thankes for the great trauell and long iourney which we tooke vpon vs in his seruice, for to giue him notice of the discouering of this great kingdome, and of other things touching the Ilands Philippinas. He straightwayes commanded that we should be prouided for of all things necessarie for our sustentation for the time that we should there remaine, and that we should go and giue account of all things (for the which we came thither) vnto the counsel of the Indies, who was Don Iuan de Obando, vnto whom his maiestie did recommend the consideration to be done with great care, and to consult vpon the same. After that they had comuned with the roiall counsell of the Indies touching that which should be requisite and conuenient, which was done as it appeared in effect, for that they gaue vs facultie in a few dayes after of all things that was requested from the said ilands, except that which did touch the ambassage vnto[166] the king of China, as a thing of greater importance, and requested longer time to consider of the same: so that they did referre it till they had a better occasion. So that with this resolution and with fortie religious men, and manie commissions from his maiestie touching the good gouernement of that new kingdome, wee departed from Syuell in the moneth of Ianuarie, the yeare following, in 1575, whereas I remained by his order and for certaine respects. But the aforesaid prouinciall did imbarke himselfe with his fortie religious persons, and departed in the moneth of Iuly with a faire winde and merrie passage, till they came vnto Newe Spaine, and from thence into the South Sea, vntill they came in sight of the ilands: whereas the wether did alter, and they were forced by the furie thereof to ariue at an iland inhabited with Gentiles, by whome they were all slaine, and none escaped but onely an Indian natural of the ilands, which wee carried from thence in our companie for Spaine. He afterwards came vnto Manilla, and gaue them to vnderstand how they were all slaine, and how the Gentiles did teare all the papers and commissions in peeces, and of all that happened to them.

This beeing knowne by the gouernor, and by the rest that dwelt in the ilands (after that they had done the rytes, with the funerall griefes, as iustice required in such a case), they finding themselues in the same necessitie that before they were in by reason of the losse of the aforesaid prouinciall and his companions, and also of the letters and prouisions sent from his maiestie, they forthwith in the same determination did write newe letters, in requesting that which in part the king had granted (although they had no knowledge thereof); they did also therein write touching the ambassage that they did request for the king of China, adding thereunto new occasions, wherby they should be moued to do them so much fauour as to send the ambassador afore requested, which was a thing of great importance for all those[167] ilands. When that these letters came in conformitie with the others before sent, the king did ordaine for gouernor of those ilands, a gentleman, who was called Don Gonsalo de Mercado y Ronquillo, a man of great valor and discretion, one that had serued the king as wel in the Peru as in Mexico with great fidelitie; who vnderstanding the earnest request wherewith those of the ilands did aske the ambassage, and how much it did import to haue it (as a man then elected for gouernor of those ilands, and a matter that touched him very much), did put the king and his counsell in memorie of the same: and in conclusion, they answered that hee should foorthwith depart with the souldiers that were prouided for those parts, for that it was conuenient so to be doone by reason of great necessitie that they had of them in the said ilands; and as for the ambassage, for that there was no such great necessitie nor haste, it should be intreated of at more leasure, when that the counsell will aduertise themselues of al that shalbe conuenient touching that matter, and that they would consult and confer with his maiestie that he may, as the right owner of them, command that which shuld be to the seruice of God and his benefite. So with this answere the said gouernor departed.

It happened that in the moneth of August, in the yeare following, before that this gouernor was ariued at the ilands, there came newe letters from thence of supplications, requesting with greater instance, that which before at other times they had requested, sending with their petition the whole relation of the entrie of Frier Martin de Herreda, prouinciall of the Augustine friers and his companions, into the kingdome of China, and of such things as they had seene and heard of (as may be seene at large in the said declaration, which is in the second parte of this booke). This being seene by his maiestie, he was resolued to send the ambassage which so many times they haue requested; this chanced at that time that he began to go vppon Portugall, a time of[168] trouble, but yet a great token that it was the will of God, in whose hands (as the wise man saith) are the hearts of kings. For the appointment of one for to go on this ambassage, the king did remit it vnto his roial counsel of the Indies, whose president was Don Antonio de Padilla y Meneses, who had communicated with me diuers times, touching matters of that kingdome and of Mexico, whereas I was alwayes resident euer since I was seueenteene yeares of age, and by reason of matters that was committed vnto me out of that country, was the occasion that I did vse to visit him the oftener: the which large conuersation and the good wil that hee did beare me, did perswade him that I could put in execution the ambassage of his maiestie, for that his will was that some religious person should do it: and they being fully perswaded that my good will and desire was for the saluation of those soules, and in all respects willing to serue his maiestie: all the which, with the knowledge that I had of that large nauigation,[133] and the qualitie of that countrie and people, was a great helpe to the accomplishing in effect the will of his maiestie, and desire of those that dwelt in Philippina.

So after this charge being committed vnto me, and his maiestie readie to depart on his voiage for Portugal as aforesaid, he did remit my dispatch vnto the lords of the royall counsell, who were at that time the Licenciado Gasca de Salaçar, and Doctor Gomez de Santisteuan, the Licenciado Espadero, the Licenciado Don Diego de Zuniga, the Doctor Vaillo, the Licenciado Eua, the Licenciado Gedeon de Hinonsosa. By whose commandement I depart from the court vnto Syuell, where as order was giuen that all such things should be prouided that I should carrie vnto the king. Whereas I was procuring the same certaine dayes, and for that they were many the which I should carrie, it was not[169] possible by any meanes that they should be made readie against the departure of the fleete. Then the Licenciado Gasca de

Salacar aforesaide, who was at that present resident in the contractation house of Syuel, gaue his maiestie to vnderstand thereof, who was at Badaioz occupied in matters touching the kingdome of Portugal as aforesaid, and requested him to giue order what his pleasure was to be done therein: who commanded that the fleete should depart, and that I should stay till such time as all things were made and concluded that I shoulde carrie with me for the king of China, as in ample manner as hee had commanded. And when that all things were in good order, that they should cause a shippe or galoon to bee made readie, wherein I should made my voyage, for to ouertake or meete at the Newe Spaine such shippes as euerie yeare dooth depart for the Ilands Philippinas, which is at Christmas time: this commandement was delayed vntill the beginning of Lent, as well for that the thinges were manie that shoulde bee made, and coulde not be dispatched in the time, as also for a generall sicknesse that was amongst them in Spaine, called the cattarre or murre. Then after that all thinges were in order, by the commandement of the Licenciado Gasca, hee deliuered vnto me the kinges letter, and all other thinges. The which, for that they were manie, and againe I haue beene tedious in this chapter, I doo not declare it; for that the prudent lector may of himselfe conceiue, if hee doo weigh the magnanimitie of the Catholike king that dooth sende them, and the mightinesse and richnesse of him to whome it is sent, of the which we haue declared enough in this small historie. I would I could particularly declare it vnto you, as also the copie of the letter that his maiestie did send vnto that Heathen or Gentile king, a thing worthie of the author: but for that it came not to effect, neither had I anye licence of him that all onelye might grant it: and againe, in place whereas I could not aske it, therefore I dare not, for that I[170] will not excede the limits of fidelitie which I owe vnto my prince. But it is sufficient that the letter and the present sent by his maiestie vnto the king of that countrey was to no other intent, but to procure him and all his subiects to acknowledge the true God, and to exhort them to receiue our Catholike faith, and to giue them to vnderstand the error wherein they are, and how ignorant they are of the knowledge of the true God, the creator of heauen and earth, and of all the creatures of the world visible and invisible, Sauiour and redeemer of all such as with a true knowledge doo beleeue in him and obey his holy lawe, declared by his worde, and confirmed by his deuine tokens, and other thinges in effect.

So being dispatched, I prosecuted my iourny, and order, till I came vnto the kingdome of Mexico, whereas I found a certaine inconuenience touching a matter needful in that voiage, whereof his maiestie, in the commission he gaue me, willed me to be well aduertised, and, if it were needfull, to giue him notice thereof before I did passe any farther.

The vizroy of that kingdome, who was the Earle of Couma,[134] thought it good that I shoulde returne vnto Lysborne, whereas the king was at that instant, and to giue him to vnderstand of the difficultie that was found, in a meeting that the vizroy had caused to bee made of the most grauest personages of all that kingdome, about the prosecuting of that ambassage.

With this resolution, I departed from that kingdome, and returned to Spaine, and left the present in Mexico, in the power of the kings officers, till such time as order was giuen what should be done therewith.

I found his maiestie in Lisborne, whereas I did deliuer him the letters that were written touching the same matter, and did declare vnto him my iudgement touching the meeting aforesaid: who incontinent did take the charge vpon him to[171] seeke occasion, for to put in effect his most Christian intent and zeale; the which I doo beleeue he had procured, and will by al waies possible: and that very shortly we shall see in that kingdome planted the Catholike faith, and their false idolatrie banished. And I hope in God it will bee very shortly, for that there be within that kingdome religious men, of the order of Saint Augustine, and barefoote friers of Saint Francis, and of the order of Jesus, or Jesuits, who are called there the fathers of Saint Paule: of whom there is placed fiue or sixe in the citie of Xanquin, whereas the vizroy doth dwell, and hath erected a couent in that citie ever since the year 1583, with a church, whereas they doo say masse ordinarily. And it is said, of a truth, that they haue got license of the saide vizroy for to passe freely thorough out all the whole kingdome of China. But if it bee so, you must thinke that hee did it after that he had consulted with the king, and doone by his authoritie: otherwise I am perswaded he durst not grant any such license.

At this present dooth there go out of Spaine, by the order and commandement of his maiestie and his royall counsell of the Indies, a companie of religious men, of the order of Saint Dominicke, for to aid and helpe the rest that are there to conclude this enterprise, from whom can proceed nothing but that which tends to great effect, by reason of their great zeale and learning, and the better if that they doo ioyne together in charitie as seruants to one Lord and master, and as they which are bounde to doo all one worke. By which meanes, with the fauour and helpe of Almightie God, putting to their diligence and industrie, they shall easily conquest their hearts and good willes, and shall frustrate the diuell from the possession that so long time he hath possessed in that kingdome, and reduce them to their true Lord by creation and redemption. It will not bee a small helpe, the manie and evident tokens which the Chinos doo giue of desire of their saluation; for as it is said that they haue read in their[172] bookes, that from the occident shall come the true and perfite law to direct them to heaven, where they shalbe angels. And they, seeing that those religious people which are come into their kingdome, doo come from the occident, they are perswaded, without doubt, that the law that they doo declare vnto them is the truth; by which meanes shall redowne vnto them great goodnesse. They are greatly affectioned vnto the commandements of the Catholike faith, and vnto the catechisme, which is translated into their language, and is abrode in manie parts of that kingdome, which is the occasion (as the fathers of the companie that are in the citie Xuquien dooth write) that many principal persons are conuerted vnto the Catholike faith, and others, being holpen by the heauens, and encited by the ensample of them, doo demande the holy baptisme, which is left undone because they will not cause any vprore in the countrie. And againe, when they shall better conceiue thereof, they may receiue it with more firme faith.

God, for his mercie, cause to go forwards, and with his diuine fauour, this good worke, for his honour and glorie, and exalting his holy faith; and that so great and infinite a number of soules, redeemed by his pretious blood, might be saued, and to put in the hart of Christian kings to proceed forwards in that which he hath begun: putting alwaies in their breasts a greater augmentation, to the concluding of the same, and to put apart from him all such perswasions as shoulde cause him to leaue it off, which the diuell will procure by all the wayes and meanes that he may. But against God and his diuine will there is neither power nor wisedome.

THE END OF VOLUME I.

FOOTNOTES:

[1] Purchas's Pilgrimes, vol. iii, p. 35, 36.

[2] Purchas's Pilgrimes, vol. iii, p. 5.

[3] Barros, dec. III, liv. ii, cap. 6.

[4] ... Mui prospero em honra, e fazenda, cousas que poucas vezes juntamente se conseguem, porque ha poucos homens que por sus trabalhos as merecem pelo modo que Fernão Peres naquellas partes as ganhava. Barros, dec. III, liv. ii, cap. 8. Goes, p. iv, cap. 24. Osorius, lib. xi, p. 317 et seq.

[5] Barros, dec. III, liv. vi, cap. 2, has further particulars concerning his regulations. Concerning his person and manners the same author says: "Como era cavalleiro de sua pessoa, muy pomposo, glorioso e gastador, todos suas obras eram com grande magestade, etc." In Osorius (lib. xi, p. 319 b) he appears more faulty and blameworthy. "... Andradii, viri sane fortis sed temerarii, et plurimum a mente fratris abhorrentis ... deinde in tyrannidem erupit: rapuit quæ voluit, intulit vim ingenuis virginibus, quibus voluit: multa præterea signa insiti furoris dedit."

[6] For the elaboration of the route of the friars, rendered difficult of solution by the changes in the form of names, the writer is indebted to the kind assistance of his learned

friend Dr. Neumann, professor of Chinese in the University of Munich.

[7] Martin de Rada, otherwise called Herrada, for an account of whom and his companions, see Introduction.

[8] Manilla.

[9] Cochinchina.

[10] Hainan.

[11] Birman Empire.

[12] Bernier, in his Lettre à Colbert sur l'étendue de l'Hindoustan, describes the Patans as "peuples mahometans, sortis du costé du Gange vers Bengale, qui avant l'invasion des Mogols dans les Indes avoient sceu se rendre puissans dans plusieurs endroits, et principalement à Dehly et faire plusieurs Rajas des environs leurs tributaires. Ces Patans ... haïssent mortellement les Mogols, souvenans toujours de ce qu'ils ont été autrefois, avant qu'ils les eussent chassez de leurs grandes principautez et les eussent obligez de se retirer deça delà, loin de Dehly et Agra dans des montagnes où ils se sont habituez."

[13] Moguls.

[14] Capital.

[15] Samarcand.

[16] Loo Choos.

[17] Cleanness.

[18] Germans.

[19] See note, page 7.

[20] Dimocarpus leechee.

[21] From fanega, Span. A measure for grain, varying in capacity in different parts of Spain and Portugal. It contains on an average one and three-fifths of an English bushel.

[22] Panic-grass.

[23] Martas zibellinas-sables.

[24] The Spanish Cuarto equals four maravedis, and is of about the same value as a French sou, or something less than an English halfpenny.

[25] Misspelt for Cansi. Probably Sin-gan-fu, capital of the province of Chen-sy is here referred to.

[26] Misspelt for Taybinco, meaning Ta-Bing-kwo, the kingdom under the great Bing (Ming) dynasty.

[27] Query li.

[28] Misspelt for Malacca. This sentence shows Olam to be Yun-nan.

[29] After a careful collation of the following illspelt and vague enumeration of the provinces of China with those given by Semedo, Heningius, Heylyn, and in a very early map of the country, as well as with some elucidatory passages in the text, the following explanations are offered as to their respective significations. The Paguia here mentioned is evidently Pe-che-lie.

[30] Fo-kien.

[31] Yun-nan, see note page 21.

[32] Quang-see.

[33] Chen-sy.

[34] Chan-si.

[35] Kiang-see.

[36] Hou-quang.

[37] This name which is spelt in the same manner as that given in the second volume to the city of Fo-cheu, would seem to mean the province of Kiang-nan, as that province is not otherwise represented in the list.

[38] Ho-nan.

[39] Chan-tung.

[40] Koei-tcheou.

[41] Che-kiang.

[42] Se-tchuen.

[43] Evidently Canton, by comparison with the list in next chapter.

[44] Quinsay or King-sze, means "the capital."

[45] Peking.

[46] Tay-ping-fu.

[47] One of the five ports opened to England by the treaty of Nanking in 1842.

[48] Ho-chow, in the province of Shen-si.

[49] The Tartar province of Leao-tung, in which the wall commences, has also the name of Quantonz: see Gutzlaff's Map of China and Biot's Dictionnaire des noms anciens et modernes des Villes, etc., dans l'Empire Chinois, fo. 86. From this it is evident that our author is now considering the work in its course from east to west, and not from west to east, as in the commencement of this paragraph.

[50] This is evidently Se-tchuen, as given in p. 22; for although it is not strictly correct to say that the great wall terminates in Se-tchuen, yet that province borders on the ancient province of Shen-si sufficiently near to justify the conclusion that it is here referred to, the whole of the geographical information gained by the writers at this early period being necessarily but vague and indefinite.

[51] Sic, hot.

[52] Germans.

[53] A mis-print for Barbosa. Duarte Barbosa, or Barbessa, a native of Lisbon, wrote in Portuguese an account of his travels in the south of Asia; but according to Antonio, they have only appeared in type in an Italian translation. An abridgement of his narrative is given in Ramusio, tom. i, p. 288. Subsequently Barbosa accompanied Magellan in his voyage round the world, and shared the melancholy fate of that great navigator in the Island of Zebu in 1521.

[54] Mexico.

[55] Saxii. This has been supposed to mean the province of Canton, the names of the other provinces having been pretty well identified. The writer may have considered that the finest porcelain was made at Canton, as it was usually exported from thence to Europe; but the chief seat of the manufacture is, in fact, the province of Kiang-see.

[56] Chincheou. One of the chief districts of Fokien, often named for the entire province.

[57] This and the following details of the striking similarity which exists between the ceremonial of the Buddhist and Roman Catholic religions, are verified by later travellers and resident missionaries, but there is no evidence from history to show that the former derived these peculiarities from the latter.

[58] The work here referred to was printed in black letter at Evora, 1569, 4to., under the title, "Tractado em que se

contam muito por estenso as cousas da China, con suas particularidades, y assi do regno dormuz."

[59] Laocon Izautey. The following particulars evidently relate, not to the Confucian or national religion of the Chinese, but to the sect of the Tao-sse. Grosier tells us, that "the sect of the Tao-see was founded by a philosopher named Lao-kiun or Lao-Tse, who came into the world in the year 603 before the Christian era." Grosier's China, vol. ii, p. 203. It is impossible to identify all the names given in this legend of Chinese superstition. Paosaos (see next page) is probably the same with Poosah, the name generally given to the Chinese idols. The Sichia, who are said to have come from Trautheyco, towards the west [Thibet? see note next page], are probably the disciples of the sect of Foe, also noticed by Grosier. "This sect, still more pernicious and much wider diffused throughout China than the preceding, came originally from India."—Vol. ii, p. 215. The description here given of the religious people who live without marrying and wear no hair, tallies exactly with the practice of the Bonzes or priests of Foe of the present day.

[60] This would seem to be Kwan-she, the same as Kwan-yin, the goddess of mercy of the votaries of Foe.

[61] This would appear to be Thibet (for there is no Chinese form that we can recognize as corresponding with the word), and Thibet is the country from which those points of belief are derived.

[62] This superstitious practice is described in much the same terms by Grosier. "The commonest way is to burn

perfumes before an idol, and to beat the earth several times with the forehead. Upon the altar which supports this idol, there is always a kind of horn, filled with small flat sticks, upon which are traced a variety of unintelligible characters. Each of these small sticks conceals an answer. The person who consults, lets fall, at random, one of these small sticks, the inscription of which is explained by the Bonze who accompanies him. When no Bonze is present, they have recourse to a paper fixed up to the wall of the pagoda, to discover the enigmatical meaning of the word. This manner of consulting is very common in China."—Grosier, vol. ii, p. 235.

[63] Pwan-koo, the Adam of the Chinese.

[64] Better known as Teen-Hwang.

[65] Also called Te Hwang.

[66] Also named Laoutsze.

[67] Also named Fuh-he-te.

[68] Also named Shin Nung.

[69] The Chinese pray to the dead, but the practice of prayers for the dead and the doctrine of the creation of man out of nothing by Tien, alluded to at page 50, are not found

in other writers; if therefore our author is correct, these may possibly have been relics of early Christian teaching.

[70] This expression is introduced by the English translator.

[71] Severely.

[72] This is the well-known lignum aloes of commerce. In some remarks by the late H. T. Colebrooke, Esq., on a paper of the late Dr. Roxburgh's recently read at the Linnean Society, occurs the following observation: "The Portuguese pao de aguila is an undoubted corruption, either of the Arabic aghaluji, or of the Latin agallochum; and it is by a ludicrous mistake that from this corruption has grown the name of lignum aquilæ, whence the genus of the plant now receives its botanic appellation, aquilaria agallocha." Roxb.

[73] It is thus spelt also in Steven's Spanish Dictionary. Query, cayolizan, a Mexican shrub, giving a perfume like incense.

[74] Rough.

[75] A mill. Wickliffe's translation of the Bible: Matthew xxiv, has: Two wymmen schulen be gryndynge in oo querne; oon schal be taken and the tother left.

[76] This sketch of the early annals of China is not altogether correct; but agrees in the main with that given by Du Halde. The names of the sovereigns are strangely misspelt; but the order of succession, and the years of their respective reigns, render it not difficult to identify them. Vitey does not seem to be the commonly reputed founder of the Chinese monarchy Fo-hi, but either his great successor Hoang-tie, who had 25 sons, or the celebrated Emperor Yao, whose reign lasted 100 years, and commenced b.c. 2357. Tzintzon is evidently the Chi-Hoang-ty of Du Halde, who built the great wall, and reigned b.c. 237. Aguisi, his son, is named by Du Halde Cul-chi. The Anchosan of our author is clearly the first emperor of the dynasty of Han, named Han-Cao-tsou by Du Halde. The years of the reigns which follow correspond very exactly with those of the several emperors of the Han dynasty; but the names are all spelt differently.

[77] Spanish. Vara-A yard.

[78] A third.

[79] Position, from Span. Estado.

[80] For the names of the following provinces, see note, p. 22.

[81] More properly "Mace". "The only coin in general use throughout China is the le or cash. Its intrinsic value may be about one-twelfth part of an English penny. The nominal names are those called fun, tsien, and leang, denominated

by foreigners candareen, mace, and tael, bearing respectively to each other a decimal proportion."—Murray's China, vol. iii, p. 93.

The mace is usually estimated at about 8d., and the tael 6s. 10d. sterling.

[82] Span. Quilates-carats.

[83] More properly "tael".

[84] Spanish. Millo or mijo-millet.

[85] Spanish. Panizo-panic-grass.

[86] This word is spelt the same in the original. Query blankets, from Portuguese Chim-Chinese, and mantas-blankets.

[87] Prevent.

[88] The military and non-military in China are usually distinguished by the terms ping and ming. The pon seems to refer to the ping or regular troops, and the cum to the ming or people; being only a species of local militia.

[89] Falchions?

[90] Billhooks

[91] Bombs.

[92] Loo chooans.

[93] Mis-spelt for Narsinga.

[94] Mis-spelt for Bengala.

[95] Query, Java.

[96] Pekin.

[97] Tsong-tuh.

[98] Laoye. See Chap. xiv on the title of Loytia.

[99] Possibly this word is confounded with Colao or Chung-tang, a minister of state.

[100] More properly To't'ung.

[101] More properly Po-ching-sz, or, as Du Halde has it, Pou-ching-ssee.

[102] More properly Too-tuh, adjutant-general.

[103] More properly Ngan-tcha-see.

[104] More properly Hai-tao. Respecting these offices see Du Halde, vol. ii, fol. 32, 33.

[105] Standard-bearer.

[106] More properly Paou-yin.

[107] This and the preceding title seem to be the same as those similarly spelt on page 103.

[108] Perhaps the Koo-ta-sze, or treasurer.

[109] Perhaps the Che-tsze, or secretary.

[110] Taou, tae, the intendant of circuits.

[111] More properly Kwan-paou, commissioner of customs. See Morrison's View of China, p. 94.

[112] Perhaps Te-paou, a police runner.

[113] Mre properly Yuen-chae, a police constable.

[114] Perhaps Ching-tang, assistant officer in a prise.

[115] Shin is the Chinese for the verb "to judge", and with the word officer added to it will be "a judging officer". Thus also leu-law, prefixed to che-to rule, or govern, may be the origin of the term Leuchi. This construction is, however, entirely conjectural.

[116] See note on page 113.

[117] This character is so vague as to be scarcely recognizable. The proper Chinese word for heaven is tien. The word here given may perhaps mean tsang, the azure sky, which is sometimes used metaphorically for heaven. At the same time the modern Chinese character for Keen, also pronounced Kan , which is likewise a very old word for heaven, appears somewhat to approximate in form to the character given in the text.

[118] Evidently hwang te, the character here given corresponding with the modern Chinese character Hwang.

[119] This character would seem to be intended for ching,—a walled city, the correct form of the character being .

[120] Fucheou, the capital of Fokien.

[121] Padrinos, Span.—Literally sponsors.

[122] A German.

[123] A misprint for Pegu.

[124] Mis-translated from the Spanish "Tudesco", a German. The reader will readily recognize the name of Johann Gutemberg or Ganzfleisch, of Mentz, who disputes with Laurens Koster, of Haarlem, the honour of having invented and first practised the art of printing with moveable types.

[125] Conrad Sweynheim, who, in partnership with Arnold Pannartz, published in 1465, at the Monastery of Subiaco, near Rome, the Lactantii Opera, 4to., the first work printed in Italy. The De Civitate Dei of St. Augustine, was printed by the same printers at Subiaco two years later. It is now known that the first book printed in Europe with metal types, was the Mazarine Bible, printed by Gutemberg and Fust, at Mentz, in 1455.

[126] Germany.

[127] Printing without moveable types does not go back, even in China, beyond the beginning of the tenth century of our era. The first four books of Confucius were printed, according to Klaproth, in the province of Sze-chuen, between 890 and 925, and the description of the technical manipulation of the Chinese printing press might have been

read in western countries even as early as 1310, in Raschid Eddin's Persian history of the rulers of Khatai. According to the most recent results of the important researches of Stanislas Julien, however, an ironsmith in China itself, between the years 1041 and 1048, a.d., or almost 400 years before Gutemberg, would seem to have used moveable types made of burnt clay. This is the invention of Pi-sching, but it was not brought into application. See Humboldt's Kosmos, translated by Otté, fol. 623. Moveable types are now no longer used, for as Sir John Davis observes, vol. ii, p. 222, "the present mode of Chinese printing with wooden stereotype blocks is peculiarly suited to the Chinese character, and for all purposes of cheapness and expedition is perfect". A complete set of the materials used by the Chinese in the process of printing, may be seen in the Museum of the Royal Asiatic Society. In the note on page 121 of Hakluyt's Divers Voyages, edited for the Hakluyt Society by J. Winter Jones, Esq., the following description is given of a book printed in 1348: "The earliest work of which we have been able to obtain an account, from one having had the opportunity of personally inspecting it, bears date the eighth year of the last period of the reign of Shun Te, or a.d. 1348. Mr. Prevost, our informant, who is at present engaged in cataloguing the splendid collection of Chinese books in the British Museum, has favoured us with the following description of the book. The title is 'Chin Tsaou Tsëen Wan, or the Thousand Character Classic'. It is one of the most popular works in China, and consists of exactly one thousand different characters, not one being repeated. It is composed in octosyllabic verses, which rhyme in couplets; each verse presenting to the student some useful Chinese notion, either in morals or in general knowledge. The object of this work is to teach the written character, both in its semi-cursive and in its stenographic form, termed Tsaou, or grass-writing: the text is, therefore, printed in parallel columns, alternately in the Chin, or correct, and the Tsaou, or cursive character. The author lived in the first half of the sixth century. This work, when seen by Mr. Prevost, was in the possession of Colonel Tynte." The Editor has also in his own possession a Chinese bank note, printed, or rather stamped, in the fourteenth century.

[128] Hou-quang.

[129] A sort of confection made of almonds, sugar, etc.

[130] Bever, probably from bevere, Ital., to drink, a small collation between dinner and supper.

[131] Vname, is probably Yew ma,—pitch, or the resin of the pine. In Morrison's Dictionary, "tar" is translated Pa ma yew: but the Editor finds nothing analogous to Ja pez, which is probably now obsolete.

[132] The Goletta of Tunis was taken from the Spaniards by Sinan Pacha, admiral of Selim II, on the 23rd of August 1574.

[133] Mistranslated for "the extensive knowledge which I had of navigation."

[134] Misspelt for Corunna.

Printed in Great Britain
by Amazon